The Lewis and Clark Expedition

Selections from the Journals, Arranged by Topic

Edited with an Introduction by

Gunther Barth

University of California, Berkeley

BEDFORD/ST. MARTIN'S   Boston   New York

To Ellen.

For Bedford/St. Martin's
History Editor: Katherine E. Kurzman
Developmental Editor: Charisse M. Kiino
Production Editor: Stasia Zomkowski
Marketing Manager: Charles Cavaliere
Copyeditor: Barbara G. Flanagan
Text Design: Claire Seng-Niemoeller
Indexer: Steve Csipke
Cover Design: Richard Emery Design, Inc.
Cover Art: Charles M. Russell, *Lewis and Clark Expedition,* 1918, oil on canvas. Courtesy of Thomas Gilcrease Institute of American History and Art, Tulsa, Oklahoma.
Composition: ComCom
Printing and Binding: Haddon Craftsmen, Inc.

President: Charles H. Christensen
Editorial Director: Joan E. Feinberg
Director of Editing, Design, and Production: Marcia Cohen
Managing Editor: Elizabeth M. Schaaf

Library of Congress Catalog Card Number: 97–74956

For information, write: Bedford/St. Martin's, 75 Arlington Street, Boston, MA 02116 (617-426-7440)

ISBN: 0–312–11118–5   (paperback)
ISBN: 0–312–12801–0   (hardcover)

Foreword

The Bedford Series in History and Culture is designed so that readers can study the past as historians do.

The historian's first task is finding the evidence. Documents, letters, memoirs, interviews, pictures, movies, novels, or poems can provide facts and clues. Then the historian questions and compares the sources. There is more to do than in a courtroom, for hearsay evidence is welcome, and the historian is usually looking for answers beyond act and motive. Different views of an event may be as important as a single verdict. How a story is told may yield as much information as what it says.

Along the way the historian seeks help from other historians and perhaps from specialists in other disciplines. Finally, it is time to write, to decide on an interpretation and how to arrange the evidence for readers.

Each book in this series contains an important historical document or group of documents, each document a witness from the past and open to interpretation in different ways. The documents are combined with some element of historical narrative—an introduction or a biographical essay, for example—that provides students with an analysis of the primary source material and important background information about the world in which it was produced.

Each book in the series focuses on a specific topic within a specific historical period. Each provides a basis for lively thought and discussion about several aspects of the topic and the historian's role. Each is short enough (and inexpensive enough) to be a reasonable one-week assignment in a college course. Whether as classroom or personal reading, each book in the series provides firsthand experience of the challenge—and fun—of discovering, recreating, and interpreting the past.

Natalie Zemon Davis
Ernest R. May

Preface

During the course of the Lewis and Clark expedition in 1804–06, two captains and seven other explorers jotted down their experiences in journals kept with varying degrees of regularity. The sheer bulk of these journals has repeatedly lured writers to use them as a source for their histories, to compose guides to them, or to make excerpts available for new generations of readers.

The best of these histories is that of Nicholas Biddle, whose work towers over all other guides to the Lewis and Clark journals. His *History* is the only book that acquainted nineteenth-century Americans with the explorers' experience as recorded in their journals.[1] A man of letters, a statesman, and the last president of the Second Bank of the United States, Biddle had his book published in Philadelphia in 1814; it went through twenty-two editions in the next ninety years. Often thought to be the words of the explorers themselves, the book established the promise of the Far West for several generations of Americans.[2]

Nineteenth-century Americans were wholeheartedly captivated by the appeal of the *History*. In 1893, the naturalist Elliott Coues prepared a new edition of Biddle's book on the basis of "a diligent study of the original manuscript journals and field notebooks of the explorers." He called Biddle's *History* "our national epic of exploration, conceived by Thomas Jefferson, wrought out by Lewis and Clark, and given to the world by Nicholas Biddle."[3]

In 1818, Thomas Jefferson deposited the Lewis and Clark journals,

---

[1]Nicholas Biddle, *History of the Expedition under the Command of Captains Lewis and Clark to the Source of the Missouri, Thence across the Rocky Mountains and down the River Columbia to the Pacific Ocean. Performed during the Years 1804–5–6. By Order of the Government of the United States. Prepared for the Press by Paul Allen, Esquire,* 2 vols. (Philadelphia: Bradford and Inskeep, 1814).

[2]See, for instance, J. Loughborough, "Lewis and Clarke's Expedition to and from the Pacific," *The Western Journal of Agriculture, Manufactures, Mechanic Arts, Internal Improvement, Commerce, and General Literature,* April 1850, 14.

[3]Elliot Coues, ed., *History of the Expedition under the Command of Lewis and Clark,* 4 vols. (New York: Francis P. Harper, 1893), 1:vi.

which Biddle had relied on for his *History*, with the American Philosophical Society. He may have hoped to see the journals in print, but not until 1901, with the centennial of the Louisiana Purchase and the Lewis and Clark expedition approaching, did the society make plans to publish the manuscripts.[4] In 1904–05, on the hundredth anniversary of the departure of the expedition, Reuben Gold Thwaites published an eight-volume edition titled *Original Journals of the Lewis and Clark Expedition.* The editor dedicated "this first publication of the Original Records of their 'Winning of the West' " to Theodore Roosevelt, alluding to the title of the twenty-sixth president's multivolume history of the settlement of Ohio and Kentucky.

Thwaites's magistral work, initially printed by Dodd, Mead became the definitive edition of the explorers' journals. In 1969 it was reprinted by Arno Press. Over time additional documents surfaced, prompting calls for a new edition. Sponsored by the Center for Great Plains Studies, University of Nebraska—Lincoln, and the American Philosophical Society, a splendid new multivolume edition edited by Gary E. Moulton began publication in 1983.

Several collections of excerpts from the Lewis and Clark journals, based on the Thwaites edition, appeared in the second half of the twentieth century. Among them, books prepared by Bernard DeVoto (1953), John Bakeless (1964), and Frank Bergon (1989) stand out. Their selections chronologically trace the explorers' day-by-day movement across the continent.

Brevity is the characteristic of the present volume, drawn from selections in the original Thwaites edition. Thwaites's eight volumes of information about the expedition have been condensed into a two-hundred-thirty-page book, without violating the essence of the experience or of the accomplishment. Chosen primarily for two reasons, the exerpts offer insight not only into the explorers' personalities but also into the tasks they mastered, the people they met, the places they saw, and the hardships they endured.

In recent decades, a laudable historiographical trend has focused attention on significant related subjects ranging from Lewis and Clark as naturalists to their relations with Native Americans.[5] In this collection, therefore, it seems particularly important to concentrate on the members of the Corps of Discovery.

---

[4]Paul Russell Cutright, *A History of the Lewis and Clark Journals* (Norman: University of Oklahoma Press, 1976), 70–71, 104.

[5]Paul Russell Cutright, *Lewis and Clark: Pioneering Naturalists* (Urbana: University of Illinois Press, 1969), and James P. Ronda, *Lewis and Clark among the Indians* (Lincoln: University of Nebraska Press, 1984) are outstanding examples.

The selections included here lend themselves to an effective organization by topic or theme, with entries arranged chronologically within each chapter. To keep pace with the linear route of the expedition, journal entries begin with the corps's location (or stage of the journey), the day, the date, and the name of the writer. Gathering together references to a particular person or subject that are scattered throughout the journals heightens the immediacy of the expedition's experience and enlivens the reader's encounter with the explorers and their frequently changing situations. The constant challenge to function within the diverse community of the expedition forged a unique cohesive bond that carried the group across the continent. The natural obstacles of rivers, plains, and mountains along with wary and sometimes hostile Native Americans gave the explorers a new awareness of both human nature and the natural world.

In the narrative of the journals, observations were frequently obscured by the explorers' accounts of their daily routines. A tired writer at the end of an exhausting day more often than not crammed the events of a day in whatever order he recalled them, interspersing descriptions of events with notes, thoughts, and measurements with no particular order.

This book groups together these dispersed statements on certain topics so the reader will become familiar and involved with the expedition's unique experience. Readers who are intrigued by the excerpts may want to turn to the complete edition of the journals to pursue a favorite subject in more detail.

A NOTE ON THE TEXT

All selections from the journals of Lewis and Clark are taken from Reuben Gold Thwaites, ed., *Original Journals of the Lewis and Clark Expedition, 1804–1806,* 8 vols. (New York: Dodd, Mead, 1904), referred to in the notes as Thwaites, *Original Journals of the Lewis and Clark Expedition.* The selections in this collection follow exactly the language of the journals as established by Thwaites. He encountered the Lewis and Clark manuscripts with interlineation by William Clark, Nicholas Biddle, Elliott Coues, and an unknown hand. Thwaites retained all emendations made by Clark and Biddle but let those by Coues stand only if they did not attempt to correct the spelling of proper names.

Thwaites styled the emendations as follows:

Italics in parentheses for corrections made by Biddle: (*Moses B. Read*). (Biddle and Clark spent some time together when

Biddle was working on the manuscript of his *History*. Some of Biddle's emendations represent Clark's own corrected recollections.)

Italics in brackets for corrections made by Clark, Coues, or an unknown hand: [*Petite Côte*].

Italics for words underlined by Lewis and Clark.

Roman in brackets for emendations and comments made by Thwaites: [Lewis].

In addition, comments made by the editor of the present volume are in brackets with the notation ED.: [Lewis outlines the course Jefferson mapped earlier.—ED.] Numbered gloss notes are by the editor of the present volume unless otherwise indicated in brackets.

Thwaites retained the spelling of the original manuscripts, and so do these selections. In an age when consistency did not yet govern orthography, the explorers' erratic spelling reflected differences in temperament, education, and rank, differences frequently obscured by the underlying uniformity of style.

The following are some of the more frequently used abbreviations in the selections:

Altd.	altitude
d.	degree
do.	ditto
Ds^t	downstream
L., Larb., Lard., Ld., Lbd. S.	larboard, or left, side
Latd.	latitude
Longtd.	longitude
opsd.	opposite
pd.	passed
S., SS., St., Star., Starbd., Stb.	starboard, or right, side
ulto., Ult.^{mo}	in the previous month (Latin, *ultimo*)

As writers, these officers, noncommissioned officers, and enlisted men relied on army prose, which focused on chronology, the orderly sequence of events, topography, and weather. In particular, the requirements of the terrain for issuing orders and the effect of a day's weather on the soldiers' morale were noted. Thus the prose sometimes weaves descriptions of strange or unusual natural sights into the narrative of routine daily events. Their attention to physical detail was often not matched by strict adherence to the calendar or the spellings of proper names.

Often a dated entry is accompanied by an incorrect day of the week. All references to days of the week, correct and incorrect, have been retained. While the explorers used many variations for the spellings of proper names, their meaning is usually clear in context. For instance, on October 17, 1804, Clark refers to his counterpart as "Louis" in the thirteenth line and as "Lewis" six lines later, but the reader is not confused. The following list of approximations of the proper spellings of explorers' names may help clarify an occasional reference.[6] (Variations found in the selections and in parentheses.)

Barter (La Liberté, La Liberty), Joseph
Boley (Boleye, Bolye), John
Bratton (Bratten), William E.
Carson, Alexander
Caugee (Cougee), Charles
Charbonneau, Baptiste (Pomp)
Charbonneau (Chabonneau, Charboneau, Charbono, Chaubonie, Shabono, Shabounar), Toussaint
Clark (Clarke), William
Collin, Joseph
Collins, John
Colter, John
Cruzatte (Crusat, Crusatte, Crouzatt), Pierre (Peter)
Dame, John
De Champs (Dechamps), Jean Baptiste
Degie, Phillipe
Dorion (Deurion, Dourion), Pierre, Sr.

Drouillard (Drewyer, Drullier, Drulyard), George
Fields (Feels, Field), Joseph
Fields (Field), Reuben
Floyd (Floid), Charles
Frazer (Frazier, Frasure, Frazure), Robert
Gass, Patrick
Gibson, George
Goodrich (Goodredge, Gutridge, Gutterage), Silas
Gravelines, Joseph
Hall, Hugh
Hébert, Charles
Howard, Thomas Procter
Labiche (Labieche, Labuche, Labuish), François (Francis, William)
La Jeunesse (La Jeunnesse, Laguness), Jean Baptiste
La Liberté. See Barter
Le Page (La Page, Lepage), Jean Baptiste
Lewis, Meriwether

[6]The list of the probable spellings of the explorers' names has benefited from the roster in Charles G. Clarke, *The Men of the Lewis and Clark Expedition: A Biographical Roster of the Fifty-one Members and a Composite Diary of their Activities from all Known Sources* (Glendale, Calif.: Arthur H. Clarke, 1970), 71.

McNeal (McNeel, Neel,
Neil, O'Nail), Hugh
Malboeuf (Mabbauf),
Étienne
Newman (Newmon), John
Ordway (Ordeway), John
Pinaut, Peter
Potts, John
Primeau (Primaut), Paul
Pryor, Nathaniel Hale
Read (Reed), Moses B.
Rivet, François
Robertson (Robinson),
John G.
Roi (Roie), Peter
Rokey (Ross, Rocque)
Sacagawea (Sacajawea,

Sahkahgarwea, Bird
Woman)
Shannon, George
Shields (Sheilds), John
Thompson, John B.
Tuttle, Ebenezer
Warfington (Warvington,
Worbington), Richard
Weiser (Wiser), Peter M.
Werner (Warner), William
White, Isaac
Whitehouse, Joseph
Willard, ALexander
Windsor (Winsor, Winser),
Richard
York

References to Indian nations in the introductions and headnotes follow the spelling of Native American groups found in John R. Swanton's classic handbook.[7] Its practice to give the name of a nation in the singular (for example, the Mandan) has also been adopted. Introductions and notes refer to the Indian nations with the names most frequently used by the explorers (for example, the Minitari, known to us as Hidatsa).

ACKNOWLEDGMENTS

I gratefully acknowledge the help that I have received from various quarters.

I benefited from the support of the Department of History and of The Bancroft Library at the University of California at Berkeley. My colleagues, Thomas G. Barnes and James H. Kettner, helped with office space and books.

At Bedford Books, I am indebted to publisher Charles Christensen and associate publisher Joan Feinberg. Sabra Scribner and Katherine Kurzman sponsored the book. I am beholden to my development editor, Charisse Kiino, who guided me through the series' requirements and commented extensively on my selections, notes, and apparatus. Two sets

---

[7]John R. Swanton, *The Indian Tribes of North America* (1952; reprint, Washington, D.C.: Smithsonian Institution Press, 1968).

of readers, among them William Deverell, University of California, San Diego; Susan Gray, Arizona State University; Stephen Innes, University of Virginia; William Lang, Portland State University; Roger Nichols, University of Arizona; and Alan Taylor, University of California, Davis, contributed their views. Bruce Jones drafted the maps, and Susan Pace and Richard Emery designed and produced the cover. I owe a special debt of gratitude to the skillful work of Elizabeth Schaaf, managing editor of the production department, Stasia Zomkowski, production editor, and Barbara Flanagan, copyeditor, who made the final stages of the project a pleasant experience.

My thanks to Richard M. Abrams, Robert L. Middlekauff, and Karl H. Schlesier for their helpful advice.

As always, Ellen W. Barth has improved my ideas and prose. Her help enabled me to finish the task.

Gunther Barth

Contents

Illustrations

Chronology of the
Lewis and Clark Expedition
(1803–1806)

1803

January 18 Jefferson presents confidential message to Congress. Lewis begins outfitting the expedition.

April 30 Louisiana Purchase treaty signed in Paris.

July 17 Clark accepts Lewis's invitation to share the command of the expedition.

August 31 Lewis embarks with his men at Pittsburgh traveling down the Ohio River.

October 15–26 Lewis and Clark meet at Clarksville, Indiana Territory, consolidating the Corps of Discovery.

December 13 Clark establishes Camp Dubois on the Illinois shore of the Mississippi, opposite the mouth of the Missouri River.

1804

May 14 Clark leaves Camp Dubois with the expedition, crosses Mississippi, and ascends the Missouri to meet Lewis in St. Charles.

July 30–August 2 Camp at Council Bluff, with Oto and Missouri.

August 21 At Sergeant Floyd's grave, present-day Sioux City, Iowa.

August 27–30 Stay with Yankton Sioux at James River.

September 24 Arrive at mouth of Teton River, present-day Pierre, South Dakota.

September 24–28 Meeting the Teton Sioux.

October 8–12 Stay at the Arikara earth lodges above the Grande River in present-day north central South Dakota.

October 26 Camp at the first of the five Mandan villages.

November 16–20 Move into winter quarters at Fort Mandan.

1805

April 7   Explorers leave Fort Mandan.

June 2–11   Explore the area of the Marias River.

June 13   Lewis sees the Great Falls of the Missouri.

June 21–July 2   Portage of the Great Falls.

July 19   Pass the Gates of the Rocky Mountains in present-day Helena National Forest, Montana.

July 25–30   Explore the Three Forks of the Missouri.

August 12   Lewis's party reaches headwaters of the Missouri; cross the Continental Divide (Lemhi Pass).

August 13–30   Stay with Cameahwait's Shoshoni at Lemhi River in present-day Idaho.

September 4–6   Camp with the Flathead, allies of the Shoshoni.

September 9   Arrive at Travelers Rest.

September 11–22   Cross Bitterroot Mountains on Lolo Trail.

September 20–October 7   Stay with the Nez Perce.

October 16   Arrive at juncture of Snake River and Columbia River.

October 18–19   Join councils with the Walla Walla.

October 22–23   Pass the Great Falls of the Columbia.

October 24–25   Traverse the Dalles.

November 1–2   Portage the Cascades, or Grand Rapids.

November 10   Arrive at Point Ellice and Camp Chinook.

November 25   View Pacific Ocean for the first time.

December 7   Build winter quarters at Fort Clatsop, five miles south of the Columbia.

1806

March 23   Leave Fort Clatsop; start the return trip.

April 27   At Wallawalla River; meet Walla Walla again.

May 3   Contact the first group of Nez Perce.

May 13–June 9   Wait at Camp Chopunnish on the Clearwater River for the snow to melt.

June 10–17   Aborted attempt to travel the snow-covered Lolo Trail without Nez Perce guides.

June 24–30   Recross the Bitterroots with Nez Perce guides.

July 3   Party divides at Travelers Rest: Lewis travels via the Great Falls to the headwaters of the Marias; Clark travels via the Three Forks to the Yellowstone River.

July 27   Lewis's Blackfeet fight at the Medicine River.

July 15–August 3   Clark explores the Yellowstone River.

August 12   Explorers reunited on the Missouri.

August 14–17   Reach the Mandan villages again.

August 30   Parley with Teton Sioux at Yankton.

September 1   Attend council with friendly Yankton Sioux.

September 23   Cross Mississippi: return visit to Camp Dubois after 2 years, 4 months, and 10 days (863 days).

September 23   Arrive at St. Louis at noon.

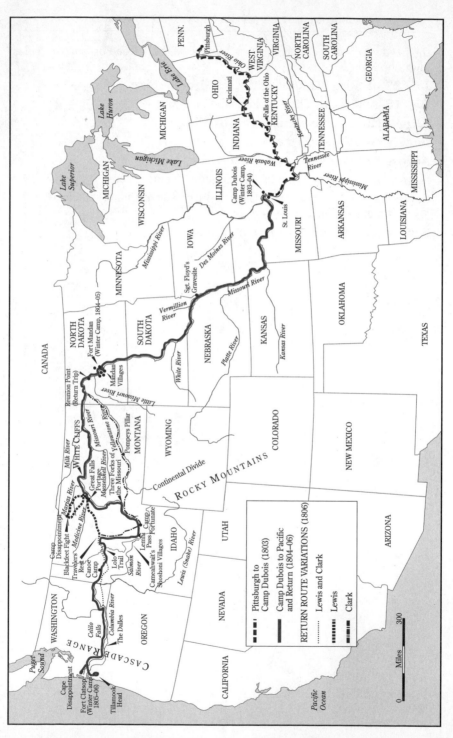

Figure 1. The Lewis and Clark Expedition, 1803–06

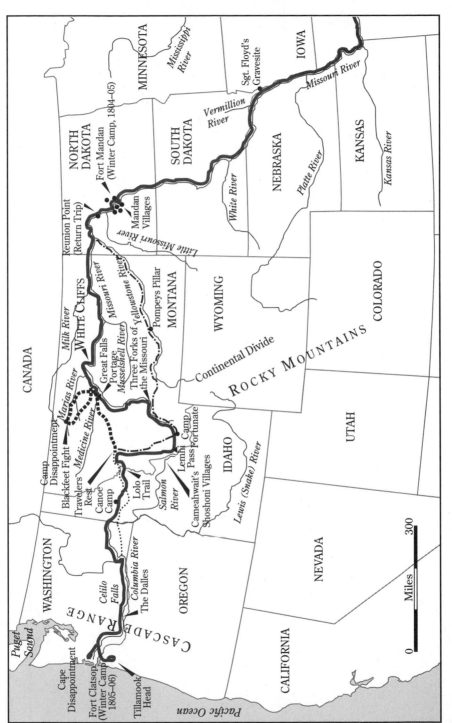

Figure 2. Enlarged Detail of the Lewis and Clark Expedition

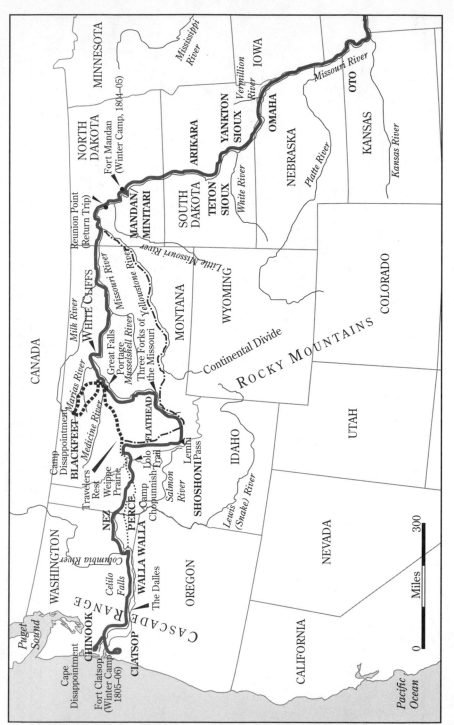

Figure 3.   Indian Nations along the Trail

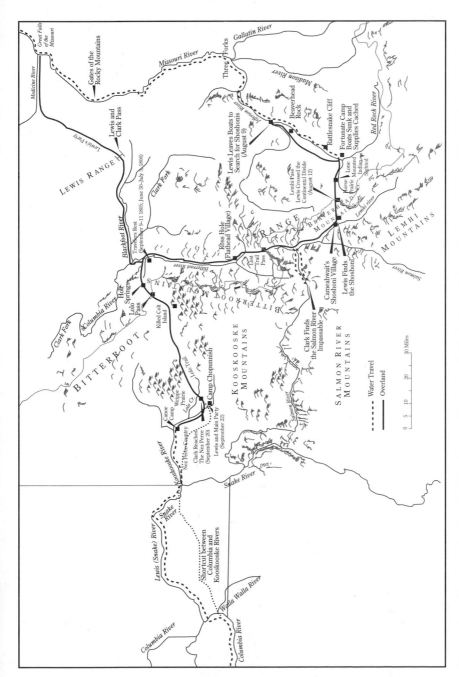

Figure 4.   Crossing the Rocky Mountains, Lewis and Clark Expedition, September 11–22, 1805; June 24–30, 1806

Introduction: Jefferson's Designs
and Western Realities

The journals of the Lewis and Clark expedition describe the continental crossing of the first United States exploring expedition between 1804 and 1806. The brainchild of President Thomas Jefferson, it was a high point in his lifelong preoccupation with the American West. The expedition produced the first decisive encounter with the people and natural resources of a part of the continent unknown to the young nation. Jefferson's idea to find a convenient waterway through North America to the Pacific Ocean fused the last phase of an old European dream with the new geopolitical concerns of the United States.

The possibility of a water route—a Northwest Passage—through North America had intrigued Europeans since the days of Columbus. In the following centuries, however, growing knowledge of the geographic configurations of the continent had narrowed the search to an unfamiliar part of the Pacific Northwest coast. By the turn of the eighteenth century, with the explorations of the mouth of the Columbia River, it seemed likely that the Columbia and the Missouri Rivers could be linked to provide such a waterway through the continent.

No European, however, had as yet traced the course of the Columbia River. In the north, Spaniards, Englishmen, Scots, Canadians, and Russians had some knowledge of the coastline. One British fur trader and explorer, Alexander Mackenzie, had actually traversed the continent in 1793, roughly along the line of the fifty-fifth parallel in present-day central Canada. In the south, the Spaniards knew much of the coast below the forty-second parallel, the northern borders of present-day California, Nevada, and Utah. In 1775, on his return voyage from Nootka Sound on the West Coast of Vancouver Island, Bruno de Hezeta, a navigator involved in a Spanish attempt to secure a foothold in the Pacific Northwest, sighted the mouth of the Columbia River. A strong current, a dangerous bar, and a sick crew kept him from entering the estuary. In the interior, in 1776, the Spanish Franciscan Silvestre Velez de Escalante set out from Santa Fe in the hope of finding a trail linking the two northern

1

outposts of the viceroyalty of New Spain, New Mexico, and Alta California. The expedition followed a northwesterly route to Utah Lake, near the present-day city of Provo, the northernmost point of Spanish penetration into North America, and then turned to the southwest in search of a pass over the Sierra Nevada to Monterey. A fall of snow caused the party to return to Santa Fe.

Between the routes of Mackenzie and Escalante, however, there remained an unknown territory vast enough to sustain the search for a waterway. In 1792, a Boston sea captain, Robert Gray, crossed the bar of the Columbia River and named it after his ship. Gray's action supported an American claim to the area; determined to assert its sphere of influence on the West Coast, the United States joined the long-standing search for a Northwest Passage. It became a distinct part of Jefferson's vision of opening a trans-Mississippi trade route to the Pacific. Instead of relying on the mythical two-thousand-mile-long River Oregon, purported to flow west from mid-America into the Pacific, Jefferson focused on the Missouri. Its big bend in present-day North Dakota seemed to point the river in the right direction. Jefferson hoped that a short portage—the transport of canoes, supplies, and trade goods overland between navigable waters—might link the Missouri to the Columbia.

In 1783, Jefferson became actively involved in the Far West. He suggested to George Rogers Clark, hero of the Revolutionary War in the Ohio Valley and older brother of William Clark, that he lead an expedition to explore the trans-Mississippi West. Clark declined. The war had bankrupted him, and the Virginia legislature would not reimburse him for his expenditures in the campaigns against Kaskaskia and Vincennes, two British strongholds in present-day Illinois and Indiana.

In 1786, as minister to Paris, Jefferson endorsed a plan from John Ledyard, who as corporal of Marines on Captain James Cook's third voyage in 1778 had recognized the commercial potential of the rich fur resources of the Pacific Northwest coast. Ledyard's plan was to cross Russia to Kamchatka, a peninsula in the northeast extending south into the North Pacific. From there he was to find his way to the Pacific Northwest, descend the coast to the latitude of the Missouri, somehow reach that river, and then follow it to the United States.

All went well after he embarked on his voyage. Several days short of reaching Kamchatka, however, Ledyard was arrested under orders from Catherine the Great and escorted back to the Polish border. The empress of Russia and her advisers had become concerned about the designs of rival nations and foreign travelers in eastern parts of the empire when they noticed that a recently published collection of Cook's North Pacific maps had replaced the Russian place-names with English ones.

Then in 1793, as secretary of state and vice president of the American Philosophical Society in Philadelphia, Jefferson advocated an expedition by the French botanist André Michaux to travel the Missouri and from there to the Pacific coast. Yet Michaux had to abandon the project when he became involved in the political schemes of the French minister to the United States, who was planning a military expedition against the Spanish possessions in the Southwest.

When Jefferson became president in 1801, the power struggle over this stretch of unknown territory escalated. Jefferson considered it essential to protect the economic and political interests of the United States along the Columbia and Missouri Rivers. The coincidence of new political interests gave him the opportunity to realize his far-reaching plans for a scientific exploration of the trans-Mississippi West.

THE LOUISIANA PURCHASE

In a confidential message to Congress on January 18, 1803, Jefferson stressed the significance of exerting control over Indian trade along the Missouri, which was dominated by British companies and free traders, men who operated independently of any fur company. Mixed-race traders and trappers, French and Spanish fur companies from St. Louis, and a few adventurers from Kentucky also sought their share of the commerce. (See p. 15.)

In order to safeguard the interests of the United States, Jefferson also requested an appropriation of $2,500 for an expedition up the Missouri and, possibly, to the Pacific Ocean. The president made his plan palatable to legislators by asking for a small sum. Since he envisioned the expedition as a military unit, much of its support would come from the Department of War. Ultimately, the total cost of the expedition amounted to about $40,000, which included the accrued army pay of the soldiers and the value of the land grants they received from Congress. The explorers were not limited, however, to the initial appropriation. Jefferson provided them with a general letter of credit in case they met ships at the mouth of the Columbia and contracted them for a passage home or for the shipment of their collections and journals.

Jefferson considered Congress's allocation of the money as its approval of the expedition and began to prepare for departure. He chose his private secretary, Meriwether Lewis, as leader of the party who acted according to the president's detailed instructions. Lewis acquired provisions, arms, trade goods, and presents. He consulted East Coast scientists and engineers for advice about his many-faceted tasks and contacted officers for the names of soldiers suitable for the expedition.

On the date of Jefferson's confidential message, the western boundary of the United States followed the Mississippi River, while the territory along the Missouri belonged to France. It was part of a large area called Louisiana, which France had given to Spain in 1762 but then reclaimed in a secret treaty in 1800. Louisiana in 1803, however, continued to be governed by Spanish officials to protect the Spanish territories of Texas, New Mexico, and California.

The capital of Lower Louisiana, New Orleans, controlled the mouth of the Mississippi and was critically important for the rapidly growing numbers of American settlers on both sides of the Ohio River. They needed to ship their crops down the Ohio and the Mississippi to the Gulf and from there to the Atlantic and the East Coast or Europe, but they worried that Spanish officials might block the route at New Orleans.

When Spanish officials closed New Orleans to American commerce in 1802, Jefferson planned to buy the city from Napoleon, the first consul of France. One year later, Napoleon surprised Jefferson's negotiators with the offer to sell *all* of Louisiana to the United States for $15 million. (See p. 23.) Napoleon, who would crown himself emperor of France in 1804, had abandoned his plan to send an army up the Mississippi to attack British Canada: Yellow fever and black freedom fighters had decimated his army on the Caribbean island of Santo Domingo. With the resumption of war with Great Britain imminent, Napoleon considered it prudent to sell Louisiana to the United States, lest it fall into British hands.

On April 30, 1803, the Louisiana Purchase treaty was signed, and news of the acquisition reached Washington on July 14. The Louisiana Purchase doubled the size of the United States. Few of its citizens understood the scope of the treaty. They knew nothing about Napoleon's intricate designs and little about the area they had acquired. They knew that New Orleans, the territory's major city, was the only part of Louisiana located east of the Mississippi. When their thoughts turned to the vast area beyond that, they generally assumed that Louisiana stretched to the watershed of the Rocky Mountains, the source of the rivers draining into the Mississippi, and reached from the Canadian line in the north to Spanish possessions in the south.

Although the purchase took Louisiana out of Spanish hands, Spanish officials in America continued to look closely at the territory and at the American expedition seeking the sources of the Missouri, especially since they believed its headwaters were much closer to New Mexico than they actually are. The Spaniards also felt threatened by the expedition's route toward the Pacific Northwest, to which Spain had a long-standing claim. Between 1804 and 1806, to protect these Spanish interests, four raiding parties were sent out from New Mexico into the Great Plains, but all failed to intercept the expedition, much less to attain their goal of blocking its advance or return.[1]

THE POLITICS OF THE PURCHASE

The Louisiana Purchase conveniently linked Jefferson's goal to explore the West with the administrative requirements inherent in acquiring such a large territory. (See p. 18.) But while Jeffersonian Republicans generally supported expansion, the Federalists generally opposed its aims and implications.

The Federalists' reaction and resistance to the Louisiana Purchase stemmed from basic differences with the Jeffersonian Republicans. Although both parties had followers in all areas of the country and in all classes, the Federalists' predominant support came from conservatives, merchants, and nationalists in New England and the Middle Atlantic states. Radicals, farmers, debtors, and states' rights advocates from the South and West generally backed the Republicans. The distinction between the parties that emerged over domestic policy assumed a definitive form over foreign policy resulting from the European Wars of the French Revolution. It followed that the Federalists often favored Great Britain, and the Republicans usually favored France.

Ardent expansionists like the Republicans, most Federalists supported the treaty with Napoleon, but credited good timing and good fortune, not the president. Yet some New England Federalists opposed expansion in general and the acquisition of Louisiana in particular. They considered the price of the purchase mind-boggling and feared that westward expansion would disperse people too widely and alter the balance between the states in favor of the West and the South. Some Federalists opposed the purchase as commercial allies of British exporters, insisting that Florida should have been acquired from Spain, not Louisiana from France, to consolidate the hold of the United States on the Atlantic coast. Jefferson felt, however, that Florida would ultimately fall into the hands of the United States as a sequel to the Louisiana Purchase. Federalist businessmen had little interest in United States control of the Mississippi and western

[1]Warren L. Cook, *Flood Tide of Empire: Spain and the Pacific Northwest, 1543–1819* (New Haven: Yale University Press, 1973), 456–83.

lands. They anticipated economic chaos as people and coin rushed into what one Federalist statesman and publicist considered "infinite space."

In addition to political opposition, Jefferson had doubts about the constitutionality of the purchase. As the leading Republican, Jefferson adhered to strict construction of the United States Constitution, which in this case meant that the federal government could not buy Louisiana because the power to buy territory was not explicitly granted by the Constitution. The president reluctantly adjusted his previously strict construction in view of the great benefits the nation would gain from this large acquisition.

In Jefferson's view, the Louisiana Purchase would extend the agricultural character of the United States and buttress all the virtues associated with a nation of farmers for centuries to come. Equally important, a large nation of yeoman farmers sustained by so much agricultural land would ensure that popular government would never be overwhelmed by a dangerously powerful federal government. Having weighed both constitutional legitimacy and national interest, Jefferson quickly pushed the treaty through Congress to prevent Napoleon from cancelling the bargain. Despite the Federalist opposition, the legislation implementing the purchase passed by large majorities early in November 1803, and the timely and prompt acquisition of Louisiana heightened the popularity of Jefferson and his party.

TIMING THE EXPEDITION

Jefferson's extraordinary success did not hasten the start of the Lewis and Clark expedition. The time gap for news and orders to travel between Europe and America demanded a wait-and-see attitude: waiting for the transfer of the vast territory to take effect and seeing who would actually be wielding power in Louisiana at the time of the expedition's departure. These uncertainties challenged the three major diplomatic tasks of the expedition: to inform the few scattered white settlements near the confluence of the Missouri and the Mississippi that they were now part of the United States; to exact from British, French, and Spanish fur traders respect for the territorial rights of the United States; and to demonstrate to the Indian nations on both sides of the Missouri the power and the goodwill of the president of the United States, the Great Father in Washington in the parlance of Indian councils.

A delicate balance of persuasion and pressure would be needed to complete all three tasks. But the most demanding was that of relating the news to Native Americans because the explorers knew so little about the complexity of the Indian cultures they would encounter. They shared the Jeffersonian view that Native Americans should be incorporated into Anglo-American society as useful yeoman farmers. When Indians resisted, the Jeffersonians believed they should be moved, by force if necessary, beyond the Mississippi, where time and segregation would strengthen and prepare them for integration into white society.[2]

Jefferson himself considered Native Americans part of the natural order. He assumed that distinctions could be ignored and Indians incorporated into the white world. As president, however, Jefferson planned for the temporary removal of Native Americans onto the lands of the Louisiana Purchase "to rehearse the arts of Civilization"[3] while white settlers migrated westward. In other words, Jefferson's Indian policy had an eastern and a western variant. East of the Mississippi, the government attempted to purchase tribal lands inexpensively and to persuade the Indians to farm more and hunt less, preferably to give up the hunt entirely, and to wear European-style clothing. Jefferson's policy was less clear west of the Mississippi. There he envisioned Native American roles in commerce and trade and seemed ready to reserve the lands for traders, including Indians, not settlers. Ultimately, these lands might even become a sanctuary for Native Americans uprooted by the westward expansion of the farmers' frontier.[4]

Like most Americans, the explorers considered Native Americans merely temporary occupants of virgin lands, destined to vanish or be removed to areas the advancing white settlers did not covet. Conflicting views about the future of Native Americans accompanied the expedition across the continent.

ENCOUNTERS WITH NATIVE AMERICANS

During the journey to the Pacific, the expedition encountered Plains, Plateau, and Northwest coast Indians, three of the eleven cultural groups in North America, and at least eight linguistic families: Algonquian, Siouan, Caddoan, Shoshonian, Salishan, Sahaptian, Chinookan, and Athapascan. Frequently, these cultural groups were divided into nations, often as a result of their previous contact with European powers. The divisions

[2]Bernard W. Sheehan, *Seeds of Extinction: Jeffersonian Philanthropy and the American Indian* (Chapel Hill: University of North Carolina Press, 1973), 6, 276.
[3]Donald Jackson, *Thomas Jefferson and the Stony Mountains: Exploring the West from Monticello* (Urbana: University of Illinois Press, 1981), 34.
[4]James P. Ronda, *Lewis and Clark among the Indians* (Lincoln: University of Nebraska Press, 1984), 4–5.

were as artificial as the notion of national loyalty they implied. One common bond the members of these diverse nations shared was their respect for the dignity of the individual; their loyalty did not extend much beyond the immediate clan or village.

Lewis and Clark's many observations often reveal as much about their own conceptual limitations and biases as they do about the Native Americans and their customs. In general, the explorers could not fully grasp Indian ways of life and patterns of population. Specifically, they did not understand the intimate bond of Native Americans with the natural and spirit worlds that shaped their lives.

At the turn of the eighteenth century, every facet of Plains Indian life depended on the grasslands of the buffalo range that stretched from the southern rim of the Canadian woodlands to the Rio Grande. In that area a new Indian culture, based on horse and buffalo, had emerged during the seventeenth and eighteenth centuries. Although European contact eventually undermined all Indian societies, a Native American culture thrived and flourished on the Great Plains.

The horse had come onto the Great Plains through Indian trade with and raids on the Spanish settlements in New Mexico. The Indians' mastery of the horse made hunting easier. They could follow buffalo closely, trailing herds within distinct areas claimed by different groups as their hunting grounds. Successful hunts meant that the Plains Indians had to give up their former semisedentary life to follow the annual buffalo movement, but the results were meat for sustenance, hide for tipis, and fur robes and blankets.

While the horse added brilliance and vibrancy to Plains culture, the movement of the buffalo determined its pattern of life. Great herds dispersed with the coming of winter, as small groups of straggling buffalo searched for scarce grass under the snow and sought shelter from blizzards in ravines or in stands of trees. Like the buffalo, the Indians faced the harsh winter on the Plains in small family units. They expanded into clans again when the snow melted, the grass turned green, and the buffalo reappeared. With the onset of summer, the great herds slowly gathered again for the rutting season in July and August, as the Indian nations gathered for the big hunt.

The slow-moving mass of huge animals, easily spooked into stampedes, challenged the hunting and social skills of the Plains Indians. Families and clans were forged into an effective striking force at the annual hunt. To ensure success, medicine men guided the hunters to seek the consent of the buffalo spirit for the hunt and to atone for killing the animal. Scouts sent out by warrior societies located herds and guided hunters to them. The so-called dog soldiers supervised the movements of the hunters, and of everyone else, to guarantee that each individual joined in the spiritual and physical demands of the hunt.

Nourishing body and spirit, the buffalo dominated the social and cultural lives of the Plains Indians. Committed to the chase, the Indians became superb horsemen, indefatigable hunters, and ferocious warriors. In an instant they could bridge the line between chase and war, fighting old enemies for hunting grounds or raiding their horse herds for the acquisition of a *remuda,* a supply of remounts, which gave status to young men yearning to distinguish themselves as warriors. The mobile way of life epitomized by the hunter-warrior fascinated the Lewis and Clark expedition.

The Indians' confidence and sagacity, their apparent indifference to pleasure, pain, or fear, and their ability to rise above the austerity of life were less obvious components of the Plains culture. Medicine men and peace chiefs instilled these attitudes and behaviors into members of their clans by reiterating the benefits of symbiosis with the world around them. Invoking spirits of the sky and earth kept families and clans in contact with buffalo, elk, pronghorn, bear, and other animal spirits, thus ensuring their well-being.

Some Plains Indians, such as the Arikara, the Mandan, and the Minitari, were middlemen in a vast network of trade relations. Although these nations continued to live in villages of earth houses and raised corn, beans, and squash, the explorers generally felt that they faced a Native American world in perpetual motion. Indian nations uprooted by the relentless advance of French Canadian fur traders and Anglo-American settlers pushed other Indian nations out of their homelands onto the Great Plains.

Physical and cultural death accompanied the white migrants, who unwittingly carried measles, whooping cough, and cholera germs, unknown to the Indians until their encounters with Europeans and their descendants. The epidemics spawned by contact decimated populations and eroded Indian cultures, which were once nourished by medicine men who now found themselves helpless in the face of unfamiliar, deadly diseases. At the same time, European trade and the Indian demand for more foreign goods steadily undermined Native American economies. Despite their spiritual strength and their physical stamina, the Plains Indians' society, economy, and culture were already seriously undermined when the expedition encountered them.

The explorers had only limited understanding of the Plains Indians' world, but they could still recognize analogous but contrasting patterns in Plateau and Pacific Northwest Indian cultures. On the westward course of their journey they noted that elk and salmon replaced the buffalo as the major source of meat. But only rarely did they realize how much buffalo, elk, or salmon shaped the total physical and spiritual features of the societies depending on them. The explorers could describe what they saw only as accurately as their vocabulary and their conceptions would allow as they tried to comprehend so much novelty.

For their time, the explorers were remarkably reliable ethnographers. Misunderstandings occurred mostly when they did not grasp the meaning of what they saw or did not know where to look for an answer. Quite often, particularly during swift canoe travel on the Columbia, exhaustion and lack of time prevented any thought of seeking insight into the makeup of an Indian group. They certainly lacked the modern and formal ethnological approach that would have led them to treat their impressions and observations dispassionately and systematically. The variety of cultural differences between groups of Native Americans they met strained their descriptive abilities. In the time-honored practice of overburdened writers before them, whether travelers, traders, missionaries, or explorers, they simply made generalizations without applying any systematic analysis.

ENCOUNTERS WITH GEOGRAPHY

The explorers knew very little geography of the lands they traversed. They knew most about the area of the lower reaches of the Missouri because it was the lifeline of the St. Louis fur trade, a pathway of commerce long before the expedition ascended it. The great unknown, a vast area familiar only to the Indian nations living there, lay beyond the earthen houses of the Mandan villages, just below the Great Bend of the Missouri in present-day North Dakota. Two of the Mandan villages were occupied by Mandan Indians and three by Minitari. In the 1730s and 1740s, the French explorer and fur trader La Vérendrye and his sons reputedly went west beyond the Mandan villages. A rumor circulated that one French trapper reached the confluence of the Missouri and the Yellowstone Rivers and for a few days journeyed up the latter. To the north the traders of the British North West Company were familiar with the Saskatchewan River route to the Rocky Mountains, but they knew little about the upper Missouri.

At the Mandan villages the expedition had access to the collective geographic knowledge of a large and established trade network. Native

Americans living on both sides of the Continental Divide had long traded and fought with other Indian nations along the Missouri's course. From several Native Americans Lewis and Clark heard of the Great Falls of the Missouri, a conspicuous site identifying the Missouri route to the Rocky Mountains.

The Missouri became the expedition's "river of destiny" because it had played a major role in Jefferson's confidential message to Congress. (See p. 17.) To gain support for his project from a Congress inclined to think it an unprofitable enterprise, he skillfully linked the proposed expedition to the establishment of additional Indian trading houses. Under the supervision of government agents, these trading houses, first established in the mid-1790s, exchanged manufactured goods for fur at fair prices. Policy required the agents to accept all fur irrespective of the current market value. That practice distinguished the Indian trading houses from fur company posts and ensured the goodwill of the Indians as well as their dependence on the government system. In addition, Jefferson argued, more trading houses would promote peace and thus save stationing an army to guarantee it.

THE ROUTE OF THE EXPEDITION

In the spring and summer of 1803, Lewis put in several months of hard work outfitting and provisioning the expedition. In May and June, the purveyor of public supplies received a draft of $1,000 and instructions from the War Department to assist Lewis by acquiring the requested supplies and articles, ranging from portable soup for explorers to blue beads for Indians.

Lewis began the expedition in Pittsburgh, where he had a fifty-five-foot keelboat adapted for use on the rivers, gathered supplies, and began to forge a crew that would be known as the Corps of Discovery. After a delay of six weeks for the boat to be finished and the Ohio River to recover from a drought, Lewis set off on August 31, 1803, in the keelboat with seven soldiers, three young men eager to join the group, and a pilot.

Nearly two months later, Lewis and his crew arrived in Clarksville, Indiana Territory, just below the falls of the Ohio River, where Captain William Clark awaited them. Clark, whom Lewis had invited to share his command, had gathered a group of woodsmen and hunters who came to be known as "the nine young men from Kentucky." Other members of the Corps of Discovery were picked up along the way down the Ohio River and from around St. Louis. The party then ascended the Mississippi and in December 1803 began building Camp Dubois on the south side of the Dubois or Wood River, on the Illinois side of the Mississippi. The captains labored hard for five winter months to turn a disparate group of men into a fit military unit.

On May 14, 1804, the date usually referred to as the start of the expedition, the Corps of Discovery left Camp Dubois for the arduous journey up the Missouri throughout the summer and well into the fall. The winter was spent at Fort Mandan, in log huts enclosed by a palisade, below the Mandan villages. Here Lewis and Clark selected the regular members of the Corps of Discovery, whose numbers clearly exceeded Jefferson's original estimate of ten or twelve men. Twenty-nine men formed the core of the group: the two captains, an interpreter, two French Canadian river men, Clark's black servant York, fourteen army regulars, and the nine young men from Kentucky. At the Mandan villages, Toussaint Charbonneau, a French Canadian interpreter, and his pregnant Shoshoni wife Sacagawea joined the group.

Before the expedition left the Mandan villages, on April 7, 1805, the two captains sent a party back to St. Louis consisting mostly of the keelboat crew under the command of Corporal Richard Warfington. The melting ice had now opened the Missouri for upstream travel, and the corps set out. In six canoes and two pirogues — large dugout canoes, one painted white with six oars and one red with seven — the explorers traveled past the junctures of the Missouri River with the Yellowstone and the Marias Rivers.

From June 22 to July 2, the explorers portaged the Great Falls of the Missouri. They cached the two pirogues, making hiding places to conceal the boats and unneeded supplies. After building two additional dugout canoes, they continued in eight canoes to the Three Forks of the Missouri, where they honored the leading men of the Jefferson administration. They named the north fork for Jefferson, the middle fork for Secretary of State James Madison, and the south fork for Secretary of the Treasury Albert Gallatin and started ascending the Jefferson River on July 30.

On August 17 the expedition reached the navigable limits of the Missouri. With Sacagawea's help they acquired crucial pack and riding horses from the long-sought Shoshoni, the first Indian nation they encountered since leaving the Mandan villages four months earlier. For the crossing of the Rocky Mountains the explorers followed Shoshoni advice: They first moved north along the Lemhi River and the north fork of the Salmon River and then turned west onto the Lolo Trail at Travelers Rest, about ten miles south of present-day Missoula, Montana; with the help of a Shoshoni guide, they struggled for eleven days as they crossed the rugged Bitterroot Mountains.

The 150-mile ordeal from the Bitterroot Valley in western Montana to the foot of the mountains on the Kooskooske River in present-day Idaho was a devastating experience for the expedition. Once back to river travel, Lewis and Clark entrusted their horses to members of the Nez Perce nation who had helped restore the health and morale of the corps, and in five newly built dugout canoes the explorers descended the Kooskooske, Snake, and Columbia Rivers to the Pacific, which they reached in November 1805.

On the south side of the Columbia, the Corps of Discovery built winter quarters, which the captains called Fort Clatsop after a nearby Indian nation. Game became scarce, and after a soggy winter devoted to repairing outfits, replenishing the salt supply, updating journals, and collecting information about the country and its inhabitants, they started their homeward journey on March 26, 1806. They retraced their Columbia route, and then with the help of the Walla Walla Indians took a shortcut overland to the Nez Perce. The Indians urged the explorers to wait until most of the snow in the Bitterroots had melted before tackling the Lolo Trail again.

The captains established camp on the east bank of the Kooskooske River. They did not name the camp, but almost a century later Elliott Coues, using the Lewis and Clark papers for a new edition of Biddle's *History*, called the site Camp Chopunnish, after one of the names Lewis and Clark used for the Nez Perce, and this name has been generally adopted.[5] The explorers stayed there from May 14 to June 10, 1806, longer than anywhere else except Fort Mandan and Fort Clatsop. When the snow began to melt, with the help of the Nez Perce the explorers recrossed the Bitterroots on the Lolo Trail to Travelers Rest. There on July 3 the expedition broke up into several groups to check on possible alternate routes and to retrieve the cached supplies and canoes along the trail.

With nine men Lewis went cross-country to the Falls of the Missouri, where he left six of them and proceeded with the other three to the headwaters of the Marias to scout its potential as a fur trading route. They then turned southeast to join the others descending the Missouri. Meanwhile, Clark followed the advice of Sacagawea who was again on familiar ground

---

[5] Elliott Coues, ed., *History of the Expedition under the Command of Lewis and Clark,* 4 vols. (New York: Francis P. Harper, 1893), 3:1010 n. 2.

and led the other group on a shorter route to the Three Forks of the Missouri. There Sergeant John Ordway took a contingent of men by canoe to the Great Falls of the Missouri. Clark with another detachment headed to the Yellowstone and descended the river to its confluence with the Missouri. A few miles below that point, the entire Corps of Discovery was reunited on August 12, 1806. The explorers stopped at the Mandan villages long enough to persuade one of the chiefs to return with them for a visit to the president of the United States. Jefferson had suggested this in his original instructions to Lewis; undoubtedly he hoped to impress the chiefs with the splendor of civilization, as the British colonial governments had tried when they brought Cherokee and Iroquois chiefs to London. With the accompanying chief, the expedition hurried down the Missouri and returned to St. Louis on September 23, 1806.

JEFFERSON'S PLAN

Even before the Louisiana Purchase made access to the Northwest easier, President Thomas Jefferson had requested congressional support for an expedition to the Pacific coast. In a confidential message to Congress in January 1803, the president showed his mastery of practical politics, emphasizing the commercial advantages of a waterway through the continent and only incidentally the advance of geographic knowledge. The growth of commerce with Indians, he stressed, would help traders who had suffered losses through the expansion of the government's Indian trading house system. It would give Native Americans access to factory goods. These would lure Indians from the hunt to the farm, open up their former hunting grounds to white settlers, and enable Native Americans to share the benefits of an enlightened United States government.

Jefferson's instructions to Lewis contain specific orders about the route, suggestions on attitudes and actions the explorers should adopt toward Europeans as well as Native Americans, and information on what specimens and information they should gather. The document shares several subjects with the congressional message: the aims of peacefully bringing Native Americans into white society through commerce and of considering peace between Indian nations and a thorough knowledge of their cultures as prerequisites for commerce. Jefferson anticipates that early contacts will lead to more complex relations that will be worked out during visits of Indian chiefs to Washington. The broad scope of the instructions emphasizes the president's determination to explore the

West, his knowledge of geography and science, his faith in Lewis, and his concern about the safety of the corps.

President Jefferson's Secret Message to Congress

JANUARY 18, 1803.

Gentlemen of the Senate and of the House of Representatives: As the continuance of the act for establishing trading houses with the Indian tribes will be under the consideration of the Legislature at its present session, I think it my duty to communicate the views which have guided me in the execution of that act, in order that you may decide on the policy of continuing it in the present or any other form, or discontinue it altogether if that shall, on the whole, seem most for the public good.

The Indian tribes residing within the limits of the United States have for a considerable time been growing more and more uneasy at the constant diminution of the territory they occupy, although effected by their own voluntary sales, and the policy has long been gaining strength with them of refusing absolutely all further sale on any conditions, insomuch that at this time it hazards their friendship and excites dangerous jealousies and perturbations in their minds to make any overture for the purchase of the smallest portions of their land. A very few tribes only are not yet obstinately in these dispositions. In order peaceable to counteract this policy of theirs and to provide an extension of territory which the rapid increase of our numbers will call for, two measures are deemed expedient. First. To encourage them to abandon hunting, to apply to the raising stock, to agriculture, and domestic manufacture, and thereby prove to themselves that less land and labor will maintain them in this better than in their former mode of living. The extensive forests necessary in the hunting life will then become useless, and they will see advantage in exchanging them for the means of improving their farms and of increasing their domestic comforts. Secondly. To multiply trading houses among

James D. Richardson, *Messages and Papers of the Presidents, 1789–1897,* 10 vols. (Washington, D.C.: GPO, 1896–99), 1:352–54, reprinted in Reuben Gold Thwaites, ed., *Original Journals of the Lewis and Clark Expedition, 1804–1806,* 8 vols. (New York: Dodd, Mead, 1904), 7:206–09.

them, and place within their reach those things which will contribute more to their domestic comfort than the possession of extensive but uncultivated wilds. Experience and reflection will develop to them the wisdom of exchanging what they can spare and we want for what we can spare and they want. In leading them thus to agriculture, to manufactures, and civilization; in bringing together their and our sentiments, and in preparing them ultimately to participate in the benefits of our Government, I trust and believe we are acting for their greatest good. At these trading houses we have pursued the principles of the act of Congress which directs that the commerce shall be carried on liberally, and requires only that the capital stock shall not be diminished. We consequently undersell private traders, foreign and domestic, drive them from the competition, and thus, with the good will of the Indians, rid ourselves of a description of men who are constantly endeavoring to excite in the Indian mind suspicions, fears, and irritations toward us. A letter now enclosed shows the effect of our competition on the operations of the traders, while the Indians, perceiving the advantage of purchasing from us, are soliciting generally our establishment of trading houses among them. In one quarter this is particularly interesting. The Legislature, reflecting on the late occurrences on the Mississippi, must be sensible how desirable it is to possess a respectable breadth of country on that river, from our southern limit to the Illinois, at least, so that we may present as firm a front on that as on our eastern border. We possess what is below the Yazoo, and can probably acquire a certain breadth from the Illinois and Wabash to the Ohio; but between the Ohio and Yazoo the country all belongs to the Chickasaws, the most friendly tribe within our limits, but the most decided against the alienation of lands. The portion of their country most important for us is exactly that which they do not inhabit. Their settlements are not on the Mississippi, but in the interior country. They have lately shown a desire to become agricultural, and this leads to the desire of buying implements and comforts. In the strengthening and gratifying of these wants I see the only prospect of planting on the Mississippi itself the means of its own safety. Duty has required me to submit these views to the judgement of the Legislature, but as their disclosure might embarrass and defeat their effect, they are committed to the special confidence of the two Houses.

While the extension of the public commerce among the Indian tribes may deprive of that source of profit such of our citizens as are engaged in it, it might be worthy the attention of Congress in their care of individual as well as of the general interest to point in another direction the enterprise of these citizens, as profitably for themselves and more usefully for the public. The river Missouri and the Indians inhabiting it are not as well known as is rendered desirable by their connection with the Mississippi, and consequently with us. It is, however, understood that the country on that river is inhabited by numerous tribes, who furnish great supplies of furs and peltry to the trade of another nation, carried on in a high latitude through an infinite number of portages and lakes shut up by ice through a long season. The commerce on that line could bear no competition with that of the Missouri, traversing a moderate climate, offering, according to the best accounts, a continued navigation from its source, and possibly with a single portage from the Western Ocean, and finding to the Atlantic a choice of channels through the Illinois or Wabash, the Lakes and Hudson, through the Ohio and Susquehanna, or Potomac or James rivers, and through the Tennessee and Savannah rivers. An intelligent officer, with ten or twelve chosen men, fit for the enterprise and willing to undertake it, taken from our posts where they may be spared without inconvenience, might explore the whole line, even to the Western Ocean, have conferences with the natives on the subject of commercial intercourse, get admission among them for our traders as others are admitted, agree on convenient deposits for an interchange of articles, and return with the information acquired in the course of two summers. Their arms and accouterments, some instruments of observation, and light and cheap presents for the Indians would be all the apparatus they could carry, and with an expectation of a soldier's portion of land on their return would constitute the whole expense. Their pay would be going on whether here or there. While other civilized nations have encountered great expense to enlarge the boundaries of knowledge by undertaking voyages of discovery, and for other literary purposes, in various parts and directions, our nation seems to owe to the same object, as well as to its own interests, to explore this the only line of easy communication across the continent, and so directly traversing our own part of it. The interests of commerce place the principal object within the constitutional powers and care of Congress, and that it should incidentally advance the geographical knowledge of our own continent can not but be an additional gratification. The nation claiming the territory, regarding this as a literary pursuit, which it is in the habit of permitting within its dominions, would not be disposed to view it with jealousy, even if the expiring state of its interests there did not render it a matter of indifference. The appropriation of $2,500 "for the purpose of extending the external commerce of the United States," while understood and considered by the Executive as giving the legislative sanction, would cover the undertaking from notice and prevent the obstructions which interested individuals might otherwise previously prepare in its way.

TH: JEFFERSON.

Jefferson's Instructions to Lewis

JUNE 20, 1803

To Meriwether Lewis, esquire, Captain of the 1ˢᵗ regiment of infantry of the United States of America: Your situation as Secretary of the President of the United States has made you acquainted with the objects of my confidential message of Jan. 18, 1803, to the legislature. . . . you are appointed to carry them into execution.

Instruments for ascertaining by celestial observations the geography of the country thro' which you will pass, have already been provided. light articles for barter, & presents among the Indians, arms for your attendants, say for from 10 to 12 men, boats, tents, & other travelling apparatus, with ammunition, medicine, surgical instruments & provisions you will have prepared with such aids as the Secretary at War can yield in his department; & from him also you will recieve authority to engage among our troops, by voluntary agreement, the number of attendants above mentioned, over whom you, as their commanding officer are invested with all the powers the laws give in such a case. . . .

Your mission has been communicated to the Ministers here from France, Spain & Great Britain, and through them to their governments: and such assurances given them as to it's objects as we trust will satisfy them. the country of Louisiana having been ceded by Spain to France, the passport you have from the Minister of France, the representative of the present sovereign of the country, will be a protection with all it's subjects: And that from the Minister of England will entitle you to the friendly aid of any traders of that allegiance with whom you may happen to meet.

The object of your mission is to explore the Missouri river, & such principal stream of it, as, by it's course & communication with the waters of the Pacific Ocean, may offer the most direct & practicable water communication across this continent, for the purposes of commerce.

From original manuscript in Bureau of Rolls, *Jefferson Papers*, ser. 1, vol. 9, doc. 269, reprinted in Thwaites, *Original Journals of the Lewis and Clark Expedition*, 7:247–52.

Beginning at the mouth of the Missouri, you will take observations of latitude & longitude, at all remarkable points on the river, & especially at the mouths of rivers, at rapids, at islands & other places & objects distinguished by such natural marks & characters of a durable kind, as that they may with certainty be recognized hereafter. . . .

The interesting points of the portage between the heads of the Missouri & the water offering the best communication with the Pacific Ocean should also be fixed by observation, & the course of that water to the ocean, in the same manner as that of the Missouri.

Your observations are to be taken with great pains & accuracy, to be entered distinctly, & intelligibly for others as well as yourself, to comprehend all the elements necessary, with the aid of the usual tables, to fix the latitude and longitude of the places at which they were taken, & are to be rendered to the war office, for the purpose of having the calculations made concurrently by proper persons within the U.S. several copies of these, as well as your other notes, should be made at leisure times & put into the care of the most trustworthy of your attendants, to guard by multiplying them, against the accidental losses to which they will be exposed. a further guard would be that one of these copies be written on the paper of the birch, as less liable to injury from damp than common paper.

The commerce which may be carried on with the people inhabiting the line you will pursue, renders a knoledge of these people important. you will therefore endeavor to make yourself acquainted, as far as a diligent pursuit of your journey shall admit,

with the names of the nations & their numbers;
the extent & limits of their possessions;
their relations with other tribes or nations;
their language, traditions, monuments;
their ordinary occupations in agriculture, fishing, hunting, war,
   arts, & the implements for these;
their food, clothing, & domestic accomodations;
the diseases prevalent among them, & the remedies they use;
moral & physical circumstances which distinguish them from the
   tribes we know;
peculiarities in their laws, customs & dispositions;
and articles of commerce they may need or furnish, & to what extent.

And considering the interest which every nation has in extending & strengthening the authority of reason & justice among the people around them, it will be useful to acquire what knolege you can of the state of morality, religion & information among them, as it may better enable those who endeavor to civilize & instruct them, to adapt their measures to the existing notions & practises of those on whom they are to operate. Other object worthy of notice will be

the soil & face of the country, it's growth & vegetable productions; especially those not of the U.S.

the animals of the country generally, & especially those not known in the U.S.

the remains and accounts of any which may deemed rare or extinct;

the mineral productions of every kind; but more particularly metals, limestone, pit coal & saltpetre; salines & mineral waters, noting the temperature of the last, & such circumstances as may indicate their character.

Volcanic appearances.

climate as characterized by the thermometer, by the proportion of rainy, cloudy & clear days, by lightening, hail, snow, ice, by the access & recess of frost, by the winds prevailing at different seasons, the dates at which particular plants put forth or lose their flowers, or leaf, times of appearance of particular birds, reptiles or insects.

Altho' your route will be along the channel of the Missouri, yet you will endeavor to inform yourself, by inquiry, of the character & extent of the country watered by it's branches, & especially on it's Southern side. the North river or Rio Bravo which runs into the gulph of Mexico, and the North river, or Rio colorado, which runs into the gulph of California, are understood to be the principal streams heading opposite to the waters of the Missouri, and running Southwardly. whether the dividing grounds between the Missouri & them are mountains or flatlands, what are their distance from the Missouri, the character of the intermediate country, & the people inhabiting it, are worthy of particular enquiry. The Northern waters of the Missouri are less to be enquired after, because they have been ascertained to a considerable degree, and are still in a course of ascertainment by English traders & travellers. but if you can learn anything certain of the most Northern source of the Missisipi, & of it's position relative to the lake of the woods, it will be interesting to us. some account too of the path of the Canadian traders from the Missisipi, at the mouth of the Ouisconsin river, to where it strikes the Missouri and of the soil & rivers in it's course, is desireable.

In all your intercourse with the natives treat them in the most friendly & conciliatory manner which their own conduct will admit; allay all jealousies as to the object of your journey, satisfy them of it's innocence, make them acquainted with the position, extent, character, peaceable &

commercial dispositions of the U. S. of our wish to be neighborly, friendly & useful to them, & of our dispositions to a commercial intercourse with them; confer with them on the points most convenient as mutual emporiums, & the articles of most desireable interchange for them & us. if a few of their influential chiefs, within practicable distance, wish to visit us, arrange such a visit with them, and furnish them with authority to call on our officers, on their entering the U. S. to have them conveyed to this place at public expence. if any of them should wish to have some of their young people brought up with us, & taught such arts as may be useful to them, we will receive, instruct & take care of them. such a mission, whether of influential chiefs, or of young people, would give some security to your own party. carry with you some matter of the kine-pox,[1] inform those of them with whom you may be of it's efficacy as a preservative from the small-pox; and instruct & incourage them in the use of it. this may be especially done wherever you winter.

As it is impossible for us to foresee in what manner you will be recieved by those people, whether with hospitality or hostility, so is it impossible to prescribe the exact degree of perseverance with which you are to pursue your journey. we value too much the lives of citizens to offer them to probably destruction. your numbers will be sufficient to secure you against the unauthorised opposition of individuals, or of small parties: but if a superior force, authorised or not authorised, by a nation, should be arrayed against your further passage, & inflexibly determined to arrest it, you must decline it's further pursuit, and return. in the loss of yourselves, we should lose also the information you will have acquired. by returning safely with that, you may enable us to renew the essay with better calculated means. to your own discretion therefore must be left the degree of danger you may risk, & the point at which you should decline, only saying we wish you to err on the side of your safety, & bring back your party safe, even if it be with less information. . . .

Should you reach the Pacific ocean . . . inform yourself of the circumstances which may decide whether the furs of those parts may not be collected as advantageously at the head of the Missouri (convenient as is supposed to the waters of the Colorado & Oregon or Columbia) as at Nootka sound or any other point of that coast; & that trade be consequently conducted through the Missouri & U. S. more beneficially than by the circumnavigation now practised.

On your arrival on that coast endeavor to learn if there be any port within your reach frequented by the sea-vessels of any nation, and to send

---

[1]Cowpox (Jefferson used the Scottish noun *kine* for cattle), a serum used as vaccine against smallpox.

two of your trusty people back by sea, in such way as shall appear practicable, with a copy of your notes. and should you be of opinion that the return of your party by the way they went will be eminently dangerous, then ship the whole, & return by sea by way of Cape Horn or the Cape of good Hope, as you shall be able. as you will be without money, clothes or provisions, you must endeavor to use the credit of the U. S. to obtain them; for which purpose open letters of credit shall be furnished you authorising you to draw on the Executive of the U. S. or any of its officers in any part of the world. . . .

Should you find it safe to return by the way you go, after sending two of your party round by sea, or with your whole party, if no conveyance by sea can be found, do so; making such observations on your return as may serve to supply, correct or confirm those made on your outward journey.

In re-entering the U. S. and reaching a place of safety, discharge any of your attendants who may desire & deserve it, procuring for them immediate paiment of all arrears of pay & cloathing which may have incurred since their departure; & assure them that they shall be recommended to the liberality of the legislature for the grant of a soldier's portion of land each, as proposed in my message to Congress & repair yourself with your papers to the seat of government. . . .

TH. JEFFERSON
Pr. U S. of America

THE LOUISIANA AFFAIR

The Louisiana Purchase treaty, dated April 30, 1803, in Paris, arrived in Washington on July 14, 1803. The document had far-reaching consequences for the expedition and gave Jefferson another chance to voice his commercial interest in the Columbia River. He also sent Lewis an excerpt of a French naturalist's letters that stressed the preeminent role of a settlement at the mouth of the Columbia for global commerce. The possibilities pleased Jefferson and his French correspondent because they could potentially damage the British fur trade. A settlement could control the flow of far western fur to China and Europe, enabling Americans to outdo their British competitors, who would have to pay duties or depend on inferior routes.

Jefferson anticipated a delay in the transfer of Louisiana, while Spanish officials observed diplomatic etiquette and placed the territory briefly into the hands of French representatives before turning it over to American officers. A month after the United States took possession of New Orleans on December 20, 1803, Jefferson instructed Lewis to notify the

Louisiana Indians of the transfer of authority and of the Americans' intention to establish commercial relations with them.

Jefferson to Lewis

JULY 15, 1803.

DEAR SIR: . . . last night . . . we recieved the treaty from Paris ceding Louisiana according to the bounds to which France had a right. price 11¼ millions of Dollars, besides paying certain debts of France to our citizens which will be from 1, to 4, millions. I received also from M.ʳ La Cepede,[1] at Paris, to whom I had mentioned your intended expedition a letter of which the following is an extract. " M.ʳ Broughton, one of the companions of Mr. Vancouver went up Columbia River 100 miles, in December 1792. he stopped at a point which he named Vancouver. . . . here the river Columbia is still a quarter of a mile wide & from 12 to 36 feet deep. It is far then to it's head. . . . if your nation can establish an easy communication by rivers, canals & short portages between N. York for example & the city (they were building) or (to be built) (for the badness of the writing makes it uncertain which is meant, but probably the last) at the mouth of the Columbia, what a route for the commerce of Europe, Asia & America." Accept my affectionate salutations.

TH. JEFFERSON.

[1]Bernard Germain Etienne de Laville, Comte de Lacépède, a distinguished French naturalist. [Thwaites's note.]

From original manuscript in Bureau of Rolls, *Jefferson Papers,* ser. 2, vol. 51, doc. 115, reprinted in Thwaites, *Original Journals of the Lewis and Clark Expedition,* 7:258.

Jefferson to Lewis

NOVEMBER 16, 1803.

DEAR SIR: . . . I enclose . . . copies of the treaties for Louisiana. . . . orders went from hence signed by the King of Spain & the first Consul of France, so as to arrive at Natchez yesterday evening and we expect the delivery

From original manuscript in Bureau of Rolls, *Jefferson Papers,* ser. 1, vol. 9, doc. 305, reprinted in Thwaites, *Original Journals of the Lewis and Clark Expedition,* 7:281–82.

of the province at New Orleans will take place about the close of the ensuing week, say about the 25th inst. . . . at the moment of delivering over the posts in the vicinity of N. Orleans, orders will be dispatched from thence to those in Upper Louisiana to evacuate & to deliver them immediately. you can judge better than I can when they may be expected to arrive at these posts, considering how much you have been detained by low waters, how late it will be before you can leave Cahokia, how little progress up the Missouri you can make before the freezing of the river; that your winter might be passed in gaining much information by making Cahokia or Kaskaskia your head quarters, & going to S! Louis & the other Spanish posts that your stores &ᶜ would thereby be spared for the winter, *as your men would draw their military rations,* all danger of Spanish opposition avoided. we are strongly of the opinion here that you had better not enter the Missouri until the spring, but as you have a view of all circumstances on the spot, we do not pretend to enjoin it, but leave it to your own judgment in which we have entire confidence. . . . By having mr. Clarke with you we consider the expedition double manned, & therefore the less liable to failure. . . .

The votes of both houses on ratifying and carrying the treaties into execution have been precisely party votes. . . .

TH. JEFFERSON.

Jefferson to Lewis

JANUARY 22, 1804

DEAR SIR: . . . N. Orleans was delivered to us on the 20th of Dec. and our garrisons & government established there. the order for the delivery of the Upper posts were to leave N. Orleans on the 28th and we presume all those posts will be occupied by our troops by the last day of the present month. when your instructions were penned, this new position was not so authentically known as to effect the complection of your instructions. being now become sovereigns of the country, without however any diminution of the Indian rights of occupancy we are authorised to propose to them in direct terms the institution of commerce with them. it will now be proper you should inform those through whose country you

From original manuscript in Bureau of Rolls, *Jefferson Papers,* ser. 1, vol. 10, doc. 8, reprinted in Thwaites, *Original Journals of the Lewis and Clark Expedition,* 7:292–93.

will pass, or whom you may meet, that their late fathers, the Spaniards have agreed to withdraw all their troops from all the waters & country of the Missisipi and Missouri, that they have surrendered to us all their subjects Spanish and French settled there, and all their posts & lands: that henceforward we become their fathers and friends, and that we shall endeavor that they shall have no cause to lament the change: that we have sent you to enquire into the nature of the country & the nations inhabiting it, to know at what places and times we must establish stores of goods among them, to exchange for their peltries: that as soon as you return with the necessary information we shall prepare supplies of goods and persons to carry them and make the proper establishments: that in the meantime, the same traders who reside among or visit them, and who are now a part of us, will continue to supply them as usual: that we shall endeavor to become acquainted with them as soon as possible and that they will find in us faithful friends and protectors. . . .

TH. JEFFERSON.

1

The Two Captains

Jefferson chose fellow Virginian Meriwether Lewis as the leader of the expedition only after he failed to find a scientist with both wilderness experience and an ability to lead men. Lewis had been his private secretary since the spring of 1801 and was familiar with Jefferson's objectives for the expedition. As private secretary, however, Lewis served primarily as Jefferson's liaison to the army. "Brave, prudent, habituated to the woods, & familiar with Indian manners and character," Jefferson described him in a letter to the Philadelphia physician Benjamin Rush in February 1803. "He is not regularly educated," Jefferson added, "but he possesses a great mass of regular observation on all the subjects of nature which present themselves here, & will therefore readily select those only in his new route which shall be new."[1]

To prepare him for the rigors of scientific observation, Jefferson introduced Lewis to the scientific elite, members of the American Philosophical Society in Philadelphia. They familiarized Lewis with some aspects of medicine, mathematics, and astronomy and taught him to use the sextant and the chronometer to observe latitude and longitude and to record his position during the expedition.

Lewis was born in Albemarle County in 1774 as a neighbor of the Jeffersons and other distinguished families. During the Whiskey Rebellion in 1794, Lewis joined the militia and served in western Maryland and Pennsylvania. In May of the following year he enlisted in the regular army but "fought neither Indian nor white man."[2] He was present as an ensign when General Anthony Wayne signed the Treaty of Greenville in August 1795, ending his campaign against the major Indian nations north of the Ohio River. The only "West" Lewis actually saw were the army forts of the Ohio Valley.

[1]Thomas Jefferson to Dr. Benjamin Rush, February 28, 1803, Thwaites, *Original Journals of the Lewis and Clark Expedition*, 7:211.
[2]Donald Jackson, *Thomas Jefferson and the Stony Mountains* (Urbana: University of Illinois Press, 1981), 118.

Lewis's military career proved useful to Jefferson when he became the president's private secretary. From his personal knowledge of the officer corps Lewis advised Jefferson on how to retain competent officers across party lines when he reduced the army as he had promised during the presidential campaign of 1800. Lewis's close association with Jefferson lasted through the expedition and his brief service as governor of the territory of Louisiana after his return from the Pacific in 1806. Sometime after that, Lewis seemed to lose some of the traits that had long characterized him, particularly his sense of mission, of pursuing a noble goal despite the personal cost. He engaged increasingly in land speculation, political fighting, and hard drinking; after much emotional turmoil, he committed suicide in 1809. Jefferson's memoir of Lewis, written in August 1813 as the introduction to Biddle's *History,* attests to Jefferson's lasting esteem and the durability of his friendship with Lewis:

> Of courage undaunted; possessing a firmness and perseverance of purpose which nothing but impossibilities could divert from its direction; careful as a father of those committed to his charge, yet steady in the maintenance of order and discipline; intimate with the Indian character, customs, and principles; habituated to the hunting life; guarded, by exact observation of the vegetables and animals of his own country, against losing time in the description of objects already possessed; honest, disinterested, and liberal, of sound understanding and fidelity to truth so scrupulous that whatever he should report would be as certain as if seen by ourselves — with all these qualifications, as if selected and implanted by nature in one body for this express purpose, I could have no hesitation in confiding the enterprise to him.[3]

When Lewis proposed co-leadership of the expedition to William Clark, friendship reinforced by mutual respect determined his choice. Clark, born in 1770 in Caroline County, Virginia, grew up in Kentucky where his family had moved after the Revolutionary War. At age nineteen he fought against the Indians north of the Ohio River, and in 1792 he was commissioned a lieutenant of infantry. Two years later he fought in the battle of Fallen Timbers, where General Wayne defeated the so-called northern Indians of the Ohio Valley. Clark was noted for his courage and resourcefulness during his four-year service in the Western Army. The Fallen Timbers campaign forged Lewis's friendship with Clark, who was briefly his commanding officer. In 1796 Clark retired from the army and settled with his family in Kentucky, where he sought to straighten out the tangled financial affairs of his older brother George Rogers Clark.

[3]Thwaites, *Original Journals of the Lewis and Clark Expedition,* 1: xxvi.

In July 1803, Clark accepted Lewis's proposal to join him in the western expedition. (See p. 35.) After the return of the expedition, Clark resigned from the army, and Jefferson appointed him brigadier general of militia for Louisiana Territory and superintendent for Indian affairs at St. Louis. He died in St. Louis in 1838.

In the course of the intervening two hundred years, the personalities of Meriwether Lewis and William Clark have been almost fused into one. An attempt to pull them apart would be pedantic if it were to stereotype one captain or the other as leader, thinker, river man, physician, Indian expert, or scout. Their journals show that both shared many talents and tasks.

When James Kendall Hosmer, the author and librarian, published his edition of Biddle's *History* in 1902, he referred to Lewis and Clark as the "Dioscuri of American tradition," alluding to Castor and Pollux, the inseparable heroes of Greek and Roman mythology. Among their many exploits, they took part in the expedition of the Argonauts, the Greek heroes who sailed to Colchis on the Black Sea to seek the Golden Fleece. The image appealed to a generation of Americans that still recognized the Founding Fathers' affinity for antiquity and the Greek and Roman classics. The story of two brothers who side by side surmounted their trials and helped to bring the Golden Fleece to Greece seemed to evoke the two captains who shared equally in the success of an expedition opening a new world to Americans.

Lewis himself created and sustained the view of the two captains as co-leaders. When Clark agreed to join the expedition, Lewis and Jefferson promised him a captaincy, the same rank as Lewis's. (See p. 35.) The army, however, had no opening in that rank, and his commission designated Clark a second lieutenant of artillery. Lewis insisted firmly that Clark would nevertheless be in every respect his equal and eased his disappointment.

"I did not think myself very well treated," Clark recalled on August 15, 1811, in a letter to Biddle, who had raised the issue when writing his *History,* "as I did not get the appointment promised to me." Clark assured Biddle that he himself had never spoken about the matter "and must request you not to mention my disappointment & the cause to any one. ... Be so good," Clark concluded his explanation, "as to place me on equal footing with Cap. Lewis in every point of view without exposing any thing which might have taken place or even mentioning the commission at all."[4]

---

[4]William Clark to Nicholas Biddle, August 15, 1811, Donald Jackson, ed., *Letters of the Lewis and Clark Expedition, with Related Documents, 1783–1854,* 2nd ed., 2 vols. (Urbana: University of Illinois Press, 1978), 2:571, 572.

Lewis ignored the official rank and introduced Clark as captain and always shared responsibility equally. He thus forged a partnership that was fundamental to the cohesion of the expedition and ultimately to its success.

Theirs was more than an ordinary partnership that might bring two unlike men together in pursuit of a shared goal. Their success rested on a relationship that yielded results far greater than those each captain might have achieved alone. Before and after the expedition, the differences were noticeable, but during the two years, four months, and ten days of exploration, their partnership in discovery subsumed those distinctions.

Their journals, however, reveal that they looked at the world with quite different eyes. Lewis saw it as an artist, Clark as a craftsman. Equally drawn to the rivers they traveled, Lewis experimented with his iron boat while Clark built canoes. In their responses to Jefferson's questions about Native Americans, Lewis showed a strong interest in Indian material culture while Clark dealt extensively with the political structure of the Indian nations. Lewis and Clark also had considerable differences in physical appearance. The painter and naturalist Charles Willson Peale portrayed both men: Lewis in half profile, aloof and distant, his eyes bypassing the viewer and gazing into space; Clark facing the onlooker directly, self-assured and confident, the complement of his cocaptain.[5]

Yet the minds of both men were geared to action as well as to reflection. And both partners reacted well in emergencies; they could unhesitatingly replace each other when the situation demanded it.

Disagreements seemed to have been rarely recorded; they involved only minor matters. Referring to them is useful, however, because they show distinctions between the captains. In the few times the two explorers expressed differences, it usually appeared that Clark voiced views or made decisions with too little forethought.

On April 27, 1805, at the confluence of the Yellowstone and Missouri Rivers, Clark considered the "lower extremity of the low plane" close to both rivers as the best place for a trading post. Lewis, however, thought "it reather too low to venture a permanent establishment . . . at any considerable expense; for so capricious and versatile are these rivers, that it is difficult to say how long it will be, untill they direct the force of their currents against this narrow part of the low plain, which when they do must shortly yeald to their influence." In another instance, when Clark administered "a dose of tartar emetic," a compound of potassium, antimony, carbon, hydrogen, and oxygen, to his sick servant York on July 7,

---

[5]Reproductions of the portraits can be found in ibid., vol. 1, between 132 and 133.

1805, Lewis considered it "a discription of medecine that I never have recourse to in my practice except in cases of the intermittent fever."

Inspired by Lewis's sense of mission, the two captains felt themselves pledged to a major undertaking for the benefit of humankind. When they set off from Fort Mandan on April 7, 1805, up the Missouri River, they compared their six small canoes and two pirogues to the fleets of Columbus and Captain Cook. Their little flotilla did not seem quite so respectable, Lewis reflected, but was "still viewed by us with as much pleasure as those deservedly famed adventurers ever beheld theirs."

Adventure was a key word for an understanding of the explorers' sense of mission. Like their role models, they hoped that their destiny would lead them to discover inexhaustible treasures for their nation and people. The magnitude of the task, in their eyes, justified comparisons with Columbus and Cook. They were "now about to penetrate a country at least two thousand miles in width," Lewis remarked, "on which the foot of civilized man had never trodden." The euphoria of the moment swept him away. "Entertaining as I do, the most confident hope of succeeding in a voyage which had formed a darling project of mine for the last ten years"—Lewis evidently dated his commitment to the enterprise back to the year he joined the army—"I could but esteem this moment of my departure as among the most happy of my life."

Lewis and Clark found their companions equal to the promise of the momentous day. Unyielding necessity and military discipline had unified the unruly lot of men they had gathered during the winter of 1803–04. The captains had turned a mixed collection of soldiers, backwoodsmen, and guides into an extraordinary unit that measured up to their expectations. The party "was in excellent health and sperits, zealously attached to the enterprise, and anxious to proceed," Lewis noted, concluding, "Not a whisper of murmur or discontent to be heard among them, but all act in unison, and with the most perfect harmony."

Remembering the ideals of the expedition lifted Clark's spirit even as he recognized the ordeal ahead when he first saw the Rocky Mountains on May 26, 1805. What follows are Lewis's words, but Clark copied them so faithfully into his journal that one can assume they express his feelings, too, only more eloquently put: "I felt a secret pleasure in finding myself so near to the head of the heretofore conceived boundless Missouri." His words anticipated the great moment by about three months, but the emotional reference was immediately qualified by a healthy measure of realism: "When I reflected on the difficulties which this snowey barrier would most probably throw in my way to the Pacific Ocean, and the sufferings and hardships of my self and the party in them, it in some measure counterbalanced the joy I had felt in the first moments in which I gazed on them." His faith in the expedition's objectives saved him from despondency at the arduous prospect: "As I always held it little Short of criminality to anticipate evils," he resolved, "I will allow it to be a good comfortable road until I am compelled to believe otherwise."

The unexpected hardships of the journey heightened Lewis's dedication to the mission. His thirty-second birthday provoked him to an eloquent statement about the spirit that guided him. The birthday came after the corps had endured the subzero winter of the Mandan villages, portaged the Great Falls of the Missouri, and made contact with the Shoshoni Indians. "I reflected that I had done little, very little indeed, to further the happiness of the human race, or to advance the information of the succeeding generation," Lewis admitted on August 18, 1805. "I viewed with regret the many hours I had spent in indolence," he added dejectedly, "and now soarly feel the want of that information which those hours would have given me had they been judiciously expanded." Overcoming the gloom, he rallied his spirits by reminding himself that the past cannot be recalled and "resolved in future to redouble my exertions and . . . to live *for mankind,* as I have heretofore lived *for myself.*"

As a tribute to Lewis's strength and perseverance, he was able to cover and control some very troubled emotions. His journal entries reveal him as a man of sudden mood changes who slipped quickly from euphoria to gloom. Eloquence and silence marked his behavior and speech. Despite his mercurial temper, the success of the expedition attested to his admirable skills as a leader. He kept his worries and insecurities hidden from the corps, exposing his fallibility in journal entries that read like soliloquies. The complexity of his personality coupled with the strength of his will allowed him to be both leader *and* partner in the expedition.

Lewis acquitted himself superbly in a vital encounter with the Shoshoni, the first Indians the expedition had seen in three months and the only possible source of horses for crossing the Rockies. After the first contact with Lewis, the Shoshoni became apprehensive and feared an ambush, but Lewis acted swiftly and decisively to counter their suspicion, entrusting his gun to the Shoshoni chief Cameahwait, making himself a hostage, and pledging the peaceful aims of the expedition. (See p. 38.) In other dangerous situations Lewis had the ability to survive by distancing himself mentally from his plight. In a hunting accident he used willpower to distract himself from a gunshot wound. In great pain, he devoted a journal entry not to his condition but to the description of a nearby cherry tree. (See p. 40.)

Clark's writing, as has often been observed, differs from Lewis's elegant prose, but during periods when Lewis was not writing and Clark could not copy him, Clark, with unflagging realism, recorded the events of the day and expressed feelings shared by the others. "The squar gave me a piece of bread made of flour which She had reserved for her child and carefully Kept untill this time, which has unfortunately got wet, and a little Sour," Clark wrote on November 30, 1805. "This bread I eate with great satisfaction, it being the only mouthfull I had tasted for Several months."

Clark's report of an event or his description of a landscape assembled so many facts that a reader can easily reconstruct the scene and action. Sometimes Clark's phrases are compact and his words are succinct, but the low-key language is expressive in the laconic manner of country folk gathered around a stove. The sheer number of sights he had never seen or heard of frequently forced Clark to interrupt his favorite linear narrative of daily events and insert detailed descriptions of unknown natural phenomena.

Clark also paused in his methodical accounts to relate incidents where human feeling transcended differences of culture; clearly, he did not feel these were out of place in a chronicle of the expedition. On his way back to Fort Clatsop with a party carrying blubber and oil from a beached whale, on January 9, 1806, Clark overtook several Indians with similar loads. The pack of a woman descending a steep cliff slipped off her back. Clark took her pack, which was so heavy that he could barely carry it, until she got her footing again. A little later, he and his party were so exhausted they decided to camp overnight. But the Indians shouldered their load and "proceeded on." His acknowledgment of the affinity of the two groups is evident in his use of the words *proceeded on*— the very words usually used in the journals to refer to the expedition's progress.

Occasionally the captains' determination overcame their better judgment. On the return voyage, they left the Nez Perce villages to start the march on the Lolo Trail despite the Indians' warnings that it was too early. They found the path across the Bitterroots still under twelve feet of snow and were forced to order the expedition's only retreat of the entire trip.

The partnership of Lewis and Clark unfailingly united them as leaders without eroding their individuality. Indeed, their writings display their differences in temperament and disposition. During the venture, as partners in discovery, they often profited from their differences. Their journal entries reflect both their unity of purpose and each man's distinct identity.

CLARK JOINS THE EXPEDITION

On June 19, 1803, Lewis sent Clark a lengthy letter inviting him to join the expedition. The letter sketches the proposed route and objectives of the trip in amazing detail and distinguishes the true aim of the voyage — exploring the Missouri River to the Pacific—from Jefferson's publicly stated aim—exploring the upper Mississippi. Lewis's letter offers Clark the rank of captain for his role in the expedition, but this was a promise that neither Jefferson as president nor Lewis as leader could deliver. Both men may have been so eager to get on with the expedition that they overlooked the red tape that would preclude the offer. Clark's letter of ready and enthusiastic acceptance of the cocaptaincy contrasts vividly with Lewis's detailed letter, studded with explicit inside information, specific knowledge of the probable route, and keen awareness of all the goals. Clark cheerfully embraces all possible dangers of the expedition and looks forward to the joint adventures of two colleagues and friends.

Lewis Invites Clark to Join Him

WASHINGTON, JUNE 19TH, 1803.
DEAR CLARK: . . . From the long and uninterrupted friendship . . . which has subsisted between us I feel no hesitation in making to you the following communication under the fulest impression that it will be held by you inviolably secret untill I see you, or you shall hear again from me.

During the last session of Congress a law was passed in conformity to a private message of the President . . . intiled "An Act making an appropriation for extending the external commerce of the United States." The object of this Act . . . was to give the sanction of the government to exploreing the interior of the continent . . . or that part of it bordering on the Missourie & Columbia Rivers. This enterprise has been confided to me by the President, and . . . since the begining of March I have been engaged in making the necessary preparations for the tour, these arrangements being now nearly completed, I shall set out for Pittsburgh (the intended point of embarcation) about the last of this month, and as soon after . . . I shall be with you, say about the 10th of August. To aid me in this enterprise I have the most ample . . . support that the government can give. . . . I am armed

From original manuscript, reprinted in Thwaites, *Original Journals of the Lewis and Clark Expedition,* 7:226–30.

with the authority of the Government . . . for my protection . . . in addition to which, the further aid has been given me of liberal pasports from the Ministers both of France and England: I am instructed to select from any corps in the army a number of noncommissioned officers and privates not exceeding 12, who may be disposed voluntarily to enter into this service; and am also authorized to engage any other men not soldiers that I may think usefull in promoting the . . . success of this expedition. I am likewise furnished with letters of credit, and authorized to draw on the government for any sum necessary for the comfort of myself or party. To all the persons engaged in this service I am authorized to offer the following rewards . . . —1st the bounty (if not a soldier) but in both cases six months pay in advance; 2dly to discharge them from the service if they wish it, immediately on their return . . . giving them their arrears of pay clothing &c. & 3dly to secure to them a portion of land equal to that given by the United States to the officers and soldiers who served in the revolutionary army. . . . I will now give you a . . . sketch of my plan of operation: I shall embark at Pittsburgh with a party of recruits eight or nine in number, intended only to manage the boat . . . ; when descending the Ohio it shall be my duty . . . to . . . engage some good hunters, stout, healthy, unmarried men, accustomed to the woods, and capable of bearing bodily fatigue in a pretty considerable degree: should any young men answering this description be found in your neighborhood I would thank you to give information of them on my arivall at the falls of the Ohio; and if possible learn the probability of their engaging in this service, this may be done perhaps by holding out the idea that the direction of this expedition is up the Mississippi to its source, and thence to the lake of the Woods, stating the probable period of absence at about 18 months; if they would engage themselves in a service of this discription there would be but little doubt that they would engage in the real design when it became necessary to make it known to them, which I should take care to do before I finaly engaged them: — The soldiers that will most probably answer this expedition best will be found in some of the companies stationed at Massac, Kaskaskias & Illinois: pardon this digression from . . . my plan: [Lewis outlines the course Jefferson mapped earlier, along with his instructions.—ED.] You must know in the first place that very sanguine expectations are at this time formed by our Government that the whole of that immense country wartered by the Mississippi and it's tributary streams, Missourie inclusive, will be the property of the U. States in less than 12 Months from this date: but here let me again impress you with the necessity of keeping this matter a perfect secret. In such a state of things therefore as we have every reason to hope, you will readily concieve the importance to the U. States of an early friendly and intimate acquaintance with the tribes that inhabit that country, that they should be early impressed with a just idea of the rising importance of the U. States and of her friendly dispositions towards them, as also her desire to become usefull to them by furnishing them through her citizens with such articles by way of barter as may be desired by them. . . . The other objects of this mission are scientific, and of course not less interesting to the U. States than to the world generally. . . .

Thus my friend you have . . . a summary view of the plan, the means and the objects of this expedition, if . . . there is anything . . . in this enterprise, which would induce you to participate with me in it's faticgues, it's dangers and it's honors, believe me there is no man on earth with whom I should feel equal pleasure in sharing them as with yourself; I make this communication to you with the privity of the President, who expresses an anxious wish that you would consent to join me in this enterprise; he has authorized me to say that in the event of your accepting this proposition he will grant you a Captain's commission which of course will intitle you to the pay and emoluments attached to that office and will equally with myself intitle you to such portion of land as was granted to offers of similar rank for their Revolutionary services; the commission with which he proposes to furnish you is not to be considered temporary but permanent if you wish it; your situation if joined with me in this mission will in all respects be precisely such as my own. Pray write to me on this subject as early as possible and direct to me at Pittsburgh. Should you feel disposed not to attatch yourself to this party in an official character, and at the same time feel a disposition to accompany me as a friend any part of the way up the Missourie I should be extremely happy in your company, and will furnish you with every aid for your return from any point you might wish it.

With sincere and affectionate regard your friend & Humb^l sev^t

MERIWETHER LEWIS.

Clark Accepts Lewis's Invitation

CLARKSVILLE 17TH JULY 1803

DEAR LEWIS: I received by yesterday's Mail your letter of the 19th ulto: the contents of which I received with *much pleasure.* The enterprise & Mission is such as I have long anticipated & am much pleased with and as

Rough draft by Clark, from original manuscript, reprinted in Thwaites, *Original Journals of the Lewis and Clark Expedition,* 7:259.

my situation in life will admit of my absence the length of time necessary
to accomplish such an undertaking, I will cheerfully join you in an "official character" as mentioned in your letter and partake of all the Dangers
Difficulties & fatigues, and I anticipate the honors & rewards of the result
of such an enterprise should we be successful in accomplishing it. This
is an imense undertaking fraited with numerous dificulties, but my friend
I can assure you that no man lives with whom I would prefer to undertake and share the Dificulties of such a trip than yourself. I reserve nothing from you that will add either to y^r profit or satisfaction and shall
arrange my matters as well as I can against your arrival here.

It may be necessary that you inform the president of my acceding to
the proposals, so that I may be furnished with such credentials, as the
nature of the Tour may require. . . .

I shall endeavor to engage temporally such men as I think may answer
our purpose but, holding out the Idea as stated in your letter—the subject of which has been mentioned in Louisville several weeks ago.

Pray write to me by every post, I shall be exceedingly anxious to know
where you are and how you proceed.

With every assurance of sincerity in every respect, and with aff^n y^r f^d
& H. Srv

W. C.

RESOURCEFUL AND PRUDENT LEWIS

Many times both captains could have jeopardized the entire expedition
if they had acted impulsively, but for the most part they kept their heads
and responded as leaders without whom the mission would not be completed. Lewis recounts an incident on May 14, 1805, when a canoe almost
capsized on the Missouri and he was momentarily tempted to jump in the
rapids himself and right it.

Lewis's diplomatic skills were crucial to the expedition's success.
When he finally met Chief Cameahwait's Shoshoni group on August 16,
1805, at the Lemhi River in present-day Idaho, he realized that the fate of
the expedition hung in the balance. If he failed to initiate the trade for
horses with Indians who had never seen a white man, Lewis feared that
the resulting delay of the voyage would discourage his men and ruin the
expedition altogether. Although he claimed that its progress depended
on "the caprice of a few savages who are ever as fickle as the wind," it
actually depended on his skill as a consummate negotiator.

Lewis also had a leader's ability to ignore his own shock and pain and
keep the expedition moving. In present-day North Dakota, on August 11,

1806, when Cruzatte, who had poor eyesight, accidentally shot the captain in his buttocks, Lewis had to treat the painful injury himself and wait two days until the expedition reunited and Clark could dress the wound. Lewis distracted himself from the pain by writing a detailed botanical account of a cherry tree he noticed ashore.

Yellowstone to Musselshell

LEWIS   TUESDAY MAY 14TH 1805.
It happened unfortunately for us this evening that Charbono was at the helm of this Perogue, in stead of Drewyer, who had previously steered her; Charbono cannot swim and is perhaps the most timid waterman in the world; perhaps it was equally unluckey that Capt C. and myself were both on shore . . . , a circumstance which rarely happened; and tho' we were . . . opposite to the perogue, were too far distant to be heard or to do more than remain spectators . . . ; in this perogue were embarked, our papers, Instruments, books medicine, a great part of our merchandize and in short almost every article indispensibly necessary to . . . insure the success of the enterprize in which we are now launched to the distance of 2200 miles. . . . the Perogue was under sail when a sudon squawl of wind struck her obliquely, and turned her considerably, the steersman allarmed, in stead of puting, her before the wind, lufted her up into it, the wind was so violent that it drew the brace of the squarsail out of the hand of the man who was attending it, and instantly upset the perogue and would have turned her completely topsaturva, had it not have been from the resistance mad[e] by the oarning [awning] against the water; in this situation Capt. C. and myself both fired our guns to attract the attention . . . of the crew and ordered the halyards to be cut and the sail hawled in, but they did not hear us; such was their confusion . . . that they suffered the perogue to lye on her side for half a minute before they took the sail in, the perogue then wrighted but had filled within an inch of the gunwals; Charbono still crying to his god for mercy, had not yet recollected the rudder, nor could the repeated orders of the Bowsman, Cruzat, bring him to his recollection untill he threatend to shoot him instantly if he did not take hold of the rudder and do his duty, the waves by this time were runing very high, but the . . . good conduct of Cruzat saved her; he ordered 2 of

the men to throw out the water with some kettles that fortunately were convenient, while himself and two others rowed her as[h]ore, where she arrived scarcely above the water; we now took every article out of her and lay them to drane . . . , baled out the canoe and secured her. there were two other men beside Charbono on board who could not swim, and who of course must also have perished had the perogue gone to the bottom. while the perogue lay on her side, finding I could not be heard, I for a moment forgot my own situation, and involluntarily droped my gun, threw aside my shot pouch and was in the act of unbuttoning my coat, before I recollected the folly of the attempt I was about to make; which was to throw myself into the river and inde[a]vour to swim to the perogue; the perogue was three hundred yards distant the waves so high that a perogue could scarcely live in any situation, the water excessively could, and the stream rappid; had I undertaken this project therefore, there was a hundred to one but what I should have paid the forfit of my life for the madness of my project, but this had the perogue been lost, I should have valued but little. After having all matters arranged for the evening as well as the nature of circumstances would permit, we thought it a proper occasion to console ourselves and cheer the sperits of our men and accordingly took a drink of grog and gave each man a gill of sperits.

Beaverhead to Great Divide

LEWIS   FRIDAY, AUGUST 16TH 1805.
. . . this morning . . . a considerable part of our escort became allarmed and returned 28 men and three women only continued with us. . . . being now informed of the place at which I expected to meat Capt C. and the party they insisted on making a halt . . . we now dismounted and the Chief with much cerimony put tippets about our necks such as they t[h]emselves woar I redily perceived that this was to disguise us. . . . to give them further confidence I put my cocked hat with feather on the chief and my over shirt being of the Indian form my hair deshivled and skin well browned with the sun I wanted no further addition to make me a complete Indian in appearance the men followed my example and we were so[o]n completely metamorphosed. . . . we now set out and rode briskly

within sight of the forks making one of the Indians carry the flag that our own party should know who we were. . . . I discovered to my mortification that the party had not arrived, and the Indians slackened their pace. I now scarcely new what to do and feared every moment when they would halt altogether, I now determined to restore their confidence cost what it might and therefore gave the Chief my gun and told him that if his enimies were in those bushes before him that he could defend himself with that gun, that for my own part I was not affraid to die and if I deceived him he might make what ucc of the gun he thought proper or in other words that he might shoot me. the men also gave their guns to other indians which seemed to inspire them with more confidence;
. . . when I drew near the place I thought of the notes which I had left and directed Drewyer to go with an Indian man and bring them to me which he did. the indian seeing him take the notes from the stake. . . . I now had recource to a stratagem in which I thought myself justifyed by the occasion, but which I must confess set a little awkward. it had it's desired effect. after reading the notes . . . I told the Chief that when I had left my brother Chief . . . where the river entered the mountain that we both agreed not to bring the canoes higher up than the next forks of the river above us wherever this might happen, that there he was to wait my return, should he arrive first, and that in the event of his not being able to travel as fast as usual from the difficulty of the water, that he was to send up to the first forks above him and leave a note informing me where he was, that this note was left here today and that he informed me that he was just below the mountains and was coming on slowly up, and added that I should wait here for him, but if they did not beleive me that I should send a man at any rate to the Chief and they might also send one of their young men with him, that myself and two others would remain with them at this place. this plan was readily adopted and one of the young men offered his services; I promised him a knife and some beads as a reward for his confidence in us. most of them seemed satisfyed but there were several that complained of the Chief's exposing them to danger unnecessarily and said that we told different stories, in short a few were much dissatisfyed. I wrote a note to Capt. Clark . . . and directed Drewyer to set out early being confident that there was not a moment to spare. the chief and five or six others slept about my fire and the others hid themselves in various parts of the willow brush to avoid the enimy whom they were fearfull would attack tham in the course of the night. . . . I knew that if these people left me that they would immediately . . . secrete themselves in the mountains where it would be impossible to find them . . . and that they would spread the allarm to all other

bands within our reach & . . . we should be disappointed in obtaining horses, which would vastly retard and increase the labour of our voyage and I feared might so discourage the men as to defeat the expedition altogether. my mind was in reallity quite as gloomy all this evening as the most affrighted indian but I affected cheerfullness to keep the Indians so who were about me. we finally laid down and the Chief placed himself by the side of my musquetoe bier. I slept but little . . . my mind dwelling on the state of the expedition which I have ever held in equal estimation with my own existence, and the fait of which appeared at this moment to depend in a great measure upon the caprice of a few savages who are ever as fickle as the wind. I had mentioned to the chief several times that we had with us a woman of his nation who had been taken prisoner by the Minnetares, and that by means of her I hoped to explain myself more fully than I could do signs. . . .

Lewis's Exploration

LEWIS   MONDAY AUGUST 11TH 1806.
. . . my wounds felt very stiff and soar this morning but gave me no considerable pain. there was much less inflamation than I had reason to apprehend there would be. I had last evening applyed a poltice of peruvian barks. at 1 P.M. I overtook Capt. Clark and party and had the pleasure of finding them all well. as wrighting in my present situation is extreemly painfull to me I shall desist untill I recover and leave to my fri[e]nd Capt. C. the continuation of our journal. however I must notice a singular Cherry . . . the stem is compound erect and subdivided or branching without any regular order it rises to the hight of eight or ten feet seldom puting up more than one stem from the same root not growing in cops as the Choke Cherry dose. the bark is smooth and of a dark brown colour. the leaf is peteolate, oval accutely pointed at it's apex, from one and a ¼ to 1 ½ inches in length and from ½ to ¾ of an inch in width, finely or minutely serrate, pale green and free from pubessence. the fruit is a globular berry about the size of a buck-shot of a fine scarlet red; like the cherries cultivated in the U' States each is supported by a seperate celindric flexable branch peduncle which issue from the extremities of the boughs the peduncle of this cherry swells as it approaches the fruit

being largest at the point of insertion. the pulp of this fruit is of an agreeable ascid flavour and is now ripe. the style and stigma are permanent. I have never seen it in blume.

METICULOUS AND HELPFUL CLARK

Clark often gathered and measured the dimensions of topography following his penchant for precision, while Lewis tended to paint with his words the broad sweep of scenery. Between the Kansas and the Platte Rivers the explorers noted deserted Indian villages and mounds. At a rest stop on July 12, 1804, Clark meticulously noted the details of what he saw, recording the distances to the river and even the height of the grass.

In emergencies Clark responded immediately. His swift actions took into account both the safety of the group and the protection of the equipment. On June 29, 1805, during the portage of the Great Falls of the Missouri, a sudden downpour turned a dry wash into a roaring stream within minutes. Clark managed to keep one step ahead of the rapidly rising torrent, recording the increasing depth of the water as he escaped, helping Sacagawea, her baby, and Charbonneau to safety.

Clark's helpfulness extended to Native Americans and explorers alike. At the end of May 1806, among the Nez Perce on the Kooskooske River in present-day central Idaho, he worked hard to cure a paralyzed chief whom relatives had brought to the explorers. Lewis's reports of the treatment are fuller and easier to read and so are used here for most of the descriptions, but one of Clark's accounts makes clear that he was in charge of the case.

Dubois to Platte

CLARK   JULY 12ᵀᴴ THURSDAY 1804—
. . . after going to Several Small Mounds in a leavel plain, I assended a hill on the Lower Side, on this hill Several artificial Mounds were raised, from the top of the highest of those Mounds I had an extensive view of the Serounding Plains, which afforded one of the most pleasing prospect I ever beheld, under mc a Butifull River of Clear Water of about 80 yards wide

---

Meandering thro: a leavel and extensive meadow, as far as I could See, the prospect much enlivened by the fiew Trees & Srubs which is bordering the bank of the river, and the Creeks & runs falling into it, The bottom land is covered with Grass of about 4 ½ feet high, and appears as leavel as a smoth surfice, the 2ᵈ bottom [*the upper land*] is also covered with Grass and rich weeds & flours, interspersed with copses of the Osage Plumb, on the riseing lands, Small groves of trees are Seen, with a numbers of Grapes and a Wild Cherry resembling the common Wild Cherry, only larger and grows on a small bush on the tops of those hills in every direction, I observed artifical Mounds (or as I may more justly term graves) which to me is a strong evidence [*indication*] of this Country being once thickly Settled. . . .

Great Falls Portage

CLARK   JUNE 29ᵀᴴ SATTURDAY 1805
. . . I deturmined . . . to proceed on to the falls and take the river, according we all set out, I took my servent & one man, Chabono our Interpreter & his Squar accompanied, soon after I arrived at the falls, I perceived a cloud which appeared black and threaten imediate rain, I looked out for a shelter but could see no place without being in great danger of being blown into the river if the wind should prove as turbelant as it is at some times about ¼ of a mile above the falls I obsd a Deep riveen in which was shelveing rocks under which we took shelter near the river and placed our guns the compass &ᶜ &ᶜ under a shelving rock on the upper side of the creek, in a place which was verry secure from rain, the first shower was moderate accompanied with a violent wind, the effects of which we did not feel, soon after a torrent of rain and hail fell more violent than ever I saw before, the rain fell like one voley of water falling from the heavens and gave us time only to get out of the way of a torrent of water which was Poreing down the hill in[to] the River with emence force tareing every thing before it takeing with it large rocks & mud, I took my gun & shot pouch in my left hand, and with the right scrambled up the hill pushing the Interpreters wife (who had her child in her arms) before me, the Interpreter himself makeing attempts to pull up his wife by the hand much scared and nearly without motion, we at length reached the top of

the hill safe where I found my servent in serch of us greatly agitated, for our wellfar. before I got out of the bottom of the reveen which was a flat dry rock when I entered it, the water was up to my waste & wet my watch, I scercely got out before it raised 10 feet deep with a torrent which [was] turrouble to behold, and by the time I reached the top of the hill, at least 15 feet water, I derected the party to return to the camp . . . as fast as possible to get to our Lode where Clothes could be got to cover the child whose clothes were all lost, and the woman who was but just recovering from a severe indisposition, and was wet and cold, I was fearfull of a relaps I caused her as also the others of the party to take a little spirits, which my servent had in a canteen, which revived [them] verry much. . . . Soon after the run began to rise and rose 6 feet in a fiew minets. I lost . . . in the torrent the large compas, an elegant fusee,[1] Tomahawk *Humbrallo,* [Umbrella] shot pouch & horn with powder & Ball, Mockersons, & the woman lost her childs Bear & Clothes bedding &ᶜ The Compass, is a serious loss, as we have no other large one. . . .

---

[1] Fusee or fusil, a flintlock musket.

On the Upper Kooskooske

LEWIS   SATURDAY MAY 24ᵀᴴ 1806.
. . . at 11 A.M. a canoe arrived with 3 of the natives one of them the sick man . . . having lost the power of his limbs. he is a cheif of considerable note among them and they seem extreemly anxious for his recovery. as he complains of no pain in any particular part we conceive it cannot be the rheumatism, nor do we suppose that it can be a parelitic attack or his limbs would have been more deminished. we have supposed that it was some disorder which owed it's origine to a diet of particular roots perhaps and such as we have never before witnessed. while at the village of the broken arm we had recommended a diet of fish or flesh for this man and the cold bath every morning. we had also given him a few dozes of creem of tarter and flour of sulpher to be repeated every 3ᵈ day. this poor wretch thinks that he feels himself somewhat better but to me there appears to be no visible alteration. we are at a loss what to do for this unfortunate man. we gave him a few drops of Laudanum and a little portable soup.

LEWIS   TUESDAY MAY 27TH 1806

. . . the indians were so anxious that the sick Cheif should be sweated[1] under our inspection that they requested we would make a second atte[m]pt today; accordingly the hole was somewhat enlarged and his father a very good looking old man, went into the hole with him and sustained him in a proper position during the operation; we could not make him sweat as copiously as we wished. after the operation he complained of considerable pain, we gave him 30 drops of laudanum which soon composed him and he rested very well. this is at least a strong mark of parental affection. they all appear extreemly attentive to this sick man nor do they appear to relax in their asciduity towards him notwithstand[ing] he has been sick and helpless upwards of three years. . . .

CLARK   WEDNESDAY MAY 28TH 1806

. . . The Sick Chief is much better this morning he can use his hands and arms and seems much pleased with the prospects of recovering, he says he feels much better than he has done for a great number of months. I sincerly wish that the swetts may restore him. I have consented to repeet the sweets. . . .

---

[1]"Sweating" was a typical cure for many ailments. See Lewis's detailed description of another case on page 79.

2

Forging the Corps of Discovery

In the fall of 1803, Lewis worried as much about the quality of the recruits for the expedition as he did about the delay at a Pittsburgh shipyard for a keelboat. Lewis had seven soldiers and three young men with him when he met Clark and his slave York at Clarksville, Indiana Territory. Among Clark's nine recruits were two cousins who became sergeants, Charles Floyd and Nathaniel Pryor. Other members of the corps came from army posts in Tennessee and Illinois, where Sergeant John Ordway and Private (later Sergeant) Patrick Gass were recruited at Kaskaskia. In the St. Louis area Lewis found enough men to complete the initial roster of the corps. The effectiveness of the mixed party, however, remained in question.

Camp Dubois, established on December 13, 1803, served as winter quarters and boot camp. Here the recruits spent the winter just opposite the mouth of the river that would figure so prominently in the expedition: the Missouri. The remarkable scenery did little to shape the motley party into an intrepid unit of like-minded men. That task was up to the captains during the four-month stay and once the expedition started to move, during the six-month ascent of the lower Missouri. They often lectured the men on the fatal consequences of disobedience, negligence, and drunkenness both for themselves and for the outcome of the expedition. Their constant advice eventually sank in, and the need to be alert at all times became habitual. (See p. 51.)

Somehow the captains had to combine the conventional tools of military authority with the spontaneity of expeditionary leadership. They realized that their task distinguished the Corps of Discovery from any army or militia unit. At the turn of the eighteenth century, the standard army methods, which relied on uniforms and sergeants to control recruits, did not suit this assignment. Drill sergeants would be of little use throughout the voyage and, although the men would appear more cohesive and formidable in uniforms, wearing them would not further their job.

As a newly formed army unit in search of the proper conduct, the expe-

45

dition could rely on precedents going back to the Revolutionary War, which determined the chain of command, the regulations reinforcing discipline, and the punishment following violations of the rules and regulations observed by troops who garrisoned the forts of the Ohio Valley and other military installations. The area of operation of the corps, however, was far removed from its base. Its field of action lay in parts of the continent unknown to the captains and the men, and that placed the new unit outside army convention.

During the French and Indian War the far-flung exploits of Major Robert Rogers's Rangers had created an unconventional military unit. Its esprit de corps sustained operating in no-man's-land by providing an effective substitute for the customary British floggings to enforce discipline. Rogers outlined his plan of discipline in twenty-eight articles, replacing senseless harshness with sensible advice for conduct that would ensure success and survival.[1]

The diverse origins of the explorers kept Lewis and Clark from using an authority structure like that of the community-based colonial volunteers, the so-called Provincials. While the latter had served Massachusetts, the Corps of Discovery served the nation.[2] Serving their country was a significant attitude the men acquired during the early stages of the journey. (See p. 59.) Soon after the expedition's return, Americans followed Jefferson's example and acknowledged the corps's national status by referring to it as the first United States exploring expedition.

The Rogers's Rangers analogy shows how the corps maintained duty and discipline within an unusual military unit; however, the corps's order to be at peace with everyone set it apart from the Rangers, whose commitment to and pride in their unit were recharged in combat. The corps could not rely on skirmishes and battles for bonding. Its unity stemmed from the sense of mission and the models provided by Lewis and Clark.

A degree of freedom unknown to ordinary enlisted men at the turn of the eighteenth century characterized the modified army routine of the expedition. An inherited practice from the Revolutionary Army, courts-martial were considered a standard part of army discipline. With the help of six courts-martial, the captains turned a mixed lot of soldiers, backwoodsmen, and guides into a special corps, with sensible discipline and total loyalty. (See p. 55.) Unlike regular procedure, however, Lewis and Clark insisted that enlisted men sit on the court with a sergeant presid-

---

[1] *Journals of Major Robert Rogers, Reprinted from the Original Edition of 1765* (New York: Corinth Books, 1961), 43–51.
[2] Fred Anderson, *A People's Army: Massachusetts Soldiers and Society in the Seven Years' War* (Chapel Hill: University of North Carolina Press, 1984), 170–74.

ing, except in trials involving crimes punishable by death, when the captains served.

The shared hardships of the trail also altered army routine. The severe North Dakota winter enforced the physical closeness of the expedition. Fort Mandan's palisades set the Indians living in nearby villages apart from the explorers. In turn, the fort gave the explorers a place of retreat when further ventures into the Indian world proved hazardous. These four months of shared experiences in tight winter quarters strengthened the men's loyalty to one another, their compliance with regulations, and their commitment to the goals of the expedition. Courts-martial were no longer deemed necessary.

As the Corps of Discovery took shape, Lewis and Clark went ahead with the plan to send the keelboat crew back to St. Louis. This group of predominantly French Canadian boatmen, called *engagés* in the fur trade, had accompanied the expedition up the Missouri, masterly navigating the keelboat to the Mandan villages. In the spring of 1805, under the command of Corporal Richard Warfington, the boatmen returned the keelboat to St. Louis, taking back specimens the explorers had collected and Lewis's report to Jefferson. (See p. 62.) The keelboat had served well on the Missouri so far, but it would not have been as useful on the lesser-known part of the river. In addition, managing the culturally homogeneous keelboat crew put a strain on the special military procedures.

The captains found that an egalitarian approach to discipline united the expedition. At their request, two days after Sergeant Charles Floyd died of a ruptured appendix on August 20, 1804, the soldiers held an election for his successor. Private Gass was duly promoted sergeant. Gass did not mention this election in his journal at all. Perhaps the procedure struck him as unusual; perhaps he preferred to think of himself as a "regular" sergeant whose merits had been recognized by his superior officers rather than the vote of his comrades.

On another occasion, November 24, 1805, all members of the expedition, including York and Sacagawea, were given the chance to vote on the location of the winter quarters on the Pacific coast. In his account of the voting Gass merely said that "the party were consulted by the Commanding Officers as to the place most proper for winter quarters."[3] Clark recorded each vote in his account of the election.

The expedition's limited democracy ended with the trip. York, the

<hr>

[3]Patrick Gass, *A Journal of the Voyages and Travels of a Corps of Discovery, under the Command of Capt. Lewis and Capt. Clarke of the Army of the United States* (Pittsburgh: David M'Keehan, 1807), 169–70.

slave who accompanied his master on the journey, did not appear on the roster of men that Lewis submitted to the secretary of war on January 15, 1807, and consequently received no pay. The omission could hardly have been an oversight; more likely, as a slave York was not recognized as a member of a military unit. Earlier, Sacagawea had disappeared from official sight with no payment when Charbonneau and his family left the returning expedition at the Mandan villages. If York and Sacagawea had obtained remuneration, master and husband would have stripped them of the money.

Their legal status brought York and Sacagawea to the expedition incidentally. One followed his master; the other followed her husband. Both stood out immediately, York on account of the color of his skin, Sacagawea on account of her sex. Both proved invaluable to the expedition, supplying resources that no planning could have foreseen the need for. The presence of York gave the corps a special aura in the eyes of Native Americans, who had never seen a black man. Expert with a rifle, York was a much valued member of the expedition who worked hard as hunter and scout. Lewis also praised him and a companion for trading with the Indians for much needed supplies before the dreaded return crossing of the Bitterroots.

Sacagawea appeared at Fort Mandan when Lewis and Clark enlisted her husband, Toussaint Charbonneau, as an interpreter. A French Canadian who spoke Minitari, Charbonneau had served the North West Company, a Montreal-based fur company, as a trader. The Shoshoni Sacagawea, pregnant when she joined the expedition, gave birth to Baptiste, nicknamed "Pomp," fifty days before the explorers resumed their voyage. The presence of mother and son shielded the corps from being mistaken as a war party, which in Native American practice consisted only of warriors.

Sacagawea's greatest assets were her Shoshoni origin, her familiarity with the upper reaches of the Missouri, and her presence as an interpreter and teacher of the Shoshoni language and customs. In particular, she assisted in negotiations with the Shoshoni to acquire the horses the expedition so desperately needed to continue the journey across the Rockies. (See p. 66.) Her many contributions captured the imagination of twentieth-century writers who have made her the best-known member of the expedition, next to the captains.

The differences among the party in origin, background, and experience as well as the cultural diversity sometimes served as a hurdle to creating an effective unit. The range of people they represented had not much more in common than the urge to join a great adventure. Many of the values of farmers and blacksmiths differed from those of boatmen and backwoodsmen. Professional soldiers and volunteers, illiterate and educated men, Yankees and southerners, immigrants and mixed-bloods, young and old men were forced to recognize their mutual bonds as members of an exploring expedition charged with performing demanding tasks.

George Shannon, eighteen, was the youngest and John Shields, thirty-five, the oldest, followed by Clark and Gass. Only Shields and Pryor seem to have been married. Shannon and John Ordway had more formal education than many of the others. Those lacking book learning brought different skills, however, especially the resourcefulness bred on the frontier. The captains could rely on a cumulative store of knowledge, experience, and versatility. Their constant task was to direct those resources of body and mind first and foremost to the purposes of the expedition.

Ethnically the party was predominantly American. York, the black slave, and Sacagawea, the Shoshoni woman, were distinctly "different." Shadings of the racial-ethnic spectrum were provided by men like Pierre Cruzatte and François Labiche, both half French and half Omaha; George Drouillard, son of a French Canadian father and a Shawnee mother; the Irishman Patrick Gass; John Potts, a German immigrant; Peter Weiser, a Pennsylvania Dutch; Ebenezer Tuttle, a Connecticut Yankee; and John Colter, a Virginian. They and the other explorers were listed merely by name on the expedition's roster. Only the journal entries referring specifically to the exploits of some provided those few with an identity. (See p. 72.)

The captains took in stride the mixed racial-ethnic composition and evenhandedly dealt out rewards and punishments. An extra gill of whiskey and a sentence of one hundred lashes by a court-martial were the extremes of their sanctions. Reinforcing the significance of the lessons through their own exemplary conduct, they exposed a motley group of men to the value of a soldier's mind dedicated to service.

As the journey continued, actual experiences forged the corps into an efficient team run along military lines, even more so than the drills at Camp Dubois or the courts-martial along the trail. On the eve of a move into an area populated by Native Americans seeking to retain control of their lands, the men became keenly aware that sleeping on guard duty was not just a breach of army regulations but a folly that could endanger everyone's life. It followed that a drunken sentry, befuddled by whiskey stolen from the supplies, could also be a disaster for all.

The captains recognized the danger and the benefit of the liquor the expedition carried among its supplies. At Camp Dubois, the neighboring whiskey shop had an almost irresistible attraction for the wild young men turned soldiers who thought their new calling justified liquored-up bragging. Their fervent hope to be taken as "real men" found fulfillment in another dram of whiskey. Lewis and Clark issued liquor as medicine, inducement, or reward and by rationing it persistently sought to counter the men's habits coming from a hard-drinking society. Dispersing liquor became a difficult task for the captains when the supply began to dwindle. Celebrating New Year's Day at Fort Clatsop, a somewhat dejected Lewis pointedly referred to pure water as the only beverage.

Irrespective of the significant role liquor played in a soldier's life as a cure-all for insecurity, hunger, pain, cold, heat, loneliness, and fear, the men's carefree attitude toward whiskey pointed at another habit that the captains also sought to control or, at least, to limit. They attempted to curb the waste of meat, which usually had been divided between the messes as long as it was plentiful. At Fort Clatsop on January 12, 1806, Lewis noticed "such prodigal use" of meat that the captains decided to issue it only in small quantities when a plentiful supply was doubtful.

The shifting duties of the men, as the stages and purposes of the expedition advanced, called for flexible measures to keep the corps united. The men celebrated holidays such as the Fourth of July, Christmas, New Year's, and Lewis's birthday not only for the sake of the events commemorated but also to strengthen community spirit. The captains issued an extra gill of whiskey as a treat after a particularly strenuous day. (See p. 75.) Lewis and Clark showed their consideration for each member's well-being by treating sick men and dispensing medicine, thereby heightening the men's loyalty to them. (See p. 78.) These acts served the captains well in successfully completing the voyage.

"Our little Community," as the captains called the party, contrasted sharply with the solitary traders, freewheeling trappers, canny interpreters, and cagey representatives of the Montreal-based North West Company whom the explorers encountered during the opening and closing phases of the expedition. Each of these men pursued his own interests or those of his distant employer. The explorers received the traders with some misgivings, while the captains suspected that a few of the traders were trying to block their progress. Indeed, some traders did view the expedition with alarm, regarding it as the vanguard of a new authority in upper Louisiana introducing new trading practices. Others assumed that the United States would now block their advance into the upper Missouri.

On the whole, traders were a great asset to the expedition since they provided good information about the lay of the land and its inhabitants, the conditions of Indian trade, and the strategies of large fur companies. At different times Lewis and Clark used white traders living in Indian nations as interpreters to help further the expedition's diplomatic aims of peace and trade. During the last stage of the voyage, traders also supplied welcome news of recent events back home.

The success of the expedition indicated that the captains' resourcefulness had created a strong expeditionary force by infusing a democratic spirit into army routine. Their practical adaptations gave scope to the men's creativity, sustained their confidence in each other, and linked the diverse group of explorers into a national expedition. Fusing men and methods, the captains proved that the search for unity in the context of diversity is the essence of the American experience.

ADAPTING ARMY ROUTINE

Turning raw recruits into seasoned soldiers kept the captains busy at Camp Dubois during the winter of 1804 and during the early stages of the expedition. Half of the men were unfamiliar with, or did not much care for, army regulations and the chain of command. But these men, who were used to acting on their own, had to be taught to respect a sergeant's authority. Work details, such as cutting planks or making sugar, interfered with what they thought was a real soldier's training. Men and sergeants had to work together on tasks that the recruits did not consider part of a soldier's adventurous life. An extra gill of whiskey to reward the recruits could sometimes disguise authority with camaraderie. However, creating an effective military unit required strict organization—men into squads, squads into messes, and a cook for each mess—and the execution of all orders and details.

Throughout the voyage the captains made adjustments to conventional army routine as circumstances demanded. During the first weeks on the river they adapted the size of the squads to suit boat travel. At Fort Mandan in 1805, the captains listed the duties of the winter quarters much as they did in 1806 at Fort Clatsop. The forts often attracted Indians, and the captains warned the men not to harm any visitors lest any fight endanger the expedition. At Fort Clatsop a sergeant, an interpreter, and two soldiers on guard ordered all Native Americans out of the fort at sundown to preclude the men from molesting Indian women.

Dubois to Platte

DETACHMENT ORDERS
LEWIS   CAMP RIVER DUBOIS, FEB: 20TH 1804.
The Commanding officer directs that During the absence of himself and Cap: Clark from Camp, that the party shall consider themselves under

Thwaites, *Original Journals of the Lewis and Clark Expedition*, 1:8–10.

the immediate command of Serg.ͭ Ordway, who will be held accountable for the good . . . order of the camp . . . and will also see the subsequent parts of this order carried into effect.

The sawyers will continue their work untill they have cut the necessary quantity of plank, the quantity wanting will be determined by Pryor; during the days they labour they shall recieve each an extra gill of whiskey p.ͬ day and be exempt from guard duty; when the work is accomplished, they will . . . do duty in common with the other men.

The Blacksmiths will also continue their work untill they have completed the articles contained in the memorandom . . . and during the time they are at work will recieve each an extra gill of whiskey p.ͬ day and be exempt from guard duty; when the work is completed they will . . . do duty in common with the detatc[h]ment.

The four men who are engaged in making sugar will continue . . . untill further orders, and will recieve each a half a gill of extra whiskey p.ͬ day and be exempt from guard duty.

The practicing party will in futer discharge only one round each p.ͬ day . . . under the direction of Serg.ͭ Ordway, all at the same target and at the distance of fifty yards off hand. The prize of a gill of extra whiskey will be recieved by the person who makes the best shot at each time of practice.

Floyd will take charge of our quarte[r]s and store and be exempt from guard duty untill our return, the commanding Officer hopes that this proof of his confidence will be justifyed by the rigid performance of the orders given him on that subject.

No man shal absent himself from camp without the . . . permission of Serg.ͭ Ordway, other than those who have obtained permission from me to be absent on hunting excurtions, and those will not extend their absence to a term by which they may avoid a tour of guard duty, on their return they will report themselves to Serg.ͭ Ordway and recieve his instructions.

No whiskey shall in future be delivered from the Contractor's store except for the legal ration, and as appropriated by this order, unless otherwise directed by Cap.ͭ Clark or myself.

MERIWETHER LEWIS Cap.ͭ

1.ˢᵗ U. S. Reg.ͭ Infty.

Serg.ͭ Ordway will have the men paraded this evening and read the inclosed orders to them.

M. LEWIS

[Indorsed:] to Floyd

DETACHMENT ORDERS
LEWIS: MARCH 3ᴿᴰ 1804.

The Commanding officer feels himself mortifyed and disappointed at the disorderly conduct of Reubin Fields, in refusing to mount guard when in the due roteen of duty he was regularly warned; nor is he less surprised at the want of discretion in those who urged his oposition to the faithfull discharge of his duty, particularly Shields, whose sense of propryety he had every reason to believe would have induced him reather to have promoted good order, than to have excited disorder and faction among the party, particularly in the absence of Capᵗ Clark and himself: The Commanding officer is also sorry to find any man, who has been engaged by himself and Capᵗ Clark . . . so destitute of understanding, as not to be able to draw the distinction between being placed under the command of another officer, whose will in such case would be their law, and that of obeying the orders of Capᵗ Clark and himself communicated to them through Sergᵗ Ordway, who . . . has during their necessary absence been charged with the execution of their orders; . . . and who, is in all respects accountable to us for the faithfull observance of the same.

A moments reflection must convince every man . . . that were we to neglect the more important . . . arrangements in relation to the voyage we are now entering on, for the purpose merely of remain[in]g at camp in order to communicate our orders in person to the individuals of the party on mear points of poliece, they would have too much reason to complain; nay, even to fear the ultimate success of the enterprise in which we are all embarked. The abuse of some of the party with respect [to the] prevelege heretofore granted them of going into the country, is not less displeasing; to such as have made hunting or other business a pretext to cover their design of visiting a neighbouring whiskey shop, he cannot for the present extend this previlege; and dose therefore most positively direct, that Colter, Bolye, Wiser, and Robinson do not recieve permission to leave camp under any pretext whatever for *ten days,* after this order is read on the parade, unless otherwise directed hereafter by Capᵗ Clark or himself. The commanding officers highly approve of the conduct of Sergᵗ Ordway.

The Carpenters Blacksmiths, and in short the whole party (except Floid who has been specially directed to perform other duties) are to obey implicitly the orders of Sergᵗ Ordway, who has recieved our instructions on these subjects, and is held accountable to us for their due execution.

MERIWETHER LEWIS.
Capᵗ 1ˢᵗ U. S. Regᵗ Infty Comdᵍ Detatchment

[Indorsed:] Sergᵗ Ordway will read the within order to the men on the parade the morning after the reciept of the same.

M. LEWIS CAPᵗ

At Fort Clatsop

ORDERLY BOOK; LEWIS   FORT CLATSOP, JANUARY 1ST 1806

The fort being now completed, the Commanding officers think proper to direct: that the guard shall as usual consist of one Sergeant and three privates, and that the same be regularly relieved each morning at sunrise. The post of the new guard shall be in the room of the Sergeants rispectivly commanding the same. the centinel shall be posted, both day and night, on the parade in front of the commanding offercers quarters; tho' should he at any time think proper to remove himself to any other part of the fort, in order the better to inform himself of the desighns or approach of any party of savages, he is not only at liberty, but is hereby required to do so. It shall be the duty of the centinel also to announce the arrival of all parties of Indians to the Sergeant of the Guard, who shall immediately report the same to the Commanding officers.

The Commanding Officers require and charge the Garrison to treat the natives in a friendly manner; nor will they be permitted at any time, to abuse, assault or strike them; unless such abuse assault or stroke be first given by the natives. nevertheless it shall be right for any individual, in a peaceable manner, to refuse admittance to, or put out of his room, any native who may become troublesome to him; and should such native refuse to go when requested, or attempt to enter their rooms after being forbidden to do so; it shall be the duty of the Sergeant of the guard on information of the same, to put such native out of the fort and see that he is not again admitted during that day unless specially permitted; and the Sergeant of the guard may for this purpose imploy such coercive measures (not extending to the taking of life) as shall at his discretion be deemed necessary to effect the same.

When any native shall be detected in theft, the Sergᵗ of the guard shall immediately inform the Commanding offercers of the same, to the end that such measures may be pursued with rispect to the culprit as they shall think most expedient.

At sunset on each day, the Sergᵗ attended by the interpreter Charbono and two of his guard, will collect and put out of the fort, all Indians except such as may specially be permitted to remain by the Commanding offercers, nor shall they be again admitted untill the main gate be opened the ensuing morning.

At Sunset, or immediately after the Indians have been dismissed, both gates shall be shut, and secured, and the main gate locked and con-

Thwaites, *Original Journals of the Lewis and Clark Expedition*, 3:302–04.

tinue so untill sunrise the next morning: the water-gate may be used freely by the Garrison for the purpose of passing and repassing at all times, tho' from sunset, untill sunrise, it shall be the duty of the centinel, to open the gate for, and shut it after all persons passing and repassing, suffering the same never to remain unfixed long[er] than is absolutely necessary.

It shall be the duty of the Serg: of the guard to keep the kee of the Meat house, and to cause the guard to keep regular fires therein when the same may be necessary; and also once at least in 24 hours to visit the canoes and see that they are safely secured; and shall further on each morning after he is relieved, make his report verbally to the Command[in]g officers.

Each of the old guard will every morning after being relieved furnish two loads of wood for the commanding offercers fire.

No man is to be particularly exempt from the duty of bringing meat from the woods, nor none except the Cooks and Interpreters from that of mounting guard.

Each mess being furnished with an ax, they are directed to deposit in the room of the commanding offercers all other public tools of which they are possessed; nor shall the same at any time hereafter be taken from the said deposit without the knoledge and permission of the commanding officers; and any individual so borrowing the tools are strictly required to bring the same back the moment he has ceased to use them, and [in] no case shall they be permited to keep them out all night.

Any individual selling or disposing of any tool or iron or steel instrument, arms, accoutrements or ammunicion, shall be deemed guilty of a breach of this order, and shall be tryed and punished accordingly. the tools loaned to John Shields are excepted from the restrictions of this order.

MERIWETHER LEWIS
Cap! 1ˢᵗ U. S. Reg!
Wᴹ. CLARK Capᵗ &ᶜ

INSTILLING DISCIPLINE

The captains considered fair discipline and firm leadership essential to the expedition's success. The corporal punishments ordered by some of the six courts-martial show their resolve to keep control of the corps.

Alexander H. Willard was caught sleeping on guard duty on July 11, 1804, close to the present-day Kansas-Nebraska border. The regulation penalty for that was death, but the captains used the case to emphasize the true hazards of a surprise attack.

Moses B. Reed deserted near present-day Council Bluffs, Nebraska, on August 7, 1804. He had followed an *engagé* called La Liberté whom the captains had sent ahead to invite the Oto Indians to a council. But La Liberté and Reed did not return once the first council with Plains Indians was under way. Both were caught and brought back, but La Liberté escaped again. Reed was court-martialed and sentenced to run the gauntlet—run through two lines of men facing each other, all armed with the cat-o'-nine-tails, to lash Reed's bare back.

Unaccustomed to such harsh punishments, three Indian chiefs asked that Reed be pardoned, but they later accepted the captains' explanations for why their discipline of the men was so severe. Two months later, another Indian chief objected to the same punishment: He witnessed John Newman run the gauntlet after he was found guilty of mutinous conduct, sentenced to seventy-five lashes, and discharged on October 13, 1804, near the Arikara villages. The chief stressed that his nation never whipped anyone but conceded that the Indians would put an offender to death when necessary to make an example.

Dubois to Platte

ORDERLY BOOK; LEWIS   CAMP NEW ISLAND JULY 12TH 1804.
    A Court ma[r]tial consisting of the two commanding officers will convene this day at 1 OCk. P.M. for the trial of such prisoners as may be brought before them; one of the court will act as Judge Advocate.
                        M. LEWIS
                        WM Clark

CLARK
The Commanding officers, Capts M. Lewis & W. Clark constituted themselves a Court Martial for the trial of such prisoners as are *Guilty* of *Capatal Crimes,* and under the rules and articles of *War* punishable by DEATH.
    Alexander Willard was brought foward Charged with *"Lying down and Sleeping on his post" whilst a Sentinal, on the Night of*the 11th Instant" (by John Ordway Sergeant of the Guard)

Thwaites, *Original Journals of the Lewis and Clark Expedition,* 1:76.

To this Charge the prisoner pleads *Guilty of Lying Down, and Not Guilty, of Going to Sleep.*

The Court after Duly Considering the evidence aduced, are of oppinion that the *Prisoner* Alex.^dr Willard is guilty of every part of the Charge exhibited against him. it being a breach of the *rules* and articles of *War* (as well as tending to the probable distruction of the party) *do Sentience* him to receive *One hundred lashes, on his bear back, at four different times in equal proportion.* and Order that the punishment Commence this evening at Sunset, and Continue to be inflicted (by the Guard) every evening untill Completed

W.^M Clark
M. LEWIS

Platte to Vermilion

CLARK   17ᵀᴴ AUGUST FRIDAY 1804.—

. . . at 6 oClock this evening *Labieche* one of the Party sent to the Ottoes joined, and informed that the Party was behind with one of the Deserters M. B. Reed and the 3 principal Chiefs of the Nations. La Liberty they cought but he decived them and got away. . . .

CLARK   18ᵀᴴ AUGUST, SAT'DAY 1804.—

. . . in the after part of the Day the Party with the Indians arriv.^d we meet them under a Shade near the Boat and after a Short talk we . . . proceeded to the trial of Reed, he confessed that he "Deserted & stold a public Rifle Shot-pouch Powder & Ball" and requested we would be as favourable with him as we Could consistantly with our Oathes—which we were and only Sentenced him to run the Gantlet four times through the Party & that each man with 9 Swichies Should punish him and for him not to be considered in future as one of the Party. The three principal Chiefs petitioned for Pardin for this man after we explained the injurey such men could doe them by false representations, & explan'g the Customs of our Countrey they were all Satisfied with the propriety of the Sentence & was Witness to the punishment. . . .

Thwaites, *Original Journals of the Lewis and Clark Expedition,* 1:111–12.

CLARK   13ᵀᴴ OF OCTOBER SATTURDAY 1804.—
one man J. Newmon confined for mutinous expression . . . we Tried the
Prisoner Newmon last night by 9 of his Peers they did "Centence him 75
Lashes & Disbanded [from] the party."

ORDERLY BOOK; CLARK   ORDERS 13ᵀᴴ OF OCTOBER 1804
A Court Martial to Consist of nine members will set to day at 12 oClock
for the trial of John Newmon now under Confinement. Capᵗ Clark will
attend to the forms & rules of a president without giveing his opinion.
    Detail for the Court Martial

      Sergᵗ John Ordaway   Wᵐ Werner
  Sergeant Pat: Gass   Wᵐ Bratten
          Jo: Shields   Geo: Shannon
          H: Hall   Silas Goodrich
          Jo. Collins

                MERIWETHER LEWIS Capᵗ
                  1ˢᵗ U'S. Regᵗ Infty
                  Wᴹ Clark Capᵗ
or E. N W D [Engineer North Western Discovery.]

LEWIS
In conformity to the above order the Court martial convened this day for
the trial of John Newman, charged with "having uttered repeated expres-
sions of a highly criminal and mutinous nature; the same having a tendency not only to distroy every principle of military discipline, but also
to alienate the affections of the individuals composing this detatchment
to their officers, and disaffect them to the service for which they have
been so sacredly and solemnly engaged." The Prisonar plead *not guil*[t]*y*
to the charge exhibited against him. The court after having duly considered the evidence aduced, as well as the defence of the said prisonor, are
unanimously of opinion that the prisonor John Newman is guilty of every
part of the charge exhibited against him, and do sentence him agreeably
to the rules and articles of war, to receive seventy five lashes on his bear
back, and to be henceforth discarded from the perminent party engaged
for North Western discovery; two thirds of the Court concurring in the
sum and nature of the punishment awarded. the commanding officers

Thwaites, *Original Journals of the Lewis and Clark Expedition*, 1:190–93.

approve and confirm the sentence of the court, and direct the punishment take place tomorrow between the hours of one and two P.M. The commanding officers further direct that John Newman in future be attatched to the mess and crew of the red Perogue as a labouring hand on board the same, and that he be deprived of his arms and accoutrements, and not be permitted the honor of mounting guard untill further orders; the commanding officers further direct that in lue of the guard duty from which Newman has been exempted by virtue of this order, that he shall be exposed to such drudgeries as they may think proper to direct from time to time with a view to the general relief of the detatchment.

CLARK   14TH OF OCTOBER SUNDAY 1804.—
... at 1 oClock we halted on a Sand bar & after Dinner executed the Sentence of the Court Martial so far a[s] giveing the Corporal punishment ...

The punishment of this day allarm^d the Indian Chief verry much, he cried aloud (or effected to cry) I explained the Cause of the punishment and the necessity *(of it)* which he *(also)* thought examples were also necessary, & he himself had made them by Death, his nation never whiped even their Children, from their burth.

DEALING WITH TRADERS

In addition to Native Americans, the corps met traders on the voyage up the Missouri. The reactions of these white people to the expedition clarified and sharpened the men's image of their own unit. Whether viewed as the protector of United States traders or as the defender of new territorial rights, the expedition was clearly regarded as a national enterprise and not as a trading or private commercial exploring venture. Both the captains and men took pride in their special role.

At the Mandan villages, international diplomacy occasionally elevated the corps's status. British traders only grudgingly acknowledged the American presence. The expansion of U.S. territory would force them to find ways other than the Missouri to the Pacific. This need explained François Antoine Laroque's eagerness to know more about the West by joining the corps's "very grand plan" of finding a direct waterway to the Pacific. Understanding the precarious position he was in, Lewis put aside his dislike of the British traders and allowed the men of the North West Company to address Indians through an expedition interpreter and provided a chief trader's wife at a distant post with the silk she requested.

On the return voyage, encounters with traders again added to the expedition's prestige. Near the Yellowstone River on August 11, 1806, Clark's party met two Illinois trappers, who were curious about rumors of the fur resources seen by the corps. John Colter received his discharge to join them. Once in the home stretch, the explorers met a steady stream of traders racing upriver to probe the riches found by the expedition for the United States.

At Fort Mandan

CLARK   31ST OF OCTOBER WEDNESDAY 1804—
. . . Capt Lewis wrote to the N. W. Companys agent on the Orsiniboine River *(fort &c. there about 150 miles hence)* ab! 9 Days march North of this place

CLARK   1ST OF NOVEMBER. THURSDAY 1804—
. . . M. M: Crackin a Trader Set out at 7 oClock to the Fort on the Ossiniboin by him Send a letter, (inclosing a Copy of the British Ministers protection) to the principal agent of the Company.[1]

CLARK   27TH OF NOVEMBER TUESDAY 1804—
. . . Seven Traders arrived from the fort on the Ossinoboin from the NW. Company one of which Lafrance took upon himself to speak unfavourably of our intentions &c. the principal M! *La Rock* (& M! M: Kensey) was informed of the Conduct of their interpreter & the Consequences if they did not put a Stop to unfavourable & ill founded assursions &c. &c.

CLARK   29TH NOVEMBER THURSDAY 1804—
. . . M! *La Rock* and one of his men Came to visit us, we informed him what we had herd of his intentions of makeing Chiefs &c. and forbid him to give Meadels or flags to the Indians, he Denied haveing any Such intention, we agreed that one of our interpeters Should Speak for him on Con-

---

[1]The agent's name was Charles Chaboillez, representing the North West Company; Lewis and Clark wrote to him explaining the nature of their mission, and enclosing a copy of the passport granted them by Mr. Edward Thornton, of the British legation at Washington. [Thwaites's note.]

ditions he did not say any thing more than what tended to trade alone. he gave fair promises &c.

CLARK   4ᵀᴴ MARCH MONDAY 1805 FORT MANDAN
    . . . an Engage of the NW Co: Came for a horse, and requested in the name of the woman of the principal of his Department some Silk of three Colours, which we furnished. . . .

Clark's Exploration

CLARK   WEDNESDAY 11ᵀᴴ AUGUST 1806
. . . at Meridian I set out and had not proceeded more than 2 miles before I observed a canoe near the Shore. . . . here I found two men from the illi-noies Jos. Dixon, and [blank space in MS.] Handcock those men are on a trapping expedition up the River Rochejhone. . . . the last winter they Spent with the Tetons in company with a Mʳ *Coartong* . . . The tetons robed him of the greater part of the goods and wounded this Dixon in the leg with a hard wad. The Tetons gave Mʳ *Coartong* some fiew robes for the articles they took from him. Those men further informed me that they met the Boat . . . we Sent down from Fort Mandan near the Kanzas river on board of which was a chief of the Ricaras, that he met the Yank-ton chiefs with Mʳ Deurion, Mᶜ Clellen & Several other traders on their way down. that the Mandans and Menitarrais wer at war with the Ricaras and had killed two of the latter. the Assinniboins were also at war with the Mandans &c. and had prohibited the N W. traders from comeing to the Missouri to trade. . . . Those dificulties if true will I fear be a bar to our expectations of having the Mandan Minetarra & Ricara chief to accompany us to the U. States. Tho we shall endeaver to bring about a peace between Mandans Mennetarres & Ricaras and provail on some of their Chiefs to accompany us to the U. States. . . .

CLARK   THURSDAY (SATURDAY) 14TH AUGUST 1806
Colter one of our men expressed a desire to join Some trappers [*the two
Illinois Men we met, & who now came down to us*] who offered to become
shearers with [him] and furnish traps &c. . . . we agreed to allow him the
privilage provided no one of the party would ask or expect a Similar permission to which they all agreeed that they wished Colter every suckcess
and that as we did not wish any of them to Seperate untill we Should arive
at St. Louis they would not apply or expect it &c.[1]

SHIPMENT TO ST. LOUIS

On April 7, 1805, the return of the keelboat from Fort Mandan to St. Louis
was the only opportunity on the voyage to ship reports, letters, and specimens back to the East Coast. Lewis sent no diary to Jefferson; he may
not have written one for the trip from Camp Dubois to Fort Mandan, or
perhaps it was lost at some point along the trip. To ensure a safe trip on
the river, the captains hired a pilot, Joseph Gravelines, an Arikara-
speaking Frenchman and fur agent. He also accompanied the Arikara
chiefs who had promised to make the trip to Washington.

Returning to St. Louis were also John Newman and Moses B. Reed, who
had been court-martialed for mutinous behavior and desertion. Although
Newman had atoned for his action and pleaded for permission to continue
with the corps, Lewis did not want him along as a constant reminder of
disloyalty and subversion on a trip that would surely be difficult.

Lewis and Clark sought to reinforce the group returning to St. Louis.
They encouraged fur trader Pierre Antoine Tabeau and his men to join
and strengthen the party. Such a large group would deter a surprise
attack by the Teton Sioux, who the captains felt were hostile to the expedition. They remembered their earlier encounter with the Teton who had
mixed hospitality with insults and threats and so lent credibility to the
traders' stories of the Sioux's ferocity.

[1] Colter remained on the upper rivers and in the mountains until the spring of 1810, during which time he had many adventures — the most perilous of which was his capture by
the Blackfoot Indians, and his race against them for his life, with which he barely escaped.
On returning to St. Louis (1810) he gave valuable geographical information to William Clark,
which the latter used in his large map of the Great West, published in the Biddle edition.
Colter was the first explorer of a considerable region, including notably the Yellowstone
National Park. [Thwaites's note.]

Thwaites, *Original Journals of the Lewis and Clark Expedition,* 5:341.

Lewis to Jefferson

FORT MANDAN, APRIL 7TH 1805.

DEAR SIR: ... You will ... receive herewith inclosed a part of Cap! Clark's private journal, the other part you will find inclosed in a separate tin box. this journal (is in it's original state, and of course incorrect, but it) will serve to give you the daily detales of our progress, and transactions. (Cap! Clark dose not wish this journal exposed in it's present state, but has no objection, that one or more copies of it be made by some confidential person under your direction, correcting it's gramatical errors &c. indeed it is the wish of both of us, that two of those copies should be made, if convenient, and retained untill our return; in this state there is no objection to your submitting them to the perusal of the heads of the departments, or such others as you may think proper. a copy of this journal will assist me in compiling my own for publication after my return.) ... I have sent a journal kept by one of the Sergeants,[1] to Capt Stoddard, my agent at S! Louis, in order as much as possible to multiply the chances of saving something. we have encouraged our men to keep journals, and seven of them do so, to whom in this respect we give every assistance in our power. ...

... By reference to the Muster-rolls forwarded to the War Department, you will see the state of the party; in addition to which, we have two Interpreters, one negroe man, servant to Cap! Clark, one Indian woman, wife to one of the interpreters, and a Mandan man, whom we take with a view to restore peace between the Snake Indians, and those in this neighborhood amounting in total with ourselves to 33 persons. by means of the Interpreters and Indians, we shall be enabled to converse with all the Indians that we shall probably meet with on the Missouri. ...

From this plase we shall send the barge and crew early tomorrow morning with orders to proceed as expeditiously as possible to S! Louis, by her we send our dispatches, which I trust will get safe to hand. Her crew consists of ten ablebodied men well armed and provided with a sufficient stock of provision to last them to S! Louis. I have but little doubt but they will be fired on by the Siouxs; but they have pledged themselves to us that they will not yeald while there is a man of them living.

Our baggage is all embarked on board six small canoes and two perogues; we shall set out at the same moment that we dispatch the barge. one or perhaps both of these perogues we shall leave at the falls of the

[1]Doubtless Floyd's Journal. ... [Thwaites's note.]

From original manuscript in Bureau of Rolls, *Jefferson Papers,* ser. 2, vol. 51, doc. 107, reprinted in Thwaites, *Original Journals of the Lewis and Clark Expedition,* 7:318–21.

63

Missouri, from whence we intend continuing our voyage in the canoes and a perogue of skins, the frame of which was prepared at Harper's ferry. this perogue is now in a situation which will enable us to prepare it in the course of a few hours. as our vessels are now small and the current of the river much more moderate, we calculate on traveling at the rate of 20 or 25 miles p.r day as far as the falls of the Missouri. beyond this point, or the first range of rocky Mountains situated about 100 miles further, any calculation with rispect to our daily progress, can be little more than bare conjecture. the circumstance of the Snake Indians possessing large quantities of horses, is much in our favour, as by means of horses, the transportation of our baggage will be rendered easy and expeditious over land, from the Missouri, to the Columbia river. should this river not prove navigable where we first meet with it, our present intention is, to continue our march by land down the river untill it becomes so, or to the Pacific Ocean. The map, which has been forwarded to the Secretary at War, will give you the idea we entertain of the connection of these rivers, which has been formed from the corresponding testimony of a number of Indians who have visited that country, and who have been seperately and carefully examined on that subject, and we therefore think it entitled to some degree of confidence.

Since our arrival at this place we have subsisted principally on meat, with which our guns have supplyed us amply, and have thus been enabled to reserve the parched meal, portable Soup, and a considerable proportion of pork and flour, which we had intended for the more difficult parts of our voyage. if Indian information can be credited, the vast quantity of game with which the country abounds through which we are to pass leaves us but little to apprehend from the want of food.

We do not calculate on completeing our voyage within the present year, but expect to reach the Pacific Ocean, and return, as far as the head of the Missouri, or perhaps to this place before winter. you may therefore expect me to meet you at Montochello[2] in September 1806.

On our return we shal probably pass down the yellow stone river, which from Indian informations, waters one of the fairest portions of this continent.

I can foresee no material or probable obstruction to our progress, and entertain therefore the most sanguine hopes of complete success. As to myself individually I never enjoyed a more perfect state of good health, than I have since we commenced our voyage. my inestimable friend and companion Cap.t Clark has also enjoyed good health generally. At this

[2]Monticello, Jefferson's home in Charlottesville, Virginia.

moment, every individual of the party are in good health, and excellent sperits; zealously attatched to the enterprise, and anxious to proceed; not a whisper of discontent or murmur is to be heard among them; but all in unison, act with the most perfect harmoney. with such men I have every thing to hope, and but little to fear.

Be so good as to present my most affectionate regard to all my friends, and be assured of the sincere and unalterable attatchment of

Your most Ob.^t Servt

MERIWETHER LEWIS

Capt. 1st U' S. Reg.^t Infty.

Thomas Jefferson, President of the U' States.

[Endorsed:] Lewis Meriwether.   Fort Mandan,   Apr. 7 05 rec^d Jul. 13.

YORK'S CONTRIBUTIONS

York, Clark's slave, had been willed to him by his father in 1799. He was probably just a few years younger than his master and had been his companion since childhood. The journals stress York's courage, loyalty, humor, and kindness as well as his success as a hunter and an Indian trader. The captains also used York to distract, awe, and entertain the Indians, with great success. His later life and the date of his death are subjects of speculation.

Teton to Mandans

CLARK   RIVER MAROPA 9TH OF OCTOBER 1804. TUESDAY— many Came to view us all day, much astonished at my black Servent, who did not lose the opportunity of [displaying] his powers Strength &c. &c. this nation never Saw a black man before.[1]

---

[1]By way of amusement he told them that he had once been a wild animal, and caught and tamed by his master; and to convince them showed them feats of strength which added to his looks made him more terrible than we wished him to be. [Biddle's note.]

Thwaites, *Original Journals of the Lewis and Clark Expedition,* 1:185.

Beaverhead to Great Divide

LEWIS FRIDAY AUGUST 16ᵀᴴ 1805.
Some of the party had ... told the Indians that we had a man with us who was black and had short curling hair, this had excited their curiosity very much, and they seemed quite as anxious to see this monster as they wer[e] the merchandize which we had to barter for their horses.

Thwaites, *Original Journals of the Lewis and Clark Expedition,* 2:358.

On the Upper Kooskooske

LEWIS MONDAY JUNE 2ᴺᴰ 1806.
Mʳ Neal and York were sent on a trading voyage over the river this morning. having exhausted all our merchandize we are obliged to have recourse to every subterfuge in order to prepare in the most ample manner in our power to meet that wretched portion of our journy, the Rocky Mountains, where hungar and cold in their most rigorous forms assail the w[e]aried traveller; not any of us have yet forgotten our suffering in those mountains in September last, and I think it probable we never shall. Our traders Mʳ Neal and York were furnished with the buttons which Capᵗ C. and myself cut off our coats, some eye water and Basilicon which we made for that purpose and some Phials and small tin boxes which I had brought out with Phosphorus. in the evening they returned with about 3 bushels of roots and some bread having made a successfull voyage, not much less pleasing to us than the return of a good cargo to an East India Merchant.

SACAGAWEA'S CRUCIAL ROLE

Toussaint Charbonneau already had two other wives in the Mandan villages when he purchased Sacagawea from the Minitari who had captured her in a raid. The captains hired Charbonneau ostensibly as an interpreter, but they put up with him because they anticipated they would need Sacagawea as translator when they traded for horses with the

Thwaites, *Original Journals of the Lewis and Clark Expedition,* 5:98.

Shoshoni. Sacagawea's experiences had made her very self-reliant, so much so that Lewis on one occasion failed to understand the defenses against hardship she had acquired. When not using sign language, Sacagawea spoke Minitari with Charbonneau, who rendered it in French to be translated into English by George Drouillard. Sacagawea's later life is shrouded in uncertainty. Her death is given as 1812, at times 1884.

Sacagawea and Charbonneau eventually accepted Clark's offer to raise their son, hoping for an education that they could not provide. Afterward, Baptiste was the companion of a European prince, a mountain man, and a prospector. He died in 1866.

At Fort Mandan

LEWIS   11ᵀᴴ FEBRUARY MONDAY 1805.

... about five Oclock this evening one of the wives of Charbono was delivered of a fine boy. it is worthy of remark that this was the first child which this woman had boarn, and as is common in such cases her labour was tedious and the pain violent; Mʳ Jessome informed me that he had freequently administered a small portion of the rattle of the rattle-snake, which he assured me had never failed to produce the desired effect, that of hastening the birth of the child; having the rattle of a snake by me I gave it to him and he administered two rings of it to the woman broken in small pieces with the fingers and added to a small quantity of water. Whether this medicine was truly the cause or not I shall not undertake to determine, but I was informed that she had not taken it more than ten minutes before she brought forth perhaps this remedy may be worthy of future experiments, but I must confess that I want faith as to it's efficacy.

Marias to Great Falls

LEWIS   SUNDAY JUNE 16TH 1805.
... about 2 P.M. I reached the camp found the Indian woman extreemly
ill and much reduced by her indisposition. this gave me some concern
as well for the poor object herself, then with a young child in her arms,
as from the consideration of her being our only dependence for a friendly
negociation with the Snake Indians on whom we depend for horses to
assist us in our portage from the Missouri to the columbia river. ... one
of the small canoes was left below this rappid in order to pass and repass
the river for the purpose of hunting as well as to procure the water of the
Sulpher spring, the virtues of which I now resolved to try on the Indian
woman. ... the water to all appearance is precisely similar to that of
Bowyer's Sulpher spring in Virginia. ...
  ... I found that two dozes of barks and opium which I had given her
since my arrival had produced an alteration in her pulse for the better;
they were now much fuller and more regular. I caused her to drink the
mineral water altogether. w[h]en I first came down I found that her pulse
were scarcely perceptible, very quick frequently irregular and attended
with strong nervous symptoms, that of the twitching of the fingers and
leaders of the arm; now the pulse had become regular much fuller and a
gentle perspiration had taken place; the nervous symptoms have also in
a great measure abated, and she feels herself much freer from pain. she
complains principally of the lower region of the abdomen, I therefore continued the cataplasms of barks and laudnumn which had been previously
used by my friend Capt. Clark. I beleive her disorder originated principally from an obstruction of the mensis in consequence of taking could.

Thwaites, *Original Journals of the Lewis and Clark Expedition,* 2:162–64.

Great Falls to Three Forks

LEWIS   MONDAY JULY 22^D 1805.
... The Indian woman recognizes the country and assures us that this is
the river on which her relations live, and that the three forks are at no
great distance. this peice of information has cheered the sperits of the

Thwaites, *Original Journals of the Lewis and Clark Expedition,* 2:260.

party who now begin to console themselves with the anticipation of shortly seeing the head of the missouri yet unknown to the civilized world.

Three Forks to Beaverhead

Lewis SUNDAY JULY 28TH 1805.
... Our present camp is precisely on the spot that the Snake Indians were encamped at the time the Minnetares of the Knife R. first came in sight of them five years since. from hence they retreated about three miles up Jeffersons river and concealed themselves in the woods, the Minnetares pursued, attacked them, killed 4 men 4 women a number of boys, and mad[e] prisoners of all the females and four boys, *Sah-cah-gar-we-ah* o[u]r Indian woman was one of the female prisoners taken at that time; tho' I cannot discover that she shews any immotion of sorrow in recollecting this event, or of joy in being again restored to her native country; if she has enough to eat and a few trinkets to wear I beleive she would be perfectly content anywhere.

Lewis TUESDAY JULY 30TH 1805.
... we ... set out, ascending Jeffersons river. Sharbono, his woman two invalleds and myself walked through the bottom on the Lar.d side of the river about 4½ miles when we again struck it at the place the woman informed us that she was taken prisoner.

Thwaites, *Original Journals of the Lewis and Clark Expedition,* 2:282–83, 286.

Crossing the Divide

Lewis SATURDAY AUGUST 17TH 1805.—
... an Indian who had straggled some little distance down the river returned and reported that the whitemen were coming. . . . they all appeared transported with joy, & the ch[i]ef repeated his fraturnal hug. I felt quite as much

Thwaites, *Original Journals of the Lewis and Clark Expedition,* 2:361, 370–71.

gratifyed at this information as the Indians appeared to be. Shortly after Cap͏ͭ Clark arrived with the Interpreter Charbono, and the Indian woman, who proved to be a sister of the Chief Cameahwait. the meeting of those people was really affecting, particularly between Sah-cah-gar-we-ah and an Indian woman, who had been taken prisoner at the same time with her and who, had afterwards escaped from the Minnetares and rejoined her nation. . . .

LEWIS   MONDAY AUGUST 19͏ͭͪ 1805
The Shoshonees may be estimated at about 100 warriors, and about three times that number of woomen and children. . . . The father frequently disposes of his infant daughters in marriage to men who are grown or to men who have sons for whom they think proper to provide wives. . . . Sah-car-gar-we-ah had been thus disposed of before she was taken by the Minnetares, or had arrived to the years of puberty. the husband was yet living with this band. he was more than double her age and had two other wives. he claimed her as his wife but said that as she had had a child by another man, who was Charbono, that he did not want her.

Seeking Western Waters

CLARK   OCTOBER 19͏ͭͪ SATURDAY 1805
. . . I . . . Set my self on a rock and made signs to the men to come and Smoke with me not one come out untill the canoes arrived with the 2 chiefs, one of whom spoke aloud, and as was their custom to all we had passed. the Indians came out & Set by me and smoked They said we came from the clouds &c. &c. and were not men &c. &c. this time Cap͏ͭ Lewis came down with the canoes in which the Indian[s were], as Soon as they Saw the Squar wife of the interperter they pointed to her and informed those who continued yet in the Same position I first found them, they imediately all came out and appeared to assume new life, the sight of This Indian woman, wife to one of our interpr͏ˢ confirmed those people of our friendly intentions, as no woman ever accompanies a war party of Indians in this quarter.

Thwaites, *Original Journals of the Lewis and Clark Expedition,* 3:136.

At Fort Clatsop

LEWIS   MONDAY JANUARY 6TH 1806.

Capt Clark set out after an early breakfast with the party in two
canoes . . . ; Charbono and his Indian woman were also of the party; the
Indian woman was very impo[r]tunate to be permited to go, and was
therefore indulged; she observed that she had traveled a long way with
us to see the great waters [of the Pacific — ED.], and that now that monstrous fish was also to be seen, she thought it very hard she could not be
permitted to see either (she had never yet been to the Ocean).

Thwaites, *Original Journals of the Lewis and Clark Expedition,* 3:314–15.

Dalles to Walla Walla

CLARK   MONDAY APRIL 28TH 1806

We found a *Sho-sho-ne* woman, prisoner among those people by means
of whome and *Sah-cah-gah-weah,* Shabono's wife we found means of con-
verceing with the *Wallahwallârs.* we conversed with them for several
hours and fully satisfy all their enquiries with respect to our Selves and
the Objects of our pursute. they were much pleased.

Thwaites, *Original Journals of the Lewis and Clark Expedition,* 4:333.

Little Missouri to White

CLARK   SATURDAY 17TH OF AUGUST 1806

. . . Settled with Touisant Chabono for his services as an enterpreter the
price of a horse and Lodge purchased of him for public Service in all
amounting to 500$ 33⅓ cents . . .

. . . we . . . took our leave of T. Chabono, his Snake Indian wife and their
child [son] who had accompanied us on our rout to the pacific ocean in the

Thwaites, *Original Journals of the Lewis and Clark Expedition,* 5:344–45.

capacity of interpreter and interprete[s]s. T. Chabono wished much to accompany us in the said Capacity if we could have provailed [upon] the Menetarre Chiefs to dec[e]nd the river with us to the U. States, but as none of those Chiefs of whoes language he was Conversent would accompany us, his services were no longer of use to the U. States and he was therefore discharged and paid up.[1] we offered to convey him down to the Illinois if he chose to go, he declined proceeding on at present, observing that he had no acquaintance or prospects of makeing a liveing below, and must continue to live in the way that he had done. I offered to take his little son a butifull promising child who is 19 months old to which they both himself & wife wer willing provided the child had been weened. they observed that in one year the boy would be sufficiently old to leave his mother & he would then take him to me if I would be so freindly as to raise the child for him in such a manner as I thought proper, to which I agreeed &c.

MORE THAN JUST A NAME

Little more than names on the roster of the corps is known about the lives of most men who accompanied Lewis and Clark. Few have found biographers since there is such a dearth of detail. Sometimes a personal incident or a captain's praise fleshed out a mere name into a person.

George Shannon, the youngest soldier, was one of these exceptions. At the end of August 1804, he was detailed to move the horses overland while the explorers ascended the Missouri between the Vermilion River and the Teton River in present-day South Dakota. Afraid that he was behind the boats, he raced ahead too far and was lost for sixteen days. In another incident in 1807, after the corps had returned home, he was in a party escorting the Mandan chief whom Lewis and Clark had brought to Washington. An Arikara shot Shannon in the leg, which later had to be amputated. Clark then sent him to Biddle to help with the publication of the *History*. After legal studies, Shannon made a name for himself in Kentucky and Missouri politics.

Other men had to be satisfied with less recognition. On June 9, 1805, at the mouth of the Marias River, Lewis praised Pierre Cruzatte, a good boatman and splendid fiddler, as an expert cache builder. On the same day, Clark commended John Shields for his work as gunsmith. There were several close calls with grizzlies in the summer of 1805 at the Great Falls.

---

[1]The interpreter, who intends settling among these Indians, and to whom they [Lewis and Clark] gave the blacksmith's tools, supposing they might be useful to the nation. [Gass's note.]

A year later, lucky Hugh McNeal faced a grizzly in the same area. Recording that adventure, Lewis pondered bears, providence, and fatality.

Vermilion to Teton

CLARK   SEP. 11™ TUESDAY 1804 —
... the Man who left us with the horses 22 *(16)* days ago *George Shannon He started 26 Aug.*) and has been a head ever since joined us nearly Starved to Death, he had been 12 days without any thing to eate but Grapes & one Rabit, which he Killed by shooting a piece of hard Stick in place of a ball. This Man Supposeing the boat to be a head pushed on as long as he could, when he became weak and feable deturmined to lay by and waite for a tradeing boat, which is expected, Keeping one horse for the last resorse, thus a man had like to have Starved to death in a land of Plenty for the want of Bullitts or Something to kill his meat. . . .

Thwaites, *Original Journals of the Lewis and Clark Expedition,* 1:145.

Marias to Great Falls

LEWIS   SUNDAY JUNE 9™ 1805.
. . . we set some hands to diging a hole or cellar for the reception of our stores. these holes in the ground or deposits are called by the engages *cashes (cachés);* on enquiry I found that Cruzatte was well acquainted [with] this business and therefore left the management of it intirely to him. . . .
. . . The cash being completed I walked to it and examined it's construction. it is in a high plain about 40 yards distant from a steep bluff . . . ; the situation a dry one which is always necessary. a place being fixed on for a cash, a circle ab[o]ut 20 inches in diameter is first discribed, the terf or sod of this circle is carefully removed, being taken out as entire as possible in order that it may be replaced in the same situation when the chash is filled and secured. . . .

Thwaites, *Original Journals of the Lewis and Clark Expedition,* 2:134, 136–37, 139.

... In the evening Cruzatte gave us some music on the violin and the men passed the evening in dancing singing &c and were extreemly cheerfull.

CLARK   JUNE 9ᵀᴴ [1805] SUNDAY

... Shields renewed the main-spring of my air-gun we have been much indebted to the ingenuity of this man on many occasions; without having served any regular apprenticeship to any trade, he makes his own tools principally and works extreemly well in either wood or metal, and in this way has been extreemly servicable to us, as well as being a good hunter and an excellent waterman.

Lewis's Exploration

LEWIS   TUESDAY, JULY 15, 1806
Dispatched MᶜNeal early this morning to the lower part of portage in order to learn whether the Cash and white perogue remained untouched or in what state they were. . . . a little before dark MᶜNeal returned with his musquet broken off at the breach, and informed me that on his arrival at willow run [on the portage] he had approached a white bear within ten feet without discover[ing] him the bear being in the thick brush, the horse took the allarm and turning short threw him immediately under the bear; this animal raised himself on his hinder feet for battle, and gave him time to recover from his fall which he did in an instant and with his clubbed musquet he struck the bear over the head and cut him with the guard of the gun and broke off the breech, the bear stunned with the stroke fell to the ground and began to scratch his head with his feet; this gave MᶜNeal time to climb a willow tree which was near at hand and thus fortunately made his escape. the bear waited at the foot of the tree untill late in the evening before he left him, when MᶜNeal ventured down and caught his horse which had by this time strayed off to the distance of 2 Mˢ and returned to camp. these bear are a most tremenduous animal; it seems that the hand of providence has been most wonderfully in our favor with rispect to them, or some of us would long since have fallen a sacrifice to their farosity. there seems to be a sertain fatality attatched to the neighbourhood of these falls, for there is always a chapter of accedents prepared for us during our residence at them.

FESTIVE OCCASIONS TIGHTEN BONDS

No matter where they were, the explorers observed three holidays with impromptu ceremonies: the Fourth of July, Christmas, and New Year's. July 4, 1804, they celebrated near present-day Atchison, Kansas. Most of Independence Day 1805 was spent portaging the Great Falls, which took much longer than Lewis had expected. On the Fourth of July 1806, Clark's party was at the Yellowstone River in the vicinity of present-day Billings, Montana.

Christmas and New Year's were celebrated at Fort Mandan and Fort Clatsop. Other occasions, such as Lewis's birthday, a notable discovery, or days of particularly grueling work, were marked by issuing a dram of liquor. These small celebrations provided festive moments in the months between the great feasts. Nostalgic memories of holidays and home, good food, hard liquor, and fiddle music reinforced the camaraderie of the expedition.

As the men neared the end of their journey, just anticipating their return was enough to overcome the drudgery of hardships. One hundred fifty miles from the westernmost white settlements on the Missouri, the expedition ran out of provisions. Ordinarily this meant ordering a halt to hunt game. The men, however, were so eager to get back that they assured the captains that there was no need for meat, that they could live very well for the next three days on pawpaws, a yellowish fruit growing along the river, until the party would reach the first village.

At Fort Mandan

CLARK   25 ͭͪ DECEMBER CHRISTMASS TUESDAY— [1804]

I was awakened before Day by a discharge of 3 platoons from the Party and the french, the men merrily Disposed, I give them all a little Taffia and permited 3 Cannon fired, at raising Our flag, Some Men Went out to hunt & the others to Danceing and Continued untill 9 oClock P.M. when the frolick ended &c.[1]

[1] Biddle says: "We had told the Indians not to visit us, as it was one of our great medicine days." Gass says: "Flour, dried apples, pepper, and other articles were distributed in the different messes to enable them to celebrate Christmas in a proper and social manner." Three rations of brandy were served during the day, which was mainly spent in dancing; no women were present save Charboneau's three wives, who were only spectators. [Thwaites's note.]

Thwaites, *Original Journals of the Lewis and Clark Expedition,* 1:240, 243.

FORT MANDAN ON THE NE BANK OF THE MISSOURIES 1600 MILES UP
CLARK   TUESDAY   JANUARY THE 1ST 1805.—
The Day was ushered in by the Descharge of two Cannon, we Suffered
16 men with their Musick to visit the 1st Village for the purpose of Danceing, by as they Said the perticular request of the Chiefs of that Village,
about 11 oClock I with an inturpeter & two men walked up to the Village,
(my views were to alay Some little Miss understanding which had taken
place thro jelloucy and mortification as to our treatment towards them I
found them much pleased at the Danceing of our men, I ordered my
black Servent to Dance which amused the Croud Verry much, and Somewhat astonished them, that So large a man should be active &c. &c.

Great Falls Portage

LEWIS   THURSDAY JULY 4TH 1805
. . . our work being at an end this evening, we gave the men a drink of
Sperits, it being the last of our stock, and some of them appeared a little
sensible of it's effects the fiddle was plyed and they danced very merrily
untill 9 in the evening when a heavy shower of rain put an end to that part
of the amusement tho' they continued their mirth with songs and festive
jokes and were extreemly merry untill late at night. we had a very comfortable dinner, of bacon, beans, suit dumplings & buffaloe beaf &c. in
short we had no just cause to covet the sumptuous feasts of our coun-
trymen on this day. . . .

At Fort Clatsop

CLARK   CHRISTMAS WEDNESDAY 25ᵀᴴ DECEMBER 1805
at day light this morning we we[re] awoke by the discharge of the fire
arm[s] of all our party & a Selute, Shouts and a Song which the whole
party joined in under our windows, after which they retired to their
rooms were chearfull all the morning. after brackfast we divided our
Tobacco which amounted to 12 carrots one half of which we gave to the
men of the party who used tobacco, and to those who doe not use it we
make a present of a handkerchief, The Indians leave us in the evening
all the party Snugly fixed in their huts. I recved a pres[e]nt of Capᵗ L. of
a fleece hosrie [hosiery] Shirt Draws and Socks, a pᵣ Mockersons of
Whitehouse a Small Indian basket of Gutherich, two Dozen white weazils
tails of the Indian woman, & some black root of the Indians before their
departure. . . .
  we would have Spent this day the nativity of Christ in feasting, had we
any thing either to raise our Sperits or even gratify our appetites, our
Diner concisted of pore Elk, so much Spoiled that we eate it thro' mear
necessity,[1] Some Spoiled pounded fish and a fiew roots.

[1]And we are without salt to season that. [Gass's note.]

LEWIS   FORT CLATSOP. 1806.
                        JANUARY 1ˢᵀ TUESDAY. [WEDNESDAY]
This morning I was awoke at an early hour by the discharge of a volley
of small arms, which were fired by our party in front of our quarters to
usher in the new year; this was the only mark of rispect which we had it
in our power to pay this celebrated day. our repast of this day tho' better
than that of Christmass, consisted principally in the anticipation of the 1ˢᵗ
day of January 1807, when in the bosom of our friends we hope to participate in the mirth and hilarity of the day, and when with the zest given
by the recollection of the present, we shall completely, both mentally and
corporally, enjoy the repast which the hand of civilization has prepared
for us. at present we were content with cating our boiled Elk and wappetoe,[1] and solacing our thirst with our only beverage *pure water*. two of
our hunters who set out this morning returned in the evening having
killed two bucks elk; they presented Capᵗ Clark and myself each a
marrow-bone and tonge, on which we suped.

[1]Wappato, the root of the broad-leaved arrowhead used for food by Native Americans.
The tube is as large as an egg and resembles a potato when cooked.

Thwaites, *Original Journals of the Lewis and Clark Expedition*, 3:290–91, 301–02.

THE CAPTAINS AS MEDICS

The captains knew that health and efficiency of an army unit depended a great deal on them as commanding officers. They tried repeatedly to help each sick explorer recover from recurring illnesses, and their steady efforts had good results. Their most persistent challenge was from a mysterious back ailment that had struck Private William Bratton on February 10, 1806, when he was working at the salt-making camp, about fifteen miles southwest of Fort Clatsop.

A gunsmith, Bratton was one of the nine young men from Kentucky and the runner-up to Gass in the election for a successor to Sergeant Floyd. His greatest adventure had been meeting a grizzly and running desperately for his life. After his back injury he was scarcely able to walk for 118 days. The men carried Bratton from Oregon to Camp Chopunnish in present-day central Idaho. None of the captains' remedies helped. On May 24, 1806, John Shields, gunsmith and jack-of-all-trades, suddenly recalled seeing men in similar conditions restored by long sweats. A sweat pit was built, and after a few days of treatment Bratton was able to walk again.

The captains' limited medical knowledge meant that at times care verged on experimentation, yet they did not give up. They changed diagnoses and therapy as they sought cures, but their compassion for the sick never wavered. Their devotion to the welfare of all their men reinforced the men's dedication to completing the mission.

Dubois to Platte

CLARK   JULY 20ᵀᴴ FRIDAY 1804—
... It is worthey of observation to mention that our Party has been much healthier on the Voyage than parties of the same number is in any other Situation. Tumers have been troublesom to them all.

Thwaites, *Original Journals of the Lewis and Clark Expedition,* 1:85–86.

At Fort Mandan

CLARK   29ᵀᴴ NOVEMBER THURSDAY 1804—
Sergeant Pryor in takeing down the mast put his Sholder out of Place, we made four trials before we replaced it . . .

Thwaites, *Original Journals of the Lewis and Clark Expedition,* 1:229.

On the Upper Kooskooske

LEWIS   SATURDAY MAY 24ᵀᴴ 1806.
. . . William Bratton still continues very unwell; he eats heartily digests his food well, and has recovered his flesh almost perfectly yet is so weak in the loins that he is scarcely able to walk, nor can he set upwright but with the greatest pain. we have tried every remidy which our engenuity could devise, or with which our stock of medicines furnished us, without effect. John Sheilds observed that he had seen men in a similar situation restored by violent sweats. Bratton requested that he might be sweated in the manner proposed by Sheilds to which we consented. Sheilds sunk a circular hole of 3 feet diamiter and four feet deep in the earth. he kindled a large fire in the hole and heated well, after which the fire was taken out a seat placed in the center of the hole for the patient with a board at bottom for his feet to rest on; some hoops of willow poles were bent in an arch crossing each other over the hole, on these several blankets were thrown forming a secure and thick orning of about 3 feet high. the patient being striped naked was seated under this orning in the hole and the blankets well secured on every side. the patient was furnished with a vessell of water which he sprinkles on the bottom and sides of the hole and by that means creates as much steam or vapor as he could possibly bear, in this situation he was kept about 20 minutes after which he was taken out and suddonly plunged in cold water twise and was then immediately returned to the sweat hole where he was continued three quarters of an hour longer then taken out covered up in several blankets and suffered to cool gradually. during the time of his being in the sweat hole,

Thwaites, *Original Journals of the Lewis and Clark Expedition,* 5:60–61.

he drank copious draughts of a strong tea of horse mint. Sheilds says that he had previously seen the tea of Sinneca snake root used in stead of the mint which was now employed for the want of the other which is not to be found in this country. this experiment was made yesterday; Bratton feels himself much better and is walking about today and says he is nearly free from pain.

3

The Challenge of the Continent

Once they left the Mandan villages, Lewis and Clark faced an area of the North American continent known only to the Native Americans who lived there. It stretched from the Great Bend of the Missouri to the lower reaches of the Columbia River. The explorers hoped that the two great rivers would provide a highway on which to travel through this unknown territory. Only a few members of the party—the French Canadian boatmen—were aware of the difficulties of navigating the Missouri. Some members of the corps had heard descriptions of the mouth of the Columbia at the Pacific Ocean, but none of them could imagine the enormous range of the Rockies that lay between the Missouri and the Columbia.

The Scottish fur trader and explorer Alexander Mackenzie, who reached the Pacific north of Vancouver Island in 1793, had crossed the Rocky Mountains in several short portages. His experiences, published in 1801, led Lewis and Clark, already convinced there was a convenient water link between the Missouri and the Columbia, to assume they would meet less formidable mountains when they traveled farther south. However, the magnitude of the Bitterroot Mountains far exceeded the ranges Mackenzie described. Indeed, the Rockies continually astonished the expedition members who thought they knew mountains because they had farmed, logged, mined, soldiered, or traveled in the Appalachians. But their frame of reference did not prepare them for the Rockies. The explorers never thought that mountains would be *the* major obstacle to the expedition.

Long before the expedition ascended the Missouri River in 1804, the waterway had been a trading route used by Native Americans shuttling goods over the mountains. Although navigation proved possible for the explorers as far as the headwaters of the Beaverhead River, they faced many long arduous stretches of dragging canoes through shallow waters. Strong currents moved sediment into sandbars and weakened riverbanks, which sometimes slid down on the weary travelers. The Missouri often abandoned its channels and cut new courses. With oars, poles, tow lines, and sails, the men tackled the treacherous, muddy waters, which disguised many dangers: snags, driftwood, and sandbars. Quieter waters and stagnant pools provided other hazards — clouds of mosquitoes rose ceaselessly to attack the struggling boatmen. (See p. 85.)

In the harsh winter of 1804 the river froze solid. From November 1804 to April 1805, the expedition remained in its winter quarters at Fort Mandan. Lewis and Clark used this four-month stay in the Mandan villages to obtain information about the upper Missouri. They heard of a major tributary, the Yellowstone River, and received crucial information about their future course. In particular, the Mandan Indians identified the Great Falls of the Missouri as a trail marker the explorers could use to identify that they were on the river that would take them farthest into the mountains. (See p. 87.)

Once under way, the captains were not quite certain of their direction when a tributary joined the Missouri from the northwest. At that crucial confluence, they spent nine days scouting both forks to see which one they should follow and then cache equipment and goods to make their farther travel easier and faster. The captains' scouting made clear that the joining river, which Lewis called the Marias, was not the Missouri as the men had believed. If they had followed the wrong river, they would have missed the Great Falls and only their arrival at the distant mountains would have exposed the mistake. Then it would have been too late in the year to retrace their steps and cross the mountains before snowfall. (See p. 90.) When they reached the Great Falls, their relief and delight were quickly dampened. They realized they could not take the boats through the steep and furious cascades and rapids. The exhausting eighteen-mile portage took almost two weeks in July 1805. (See p. 94.)

Once again, at the Three Forks of the Missouri, they had to pause five days to reconnoiter rivers and determine the proper route. Scouts brought reports about the Gallatin River, and Clark surveyed the Jefferson and Madison Rivers. Together with their celestial observations and the information they had received at Fort Mandan, they concluded that only the Jefferson River pointed west, to the Columbia River, which they assumed they could reach by way of a portage.

While Clark directed the slow advance of the canoes, Lewis pushed ahead with three men on a well-traveled Indian road seeking the source of the river. On August 10, the four men reached a juncture where the river branched into two equal streams. Lewis chose the one moving in the most westerly direction, the Beaverhead River, and followed it to a spring that he proclaimed to be the source of the Missouri. (In 1969 a naturalist and historian of the expedition explained that to reach the actual source of the Missouri one must follow the other branch, present-day Red Rock Creek, "to Upper Red Rock Lake in southern Montana just west of Yellowstone Park.")[1]

At the pass, a short distance from the spring, the four men were astonished by the view of enormous, partially snow-covered mountain ranges all the way to the western horizon. They rushed down the western slope of the pass to a small creek, where Lewis and his men tasted what they assumed was the cold water of the Columbia River. The explorers were wholeheartedly convinced that the Columbia, still several tall mountain ranges away, was within reach. The water they drank actually came from a tributary of the Lemhi River, which, by way of the Salmon River and the Snake River, ultimately does find its way to the Columbia. (See p. 97.)

Clark's reconnaissance of the turbulent waters and rugged gorges of the Salmon River crushed the expedition's hopes of finding a river on which they could travel through the mountains and to the Pacific. There were no banks along the Salmon for men or horses and no timber for building canoes. The captains decided they must follow Indian advice and reach the navigable waters of the Columbia drainage by crossing the mountain barrier on a trail farther north, with a Shoshoni guide. This meant moving overland a hundred miles north to the start of the Lolo Trail, which led across the Bitterroot Mountains. (See p. 101.)

For more than a week, the explorers watched the saw-toothed, snow-capped Bitterroots to the west as they trudged north. The Indians had warned them of the hardships of the Lolo Trail. Hunger, thirst, fatigue, and despair marked the eleven days on the trail and tested the men's determination and endurance as they felt lost in the maze of ridges. When the ordeal was behind them, a good rest with the Nez Perce took care of hunger and fatigue and healed cuts and bruises. It took more time to get over the painful stomach disorders. But it was the emotional impact that lasted longest. The dreaded mountains haunted Lewis even at the Pacific Ocean as he prepared the expedition for the homeward journey in the spring of 1806. Although advice and help from the Nez Perce cut the time for the return crossing to seven days, the Lolo Trail again humbled and exhausted the explorers. (See p. 108.)

Despite the harrowing days and nights on the Lolo Trail and the fleeting hopes for an easy passage, this struggle marked the high point of the expedition. The crossing of the Bitterroots was the explorers' greatest conquest. Their final achievement was reaching the Pacific. On November 7, 1805, Clark expressed his joy when he thought he first saw the

---

[1]Paul Russell Cutright, *Lewis and Clark: Pioneering Naturalists* (Urbana: University of Illinois Press, 1969), 180.

Pacific. Later he realized he had mistaken the broad mouth of the Columbia River for the sea, and on November 18 the party actually camped in sight of the ocean. Thus they completed the westward portion of their historic trek.

In crossing the awesome mountains, the explorers had resolved one of the mysteries of the continent. They neither found the often-sought waterway through the continent nor discovered a feasible land passage linking the Missouri with the Columbia. For some people, the disappointment in not finding a Northwest or a Wilderness Passage made reaching the Pacific an anticlimax to the great adventure, but Lewis and Clark brought to Americans firsthand knowledge of an enormous chain of mountains dividing the woodlands and the prairies of North America from the plateaus and the Pacific shore. In addition, the expedition confirmed knowledge of the coastal geography near the mouth of the Columbia and its relation to other landmarks in the Pacific Northwest. The explorers also attested to the flourishing trade among Europeans, Americans, and Indians as they saw European and American trade goods in the hands of the Native Americans they passed.

As soon as Lewis and Clark arrived at the mouth of the Columbia, they began to search for a good location for winter quarters. The steady rain and the scarce game complicated their decision. Indian advice that elk and edible roots were plentiful south of the Columbia coincided with the explorers' need to replenish their salt supply and their hope of meeting traders.

On November 24, after the party voted to investigate the south side of the Columbia, Lewis found a suitable site for winter quarters ten miles south of the river. Fort Clatsop, named after the local Indian nation, was completed at the end of December just when heavy rains set in. Two blockhouses, facing each other, were linked by palisades. A few days later, a salt-making camp was established about fifteen miles to the southwest where an Indian trail made it easier to reach the shore.

The winter held many disappointments besides the damp and chilly weather. Elk became scarce. The explorers watched anxiously for trading ships hoping to purchase supplies and to restock their depleted stores, but no ship appeared. The two captains were hard put to keep their men content, and everyone grew restless to head home. The departure was moved up from April 1 to March 20. Heavy rains caused a two-day delay, but on March 22, 1806, the party was homeward bound.

On the return voyage the Bitterroot Mountains were once more the major obstacle. The explorers dreaded facing them again but were so eager to pass them quickly that they complicated the crossing. The impatient captains ignored the warnings of the Nez Perce and started too early and without a guide into the higher altitudes of the Lolo Trail. They found the trail blocked by deep snow and no food for the horses. On June 17, 1806, they retreated to the Nez Perce settlements, where they procured Indian guides who could negotiate the snowy mountains. The taxing Bitterroots were finally behind them on June 29, when the explorers relaxed at Lolo Hot Springs, relieved to be close to the Great Plains and the Missouri.

THE MIGHTY MISSOURI

The Missouri River was the first and the longest continuing challenge the explorers faced. They spent most of their travel time on the river or on its banks, constantly seeking ways to cope with its erratic flow. On some stretches the meandering river cut winding courses through the prairie, adding many miles to the distances the boats had to cover. Squalls made using sails hazardous. Strong winds necessitated layovers and sometimes increased the force of the current so much that tow ropes broke. In the steep canyons of the river's upper reaches, tow ropes frequently could not be used because there was no space for a footpath, and the explorers had to paddle the canoes against fierce currents. Despite their exhaustion, the men had to remain alert to spot sawyers, drifting trees bobbing in the current, to avoid snags and logs partially embedded in a silted channel, and to notice banks undercut by the current and threatening to crash down on the boats.

Dubois to Platte

CLARK   MAY 24TH THURSDAY 1804 —
. . . passed a verry bad part of the River Called the Deavels race ground, this is where the Current Sets against some projecting rocks for half a Mile on the Lab! Side. . . . We attempted to pass up under the Lb! Bank which was falling in so fast that the evident danger obliged us to cross between the Starb! Side and a Sand bar in the middle of the river, We *hove* up near the head of the Sand bar, the Same moveing & backing

Thwaites, *Original Journals of the Lewis and Clark Expedition*, 1:28.

caused us to run on the sand. The Swiftness of the Current Wheeled the boat, Broke our *Toe* rope, and was nearly over Setting the boat, all hands jumped out on the upper Side and bore on that Side untill the Sand washed from under the boat and Wheeled on the next bank by the time She wheeled a 3 ?ᵈ Time got a rope fast to her Stern and by the means of swimmers was Carred to Shore and when her stern was down whilst in the act of Swinging a third time into Deep Water near the Shore, we returned, to the Island where we Set out and assended under the Bank which I have just mentioned, as falling in. . . . This place I call the *retragrade* bend as we were obliged to fall back 2 miles

Vermilion to Teton

CLARK   21ˢᵀ OF SEPTEMBER FRIDAY 1804 —

at half past one o'clock this morning the Sand bar on which we Camped began to under mind and give way which allarmed the Serjeant on Guard, the motion of the boat awakened me; I got up & by the light of the moon observed that the Sand had given away both above and below our Camp & was falling in fast. I ordered all hands on as quick as possible & pushed off, we had pushed off but a few minits before the bank under which the Boat & perogus lay give way, which would Certainly have Sunk both Perogues, by the time we made the ops ?ᵈ Shore our Camp fell in, we made a 2 ?ᵈ Camp for the remainder of the night.

LEWIS   FRIDAY MAY 31ˢᵀ 1805.—

... The obstructions of rocky points and riffles still continue as yesterday; at those places the men are compelled to be in the water even to their armpits, and the water is yet very could, and so frequent are those point[s] that they are one fourth of their time in the water, added to this the banks and bluffs along which they are obliged to pass are so slippery and the mud so tenacious that they are unable to wear their mockersons, and in that situation draging the heavy burthen of a canoe and walking acasionally for several hundred yards over the sharp fragments of rocks which tumble from the clifts and garnish the borders of the river; in short their labour is incredibly painfull and great, yet those faithfull fellows bear it without a murmur. The toe rope of the white perogue, the only one indeed of hemp, and that on which we most depended, gave way today at a bad point, the perogue swung and but slightly touched a rock; yet was very near overseting; I fear her evil gennii will play so many pranks with her that she will go to the bottomm some of those days. ...
... at 12 OC.ᴹ[1] we came too for refreshment and gave the men a dram which they received with much cheerfullness, and well deserved.

THE COLD WINTER OF 1804

The explorers were spared the summer floods of the Missouri River, but its cold winters caught up with them at the beginning of November 1804 while they were building winter quarters at the Mandan villages. Dropping temperatures, ice running on the river, falling snow, and swans migrating south added urgency to long working days, which extended at times into the early morning hours, to get shelters ready. On November 19, the men moved into their quarters, and on the next day the captains occupied theirs. On December 7, the river froze solid. The thermometer dropped below zero, bad frostbites occurred, and during the following days the thermometer continued to fall to thirty-eight degrees below zero.

In the three cold months that followed, the captains were most concerned with their men's health and with the danger of ice crushing their boats. They also planned ahead, gathering information from Native

---

[1]12 o'clock meridian (noon).

Thwaites, *Original Journals of the Lewis and Clark Expedition,* 2:100.

87

Americans about the course of the Missouri and the nature of the distant mountains. On March 5, the thermometer rose to forty degrees above zero. Shortly after the ice broke up, the floes disappeared downstream, and in early April the expedition set out on the next leg of the voyage.

At Fort Mandan

CLARK   8TH. DECEMBER SATTURDAY 1804—
a verry Cold morning, the Thermometer Stood at 12$^{d.}$ below 0 which is 42$^{d.}$ below the freesing point, wind from the NW. I with 15 men turned out *(Indians joined us on horseback shot with arrows rode along side of buffaloe)* and killed 8 buffalow & one Deer, one Cow and calf was brought in, two Cows which I killed at 7 miles Ds$^{t.}$ I left 2 men to Skin & keep off the Wolves, and brought in one Cow & a calf, . . . this day being Cold Several men returned a little *frost bit,* one of [the] men with his feet badly frost bit my Servents feet also *frosted* & his P[eni]s a little, I felt a little fatigued haveing run after the Buffalow all day in Snow many Places 18 inches Deep, generally 6 or 8, two men hurt their hips verry much in Slipping down. . . . 2 reflectings Suns to day.

CLARK   10TH MONDAY DEC. 1804 FORT MANDAN—
a verry Cold Day The Thermometer to day at 10 & 11 Degrees. below 0. Capt Lewis returned, to day at 12 oClock leaveing 6 Men at the Camp to prepare the meat for to pack 4 Horse loads came in, Capt Lewis had a Cold Disagreeable night last in the Snow on a Cold point with one Small Blankett, the Buffalow crossed the river below in imence herds without brakeing in. . . . The men which was frost bit is getting better. . . .

CLARK   11TH DECEMBER TUESDAY 1804—
a verry Cold morning Wind from the north The Thermometer at 4 oClock A. M. at 21° below 0 which is 53° below the freesing point and getting colder, the Sun Shows and reflects two imigies, the ice floating in the atmospear being So thick that the appearance is like a fog Despurceing.
    Sent out three horses for meat & with Derections for all the hunters

to return to the fort as Soon as possible at 1 oClock the horses returned loaded, at night all the hunters returned, Several a little *frosted.* . . .

CLARK   12ᵀᴴ DECEMBER WEDNESDAY 1804—

a Clear Cold morning Wind from the *north* the Thermometer at Sun rise Stood at 38° below 0., moderated untill 6 oClock at which time it began to get Colder. I line my Gloves and have a Cap made of the Skin of the *Louservia* (Lynx) (or wild Cat of the North) the fur near 3 inches long . . . the weather is So Cold that we do not think it prudent to turn out to hunt in Such Cold weather, or at least untill our Constˢ are prepared to under go this Climate. I measure the river from bank to bank on the ice and make it 500 yards

LEWIS   3ᴿᴰ OF FEBRUARY SUNDAY 1805.

a fine day; . . . the situation of our boat and perogues is now allarming, they are firmly inclosed in the Ice and almost covered with snow—the ice which incloses them lyes in several stratas of unequal thicknesses which are seperated by streams of water. this [is] peculiarly unfortunate because so soon as we cut through the first strata of ice the water rushes up and rises as high as the upper surface of the ice and thus creates such a debth of water as renders it impracticable to cut away the lower strata which appears firmly attatched to, and confining the bottom of the vessels. the instruments we have hitherto used has been the ax only, with which, we have made several attempts that proved unsuccessfull from the cause above mentioned. we then determined to attempt freeing them from the ice by means of boiling water which we purposed heating in the vessels by means of hot stones, but this expedient proved also fruitless, as every species of stone which we could procure in the neighbourhood partook so much of the calcarious genus that they burst into small particles on being exposed to the heat of the fire. we now determined as the dernier[1] resort to prepare a parsel of Iron spikes and attatch them to the end of small poles of convenient length and endeavour by means of them to free the vessels from the ice. we have already prepared a large rope of Elk-skin and a windless by means of which we have no doubt of being able to draw the boat on the bank provided we can free [it] from the ice.

CLARK   26ᵀᴴ FEBRUARY TUESDAY 1805

a fine Day Commenced verry early in makeing preparations for drawing up the Boat on the bank, at Sunset by Repeated exertions the whole day,

[1]French for "last."

we accomplished this troublesom task, just as we were fixed for hauling the Boat, the ice gave way near us for about 100 yd^s in length. a number of Indians here to day to See the Boat rise on the Bank.

THE RIDDLE OF THE MARIAS RIVER

After their departure from the Mandan villages, the corps reached the mouth of the Yellowstone River at the end of April and then entered a stretch of the river where it became difficult to identify the Missouri's main course. The confluence of the Marias River and the Missouri River, in present-day northwestern Montana, was a baffling juncture that tested the men's faith in the captains' judgment. Even though extensive reconnaissance supported the captains' well-founded conviction to take the south fork, the men were not convinced; yet they cheerfully followed the captains' lead on the Missouri. The great hopes, however, that Lewis had for the Marias as a commercial water route into the Northwest were later disappointed. On the return trip Lewis himself explored the headwaters of the river, which he had named for a cousin. He found that the promising tributary of the Missouri quickly became a minor stream.

Musselshell to Marias

LEWIS   MONDAY JUNE 3RD 1805.

This morning early we . . . formed a camp on the point formed by the junction of the two large rivers. . . . An interesting question was now to be determined; which of these rivers was the Missouri . . . which the Minnetares . . . had discribed to us as approaching very near to the Columbia river. to mistake the stream at this period of the season, two months of the traveling season having now elapsed, and to ascend such stream to the rocky Mountain or perhaps much further before we could inform ourselves whether it did approach the Columbia or not, and then be obliged to return and take the other stream would not only loose us the whole of this season but would probably so dishearten the party that it might defeat the expedition altogether. convinced we were that the utmost circumspection and caution was necessary in deciding on the stream to be taken. to this end an investigation of both streams was the first thing to be done; . . . accordingly we dispatched two light canoes with three men in each up those streams; we also sent out several small parties by land with instructions . . . to discover the distant bearing of those rivers by ascending the rising grounds. . . . Capt. C. & myself stroled out to the top of the hights in the fork of these rivers from whence we had an extensive and most inchanting view; the country . . . around us was one vast plain in which innumerable herds of Buffalow were seen attended by their shepperds the wolves; the solatary antelope which now had their young were distributed over it's face; some herds of Elk were also seen; the verdure perfectly cloathed the ground, the weather was pleasent and fair; to the South we saw a range of lofty mountains . . . partially covered with snow; behind these Mountains and at a great distance, a second and more lofty range of mountains appeared to strech across the country . . . their snowey tops lost . . . beneath the horizon. this last range was perfectly covered with snow. the direction of the rivers could be seen but little way, soon loosing the break of their channels, to our view, in the common plain. on our return to camp . . . we took the width of the two rivers, found the left hand or S. fork 372 yards and the N. fork 200. The no[r]th fork is deeper than the other but it's courant not so swift; it's waters run in the same boiling and roling manner which has uniformly characterized the Missouri throughout it's whole course so far; it's waters are of a whitish brown colour very thick and terbid, also characteristic of the Missouri; while the South fork is perfectly transparent runds very rappid but with a smoth unriffled surface it's bottom composed of round and flat smooth stones like most rivers issuing from a mountainous country. the bed of the N. fork composed of some gravel but principally mud; in short the air & character of this river is so precisely that of the missouri below that the party with very few exceptions have already pronounced the N. fork to be the Missouri; myself and Capt C. not quite so precipitate have not yet decided but if we were to give our opinions I believe we should be in the minority, certain it is that the North fork gives the colouring matter and character which is retained from hence to the gulph of Mexico. . . .

. . . Capt C. and myself concluded to set out early the next morning with a small party each, and ascend these rivers untill we could perfectly satisfy ourselves of the one, which it would be most expedient for us to take on our main journey to the Pacific.

Marias to Great Falls

LEWIS SATURDAY JUNE 8ᵀᴴ 1805.—

LEWIS SATURDAY JUNE 8ᵀᴴ 1805.—

... set out about sunrise and continued our rout down the river bottoms through the mud and water as yesterday, tho' the road was somewhat better ... and we were not so often compelled to wade in the river. we passed some dangerous and difficult bluffs. ... The whole of my party to a man except myself were fully pe[r]suaided that this river was the Missouri, but being fully of opinion that it was neither the main stream, nor that which it would be advisable for us to take, I determined to give it a name and in honour of Miss Maria W——d.[1] called it Maria's River. it is true that the hue of the waters of this turbulent and troubled stream but illy comport with the pure celestial virtues and amiable qualifications of that lovely fair one; but on the other hand it is a noble river; one destined to become in my opinion an object of contention between the two great powers of America and Great Britin with rispect to the adjustment of the Northwestwardly boundary of the former; and that it will become one of the most interesting branc[h]es of the Missouri in a commercial point of view, I have but little doubt, as it abounds with anamals of the fur kind, and most probably furnishes a safe and direct communication to that productive country of valuable furs exclusively enjoyed at present by the subjects of his Britanic Majesty. ... I arrived at camp about 5 OClock in the evening much fatiegued, where I found Capᵗ Clark and the ballance of the party waiting our return with some anxiety for our safety having been absent near two days longer than we had engaged to return. ...

I now gave myself this evening to rest from my labours, took a drink of grog and gave the men who had accompanyed me each a dram. Capt. Clark ploted the courses of the two rivers as far as we had ascended them.

LEWIS SUNDAY JUNE 9ᵀᴴ 1805

... today we examined our maps, and compared the information derived as well from them as [from] the Indians and fully settled in our minds the propryety of addopting the South fork for the Missouri, as that which it would be most expedient for us to take. ... The Indian information ... argued strongly in favour of the South fork. they informed

[1]Miss Maria Wood, a cousin of Captain Lewis, who was later Mrs. Clarkson. [Thwaites's note.]

Thwaites, *Original Journals of the Lewis and Clark Expedition,* 2:130–31, 134–36.

us that the water of the Missouri was nearly transparent at the great falls, this is the case with the water of the South fork; that the falls lay a little to the South of sunset from them; this is also probable as we are only a few minutes North of Fort Mandan and the South fork bears considerably South from hence to the Mountains; that the falls are below the rocky mountains and near the No[r]thern termineation of one range of those Mountains. a range of mountains which apear behind the S. Mountains and which appear to terminate S. W. from this place and on this side of the unbroken chain of the Rocky Mountains gives us hope that this part of their information is also correct, and there is sufficient distance between this and the mountains for many and I fear for us much too many falls. another impression on my mind is that if the Indians had passed any stream as large as the South fork on their way to the Missouri that they would not have omitted mentioning it; and the South fork from it's size and complexion of it's waters must enter the R.ʸ Mountains and in my opinion penetrates them to a great distance. . . . Those ideas . . . I indevoured to impress on the minds of the party all of whom except Cap.ᵗ C. being still firm in the belief that the N. Fork was the Missouri and that which we ought to take; they said very cheerfully that they were ready to follow us any wher[e] we thought proper to direct but that they still thought that the other was the river and that they were affraid that the South fork would soon termineate in the mountains and leave us at a great distance from the Columbia. Cruzatte who had been an old Missouri navigator and who from his integrity knowledge and skill as a waterman had acquired the confidence of every individual of the party declared it as his opinion that the N. fork was the true genuine Missouri and could be no other. finding them so determined in this beleif, and wishing that if we were in an error to be able to detect it and rectify it as soon as possible it was agreed between Cap.ᵗ C. and myself that one of us should set out with a small party by land up the South fork and continue our rout up it untill we found the falls or reached the snowy Mountains by which means we should be enabled to determine this question prety accurately. this expedition I prefered undertaking as Cap.ᵗ C. [is the] best waterman &.ᶜ and determined to set out the day after tomorrow; . . . as we had determined to leave our blacksmith's bellows and tools here it was necessary to repare some of our arms, and particularly my Airgun the main spring of which was broken, before we left this place. . . . I felt myself very unwell this morning and took a portion of salts from which I feel much releif this evening.

AT LAST—THE GREAT FALLS

The Great Falls, in present-day northwestern Montana, were the crucial landmark to confirm the captains' difficult choice at the confluence with the Marias River. Lewis's decision to explore ahead brought him to the first of a series of five falls on June 13, 1805.

The arrival validated the captains' choice of route, but it also indicated that a long portage causing further delays was unavoidable. The drudgery of moving boats and supplies was made worse by rough terrain. "Sharp points of earth as hard as frozen ground" cut the men's feet, Lewis reported on June 23. The hooves of buffalo had pounded the prairie during the rainy season; afterward the sun had baked the hoofprints into a rocklike shape. The buffalo, overgrazing bluffs and bench land, had sculpted the ground and also made an ideal site for prickly pears, whose thorns shredded moccasins and tore feet.

The buffalo began their seasonal movement away from the falls just as the corps arrived. Soon hunting became uncertain. Meat was required for meals each day as well as to make pemmican, an emergency food of dried meat paste seasoned with fat and berries and pressed into cakes. A swift portage and speedy continuation of the trip seemed critical. On July 13, Lewis's party left the portage and joined Clark and his men who had gone ahead to build additional canoes. Two days later, on July 15, the expedition continued its voyage.

Marias to Great Falls

LEWIS   THURSDAY JUNE 13TH 1805.

... from the extremity of this roling country I overlooked a most beatifull and level plain of great extent or at least 50 or sixty miles; in this there were infinitely more buffaloe than I had ever before witnessed at a view.... fearing that the river boar to the South and that I might pass the falls if they existed between this an[d] the snowey mountains I altered my course nea[r]ly to the South ... I sent Feels on my right and Drewyer and Gibson on my left with orders to kill some meat and join me at the river where I should halt for dinner. I had proceded on this course about two miles with

Goodrich at some distance behind me whin my ears were saluted with the agreeable sound of a fall of water and advancing a little further I saw the spray arrise above the plain like a collumn of smoke which would frequently dispear again in an instant caused I presume by the wind which blew pretty hard from the S.W. I did not however loose my direction to this point which soon began to make a roaring too tremendious to be mistaken for any cause short of the great falls of the Missouri. here I arrived about 12 OClock having traveled by estimate about 15. Miles. . . .

. . . I retired to the shade of a tree where I determined to fix my camp for the present and dispatch a man in the morning to inform Cap! C. and the party of my success in finding the falls and settle in their minds all further doubts as to the Missouri. the hunters now arrived loaded with excellent buffaloe meat. . . . I walked down the river about three miles to discover if possible some place to which the canoes might arrive or at which they might be drawn on shore in order to be taken by land above the falls; but returned without effecting either of these objects; the river was one continued sene of rappids and cascades which I readily perceived could not be encountered with our canoes, and the Clifts still retained their perpendicular structure and were from 150 to 200 feet high; in short the river appears here to have woarn a channel in the process of time through a solid rock. . . .

My fare is really sumptuous this evening; buffaloe's humps, tongues and marrowbones, fine trout parched meal pepper and salt, and a good appetite; the last is not considered the least of the luxuries.

LEWIS   MONDAY JUNE 17ᵀᴴ 1805.

Cap! Clark set out early this morning with five me[n] to . . . survey the river and portage as had been concerted last evening. I set six men at work to p[r]epare four sets of truck wheels with couplings, toungs and bodies, that they might either be used without the bodies for transporting our canoes, or with them in transporting our baggage . . . the ballance of the party I employed first in unloading the white perogue . . . and bring the whole of our baggage together and arranging it in proper order near our camp. this duty being compleated I employed them in taking five of the small canoes up the creek which we now call portage creek about 1¾ miles. . . . we found much difficulty in geting the canoes up this creek to the distance we were compelled to take them. . . . one of the canoes overset and was very near injuring 2 men essentially. . . . we were fortunate enough to find one cottonwood tree just below the entrance of portage creek that was large enough to make our carrage wheels about 22 Inchis in diameter; fortunate I say because I do not beleive that we could find another of the same size perfectly sound within 20 miles of us. the cottonwood which we are obliged to employ in the other parts of the work is . . . soft and brittle. we have made two axeltrees of the mast of the white perogue, which I hope will answer tolerably well tho' it is reather small.

Great Falls Portage

LEWIS   SATURDAY JUNE 22ᴺᴰ 1805.
This morning early Cap: Clark and myself with all the party except Serg: Ordway Sharbono, Goodrich, York and the Indian woman, set out to pass the portage with the canoe and baggage to the Whitebear Island, where we intend that this portage shall end. Cap: Clarke piloted us through the plains. about noon we reached a little stream about 8 miles on the portage where we halted and dined; we were obliged here to renew both axeltrees and the tongues and howns of one set of wheels which took us no more than 2 hours. these parts of our carriage had been made of cottonwood and one axe[l]tree of an old mast, all of which proved deficient and had broken down several times before we reached this place we have now renewed them with the sweet willow and hope that they will answer better. after dark we had reached within half a mile of our intended camp when the tongues gave way and we were obliged to leave the canoe, each man took as much of the baggage as he could carry on his back and proceeded to the river where we formed our encampment much fortiegued. . . . we kindled our fires and examined the meat which Cap: Clark had left, but found only a small proportion of it, the wolves and taken the greater part. . . .

CLARK   JUNE 27ᵀᴴ THURSDAY 1805.
. . . I proceed to finish a rough draugh[t] of the river & Distances to leave at this place, the wormest day we have had this year, at 4 oClock the Party returned from the head of the portage soon after it began to hail and rain hard and continued for a fiew minits & ceased for an hour and began to rain again with a heavey wind from the N W. I refresh the men with a drink of grog The river beginning to rise a little the water is coloured a redish brown, the small streams, discharges in great torrents, and par-

take of the choler of the earth over which it passes, a great part of which is light & of a redish brown. Several Buffalow pass drowned in passing over the falls cloudy all night, cold. . . .

CLARK   JUNE 29ᵀᴴ SATTURDAY 1805
. . . on arrival at the camp on the willow run met the party who had returned in great confusion to the run leaveing their loads in the Plain, the hail & wind being so large and violent in the plains, and them naked, they were much brused, and some nearly killed one knocked down three times, and others without hats or any thing on their heads bloody & complained verry much, I refreshed them with a little grog. Soon after the run began to rise and rose 6 feet in a fiew minets. . . . The plains are so wet that we can do nothing this evining particularly as two deep reveens are between ourselves & Load. . . .

LEWIS   WEDNESDAY JULY 3ᴿᴰ 1805.
This morning . . . some hunters were sent out to kill buffaloe in order to make pemecon to take with us and also for their skins which we now wa[n]t to cover our baggage in the boat and canoes when we depart from hence. the Indians have informed us that we should shortly leave the buffaloe country after passing the falls; this I much regret for I know when we leave the buffaloe that we shal[l] sometimes be under the necessity of fasting occasionally. and at all events the white puddings will be irretrievably lost and Sharbono out of implyment. . . . The current of the river looks so gentle and inviting that the men all seem anxious to be moving upwards as well as ourselves. . . .

SEARCHING FOR THE SOURCE OF THE MISSOURI

Between the Great Falls and the Three Forks of the Missouri the explorers passed through the long canyon of the river. A series of gorges reduced its width and increased its current; water swirled over rapids and churned between the steep cliffs. Only a few men stayed in the boats; everyone else clambered over rocks on the shore. On July 19, 1805, the corps reached the "Gates of the Rocky Mountains," a 150-yard-wide channel through solid rock. There was no room onshore to tow the boats. The river was too deep for setting poles, but despite the strong current rowing moved the boats slowly; after six miles, not far from present-day Helena, Montana, the river broadened into a valley.

On July 22, Sacagawea recognized the country and told Lewis the Three Forks were near. Three days later Clark was the first to see them. He had gone ahead with four men to look for the Shoshoni Indians, hoping to make friendly contact before they were alarmed by gunfire from the expedition's hunters. At the confluence of the three rivers, both captains, independent of each other, picked the western fork (the Jefferson River) for the continuation of the voyage because its channel angled closest to the expedition's charted course.

The captains again separated. This time Clark directed the boats, while Lewis and three men followed an Indian trail west still seeking the Shoshoni. On August 12, the Lewis party crossed the Continental Divide at Lemhi Pass on the present-day Montana-Idaho border, and on the next day they finally met the Shoshoni.

Great Falls to Three Forks

LEWIS   SATURDAY JULY 27ᵀᴴ 1805.—
We set out at an early hour and proceeded on but slowly the current still so rapid that the men are in a continual state of their utmost exertion to get on, and they begin to weaken fast from this continual state of violent exertion. . . . the river was again closely hemned in by high Clifts of a solid limestone rock. . . . we arrived at 9. A.M. at the junction of the S.E. fork of the Missouri and the country opens suddonly to extensive and bea[u]tifull plains and meadows which appear to be surrounded in every direction with distant and lofty mountains; supposing this to be the three forks of the Missouri I halted the party on the Larᵈ shore for breakfast. and walked up the S.E. fork about ½ a mile and ascended the point of a high limestone clift from whence I commanded a most perfect view of the neighbouring country. From this point I could see the S.E. fork at about 7 miles. it is rapid and about 70 Yards wide. . . . from E. to S. between the S.E. and middle forks a distant range of lofty mountains ran their snow-clad tops above the irregular and broken mountains which lie adjacent to this beautifull spot. the extreme point to which I could see the S.E. fork

boar S. 65°. E. distant 7 M. as before observed. between the middle and
S.E. forks near their junction with the S.W. fork there is a handsom site
for a fortification. . . . the rock [r]ises from the level plain as if it had been
designed for some such purpose. the extreem point to which I can see
the bottom and meandering of the Middle fork bears S. 15.E. distant about
14 Miles. here it turns to the right around a point of a high plain and dis-
appears to my view. . . . the extreme point to which I can see the S.W.
fork bears S.30.W. distant about 12 Miles. this stream passes through a
similar country with the other two and is more divided and serpentine in
it's course than either of the others; it a[l]so possesses abundan[t]ly
more timber in it's bottoms. . . . a range of high mountains at a considerable distance appear to reach from South to West and are partially covered with snow. . . . after making a draught of the connection and mean-
ders of these streams I decended the hill and returned to the party. . . .
at the junction of the S.W. and Middle forks I found a note which had been
left by Cap! Clark informing me of his intended rout, and that he would
rejoin me at this place provided he did not fall in with any fresh sighn of
Indians, in which case he intended to pursue untill he overtook them calculating on my taking the S.W. fork, which I most certainly prefer as it's
direction is much more promising than any other. beleiving this to be an
essential point in the geography of this western part of the Continent I
determined to remain at all events untill I obtained the necessary data
for fixing it's latitude Longitude &c. . . . I walked down to the middle fork
and examined and compared it with the S.W. fork but could not satisfy
myself which was the largest stream of the two, in fact they appeared as
if they had been cast in the same mould there being no difference in character or size, therefore to call either of these streams the Missouri would
be giving it a preference w[h]ich it's size dose not warrant as it is not
larger then the other. they are each 90 y^{ds} wide. . . . at 3 P.M. Capt Clark
arrived very sick with a high fever on him and much fatiegued and
exhausted. . . . this morning notwithstanding his indisposition he pursued
his intended rout to the middle fork about 8 miles and finding no recent
sign of Indians rested about an hour and came down the middle fork to
this place. Cap! C. thought himself somewhat bilious and had not had a
passage for several days; I prevailed on him to take a doze of Rushes pills,
which I have always found sovereign in such cases and to bath his feet
in warm water and rest himself. Cap! C's indisposition was a further
inducement for my remaining here a couple of days; I therefore informed
the men of my intention, and they put their deer skins in the water in
order to prepare them for dressing tomorrow.

Beaverhead to Great Divide

MONDAY AUGUST 12TH 1805.

This morning I sent Drewyer out as soon as it was light, to try and discover what rout the Indians had taken. he followed the track of the horse we had pursued yesterday to the mountain wher it had ascended, and returned to me in about an hour and a half. I now determined to pursue the base of the mountains . . . in the expectation of finding some Indian road which lead over the Mountains, accordingly I sent Drewyer to my right and Shields to my left with orders to look out for a road or the fresh tracks of horses either of which we should first meet with I had determined to pursue. at the distance of about 4 miles . . . we saw som resent bowers or small conic lodges formed with willow brush. near them the indians had geathered a number of roots from the manner in which they had toarn up the ground; but I could not discover the root which they seemed to be in surch of. . . . near this place we fell in with a large and plain Indian road. . . . this road we now pursued to the S.W. . . . after eating we continued our rout through the low bottom of the main stream along the foot of the mountains on our right the valley for 5 M^{ls} further in a S.W. direction was from 2 to 3 miles wide the main stream now after discarding two stream[s] on the left in this valley turns abruptly to the West through a narrow bottom betwe[e]n the mountains. the road was still plain, I therefore did not dispair of shortly finding a passage over the mountains and of taisting the waters of the great Columbia this evening. . . . at the distance of 4 miles further the road took us to the most distant fountain of the waters of the Mighty Missouri in surch of which we have spent so many toilsome days and wristless nights. thus far I had accomplished one of those great objects on which my mind has been unalterably fixed for many years, judge then of the pleasure I felt in all[a]ying my thirst with this pure and ice-cold water which issues from the base of a low mountain or hill of a gentle ascent for ½ a mile. the mountains are high on either hand leave this gap at the head of this rivulet through which the road passes. here I halted a few minutes and rested myself. two miles below McNeal had exultingly stood with a foot on each side of this little rivulet and thanked his god that he had lived to bestride the mighty & heretofore deemed endless Missouri. after refreshing ourselves we proceeded on to the top of the dividing ridge from which I discovered immence ranges of high mountains still to the West of us with their tops partially covered with snow. I now decended the mountain about ¾ of

Thwaites, *Original Journals of the Lewis and Clark Expedition*, 2:334–36.

100

a mile which I found much steeper than on the opposite side, to a handsome bold runing Creek of cold Clear water. here I first tasted the water of the great Columbia river. after a short halt of a few minutes we continued our march along the Indian road which lead us over steep hills and deep hollows to a spring on the side of a mountain where we found a sufficient quantity of dry willow brush for fuel, here we encamped for the night having traveled about 20 Miles. as we had killed nothing during the day we now boiled and eat the remainder of our pork, having yet a little flour and parched meal. . . .

this morning Capᵗ Clark set out early. found the river shoally, rapid, shallow, and extreemly difficult. the men in the water almost all day. they are geting weak soar and much fortiegued; they complained of the fortiegue to which the navigation subjected them and wished to go by land Capᵗ C. engouraged them and passifyed them. one of the canoes was very near overseting in a rapid today. they proceeded but slowly. . . .

CROSSING THE ROCKY MOUNTAINS

The Shoshoni, questioned by the captains about a river leading west, called the Salmon River impassable and recommended taking an old Indian trail that crossed the Bitterroot Mountains, about a hundred miles north of the Shoshoni villages. Clark's look at the Salmon convinced the captains to follow the Shoshoni's advice. The crossing of the Rockies drained the explorers' stamina, exhausted their supplies, and humbled their pride.

For twelve days, they struggled on the Lolo Trail following a Shoshoni guide across the Bitterroots. Their horses strayed to find grass when the exhausted men forgot to hobble them at night. The party was disheartened by the harsh terrain and the elusive trail. When the explorers ran out of food, they ate the colts that they could spare.

On September 18, Clark and six hunters went ahead to find game to kill as support for Lewis and the main party. Two days later Lewis's men found in a tree a cache of horse meat, put there by Clark's advance party. Clark and his hunters had come across a stray horse that not only provided nourishment but also signaled the presence of Indians.

On September 22, both parties encamped at a hospitable Nez Perce village in present-day central Idaho, twelve days after the explorers had left Travelers Rest.

Seeking Western Waters

CLARK   AUGUST 23ᴿᴰ FRIDAY 1805
... The River ... is almost one continued rapid, five verry considerable rapids the passage of either with Canoes is entirely impossible. ... my guide and maney other Indians tell me that the Mountains Close and is a perpendicular Clift on each Side, and Continues for a great distance and that the water runs with great violence from one rock to the other on each Side foaming & roreing thro rocks in every direction, So as to render the passage of any thing impossible. those rapids which I had Seen he said was Small & trifleing in comparrison to the rocks & rapids below, at no great distance & The Hills or mountains were not like those I had Seen but like the Side of a tree Streight up. ...

Thwaites, *Original Journals of the Lewis and Clark Expedition,* 3:25–26.

The Lolo Trail

CLARK   SEPTEMBER 13ᵀᴴ WEDNESDAY (FRIDAY) 1805—
Capᵗ Lewis and one of our guides lost their horses, Capᵗ Lewis & 4 men detained to hunt the horses, I proceeded on with the partey ... passed Several Springs which I observed the Deer Elk &c. had made roads to, and below one of the Indians had made a whole to bathe, I tasted this water and found it hot & not bad tasted The last [blank space in MS.] in further examonation I found this water nearly boiling hot at the places it Spouted from the rocks ... I put my finger in the water, at first could not bare it in a Second. as Several roads led from these Springs in different derections, my guide took a wrong road and took us out of our rout 3 miles through intolerable rout, after falling into the right road I proceeded on thro [a] tolerable rout for abᵗ 4 or 5 miles and halted to let our horses graze as well as wate for Capᵗ Lewis who has not yet come up, The pine Countrey falling timber &c. &c. Continue. ... dispatched two men back to hunt Capᵗ Lewis horse, after he came up, and we proceeded over a mountain to the head of the Creek ... to where the moun-

---

Thwaites, *Original Journals of the Lewis and Clark Expedition,* 3:64, 66, 67–70, 72, 73–74, 77–79, 82–83, 88–89, 96–97.

tains Closed on either Side crossing the Creek Several times & Encamped.

CLARK   SEPTEMBER 14ᵀᴴ THURSDAY (SATURDAY) 1805

. . . in the Valies it rained and hailed, on the top of the mountains Some Snow fell we . . . Crossed a high mountain on the right of the Creek for 6 miles to the forks of the Glade Creek *(one of the heads of the Koos koos kee)* . . . and crossᵈ a verry high Steep mountain for 9 miles to a large fork from the left which appears to head in the Snow toped mountains Southerley and S.E. we Crossᵈ Glade Creek above its mouth, at a place the *Tushepaws or* Flat head Indians have made 2 *Wears* across to Catch Sammon and have but latterly left the place I could see no fish, and the grass entirely eaten out by the horses, we . . . Encamped opposit a Small Island at the mouth of a branch on the right side of the river which is at this place 80 yards wide, Swift and Stoney, here we were compelled to kill a Colt for our men & Selves to eat for the want of meat & we named the South fork Colt killed Creek, and this river we Call *Flat head* River the flat head name is Koos koos ke The Mountains which we passed to day much worst than yesterday the last excessively bad & thickly Strowed with falling timber & Pine Spruce fur . . . Steep & Stoney our men and horses much fatigued. . . .

CLARK   WEDNESDAY (SUNDAY) SEPTᴿ 15ᵀᴴ 1805

We . . . proceeded on Down the right Side of *(koos koos kee)* River over Steep points rockey & buschey as usial for 4 miles to an old Indian fishing place, here the road leaves the river to the left and assends a *mountain* winding in every direction to get up the Steep assents & to pass the emence quantity of falling timber which had [been] falling from difᵗ causes i e fire & wind and has deprived the greater part of the Southerley Sides of this mountain of its green timber, 4 miles up the mountain I found a Spring and halted for the rear to come up and to let our horses rest & feed, [in] about 2 hours the rear of the party came up much fatigued & horses more So, Several horses Sliped and roled down Steep hills which hurt them verry much the one which Carried my desk & Small trunk Turned over & roled down a mountain for 40 yards & lodged against a tree, broke the Desk the horse escaped and appeared but little hurt Some others verry much hurt, from this point I observed a range of high mountains Covered with Snow from S E. to S W with their tops bald or void of timber, after two hours delay we proceeded on up the mountain Steep & ruged as usial, more timber near the top, when we arrived at the top As we Conceved, we could find no water and Concluded to . . .

make use of the Snow we found . . . to cook the remnˢ of our Colt & make our Supe, evening verry cold and cloudy. Two of our horses gave out, pore and too much hurt to proceed on and left in the rear. nothing killed to day except 2 Phestˢ . . . with the greatest exertion we could only make 12 miles up this mountain. . . .

CLARK   SATURDAY (MONDAY) SEPTᴿ 16ᵀᴴ 1805
began to Snow about 3 hours before Day and continued all day the Snow in the morning 4 inches deep on the old Snow, and by night we found it from 6 to 8 inches deep, I walked in front to keep the road . . . as in maney places the Snow had entirely filled up the track, and obliged me to hunt Several minits for the track, at 12 oClock we halted on the top of the mountain to worm & dry our Selves a little as well as to let our horses rest and graze a little on Some long grass which I observed. . . . a thickly timbered Countrey of 8 different kinds of pine, which are so covered with Snow, that in passing thro' them we are continually covered with Snow, I have been wet and as cold in every part as I ever was in my life, indeed I was at one time fearfull my feet would freeze in the thin Mockirsons which I wore, after a Short Delay in the middle of the Day, I took one man and proceeded on as fast as I could about 6 miles to a Small branch passing to the right, halted and built fires for the party agains[t] their arrival which was at Dusk, verry cold and much fatigued, we Encamped at this Branch in a thickly timbered bottom which was scurcely large enough for us to lie leavil, men all wet cold and hungary. Killed a Second Colt which we all Suped hartily on and thought it fine meat.

I saw 4 *(Black tail)* Deer to day *(before we set out which came up the mountain)* and what is singular Snaped 7 times at a large buck. it is singular as my gun has a Steel fuzee[1] and never Snaped 7 times before, in examining her found the flint loose. to describe the road of this day would be a repitition of yesterday except the Snow which made it much worse *(to prosue as we had in maney places to derect our way by the appearence of the rubbings of the Packs[2] against the trees which have limbs quiet low and bending downwards)*

CLARK   MONDAY (WEDNESDAY) 18ᵀᴴ SEPTᴿ 1805—
a fair morning cold I proceeded on in advance with Six hunters . . . to try and find deer or Something to kill . . . we passed over . . . more fallen timber . . . from the top of a high part of the mountain at 20 miles I had a view

[1]Fuzee or fusee, a fuse for firing bullets or explosives.
[2]The burdens of the Indian horses. [BIDDLE's note.]

of an emence Plain and *leavel* Countrey to the S W. & West. at a great distance a high mountain in advance beyond the Plain, Saw but little *(no)* Sign of deer and nothing else, much falling timber, made 32 miles and Encamped on a bold running Creek passing to the left which I call *Hungery* Creek as at that place we had nothing to eate. I halted only one hour to day to let our horses feed on Grass . . . and rest

LEWIS   THURSDAY SEPTEMBER 19ᵀᴴ 1805.

Set out this morning a little after sun rise . . . when the ridge terminated and we to our inexpressable joy discovered a large tract of Prairie country lying to the S. W. and widening as it appeared to extend to the W. through that plain the Indian informed us that the Columbia river, (in which we were in surch) run. this plain appeared to be about 60 Miles distant, but our guide assured us that we should reach it's borders tomorrow the appearance of this country, our only hope for subsistance greatly revived the sperits of the party already reduced and much weakened for the want of food . . . after leaving the ridge we asscended and decended several steep mountains in the distance of 6 miles further when we struck a Creek about 15 yards wide. . . . the road was excessively dangerous along this creek being a narrow rockey path generally on the side of [a] steep precipice, from which in many places if e[i]ther man or horse were precipitated they would inevitably be dashed in pieces. Fraziers horse fell from this road in the evening, and roled with his load near a hundred yards into the Creek. we all expected that the horse was killed but to our astonishment when the load was taken off him he arose to his feet & appeared to be but little injured, in 20 minutes he proceeded with his load. this was the most wonderfull escape I ever witnessed, the hill down which he roled was almost perpendicular and broken by large irregular and broken rocks. . . . we encamped . . . in a little raviene, having traveled 18 miles over a very bad road. we took a small quantity of portable soup, and retired to rest much fatiegued. several of the men are unwell of the disentary. brakings out, or irruptions of the Skin, have also been common with us for some time.

CLARK   WEDNESDAY (FRIDAY) 20ᵀᴴ SEPTEMBER 1805

I . . . proceeded on through a Countrey as ruged as usial passed over a low mountain into the forks of a large Creek which I kept down 2 miles and assended a high Steep mountain leaveing the Creek to our left hand passed the head of several dreans[1] on a divideing ridge, and at 12 miles

[1]Drains, rivulets.

decended the mountain to a leavel pine Countrey proceeded on through a butifull Countrey for three miles to a Small Plain in which I found maney Indian lodges, at the distance of 1 mile from the lodges, I met 3 *(Indian)* boys, when they saw me [they] ran and hid themselves, *(in the grass) (I desmounted gave my gun and horse to one of the men,)* searched *(in the grass and)* found *(2 of the boys)* gave them Small pieces of ribin & Sent them forward to the village *(Soon after)* a man Came out to meet me, [*with great caution*] & Conducted me [*us*] to a large Spacious Lodge which he told me (by Signs) was the Lodge of his great Chief who had Set out 3 days previous with all the Warriers of the nation to war . . . & would return in 15 or 18 days. the fiew men that were left in the Village and great numbers of women geathered around me with much apparent signs of fear . . . those people gave us a Small piece of Buffalow meat, Some dried Salmon beries & roots in different States, Some round and much like an onion which they call Pas she co [*quamash.*[2] the *Bread or Cake is called Pas-shi-co*] Sweet, of this they make bread & Supe they also gave us, the bread made of this root all of which we eate hartily, I gave them a fiew Small articles as preasents, and proceeded on with a Chief to his Village 2 miles in the Same Plain, where we were treated kindly in their way and continued with them all night Those two Villages consist of about 30 double lodges, but fiew men a number of women & children, They call themselves *Cho pun-nish* or *Pierced noses*[3] . . .

I find myself verry unwell all the evening from eateing the fish & roots too freely

LEWIS   SUNDAY SEPTEMBER 22ND 1805.

Notwithstanding my positive directions to hubble the horses last evening one of the men neglected to comply. he plead[ed] ignorance of the order. this neglect however detained us untill ½ after eleven OCk at which time we renewed our march, our course being about west. we had proceeded about two and a half miles when we met Reubin Fields one of our hunters, whom Capt Clark had dispatched to meet us with some dryed fish and roots that he had procured from a band of Indians, whose lodges

---

[2]The quamash, or camas (with many other variants of the name), is an important article of food among the Northwestern Indian tribes. It is [a] bulbous root . . . which grows in moist places from California to Montana and British Columbia . . . and may be eaten raw or cooked. It is agreeable to the taste, nutritious, and when cooked and dried can be kept for a year or more. [Thwaites's note.]

[3]The Chopunnish, or Nez Percés, were located on the Salmon and Snake rivers; they were the principal tribe of the Shahaptian family, which formerly extended along a considerable part of the lower Columbia and its tributaries, as far east as the Bitter Root Mountains. [Thwaites's note.]

were about eight miles in advance. I ordered the party to halt for the purpose of taking some refreshment. I divided the fish roots and buries, and was happy to find a sufficiency to satisfy compleatly all our appetites. Fields also killed a crow after refreshing ourselves we proceeded to the village . . . where we arrived at 5 OCk in the afternoon. . . . the pleasure I now felt in having tryumphed over the rockey Mountains and decending once more to a level and fertile country where there was every rational hope of finding a comfortable subsistence for myself and party can be more readily conceived than expressed, nor was the flattering prospect of the final success of the expedition less pleasing. on our approach to the village which consisted of eighteen lodges most of the women fled to the neighbouring woods on horseback with their children, a circumstance I did not expect as Capt Clark had previously been with them and informed them of our pacific intentions towards them and also the time at which we should most probably arrive.[1] the men seemed but little concerned, and several of them came to meet us at a short distance from their lodges unarmed.

CLARK   TUESDAY (THURSDAY) 26TH SEPT^R 1085

. . . proceeded on down the river to a bottom opposit the forks of the river on the South Side and formed a Camp. . . . I had the axes distributed and handled and men apotn^ed [apportioned] ready to commence building canoes on tomorrow, our axes are Small & badly calculated to build Canoes of the large Pine, Capt Lewis Still very unwell, Several men taken Sick on the way down, I administered *Salts* Pils Galip, [jalap] Tarter emetic &c. I feel unwell this evening, two Chiefs & their families follow us and encamp near us, they have great numbers of horses. This day proved verry hot, we purchase fresh Salmon of the Indians

CLARK   27TH SEPT^R (FRIDAY) 1805

All the men able to work comen[c]ed building 5 Canoes, Several taken Sick at work, our hunters returned Sick without meet. J. Colter returned he found only one of the lost horses, on his way killed a Deer, half of

---

[1]There is a tradition among the Nez Percé Indians that when Lewis and Clark first visited the Chopunnish, the latter were inclined to kill the white men, — a catastrophe which was averted by the influence of a woman in that tribe. She had been captured by hostile Indians, and carried into Manitoba, where some white people enabled her to escape; and finally she returned to her own tribe, although nearly dead from fatigue and privations. Hearing her people talk of killing the explorers, she urged them to do no harm to the white men, but to treat them with kindness and hospitality—counsel which they followed. [O. D. Wheeler's note.]

which he gave the Indians the other proved nourishing to the Sick The day verry hot, we purchase fresh Salmon of them Several Indians come up the river from a Camp Some distance below *(Capt Lewis very sick nearly all the men sick. our Shoshonee Indian Guide employed himself makeing flint points for his arrows)*

CLARK   OCTOBER 6TH SATURDAY [SUNDAY] 1805
. . . had all our Saddles Collected a whole dug and in the night buried them, also a Canister of powder and a bag of Balls . . . all the Canoes finished this evening ready to be put into the water. I am taken verry unwell with a pain in the bowels & Stomach, which is certainly the effects of my diet which last all night. . . .

The river below this forks is Called *Kos-kos-kee* it is Clear rapid with Shoals or Swift places

The open Countrey Commences a fiew miles below this on each side of the river. . . .

THE SOGGY WINTER OF 1805

During their brief stay with the Nez Perce the explorers built canoes and mapped waterways to the Pacific described by their hosts. They left the rugged mountains, the heavy timber, and the severe weather behind; visions of the Columbia—the "River of the West" leading to the "Western Ocean"—lured them ahead. Progressing rapidly on the Clearwater and Snake Rivers, the explorers reached the Columbia in nine days, on October 16, 1806.

The Indians along the route remained friendly as the canoes swept down the Columbia. Two Nez Perce who accompanied the explorers for a while translated the words of the Walla Walla Indians into sign language. Approaching the hazardous fifty-mile stretch of falls, cataracts, and cascades made by the Columbia River as it cuts its way through the Cascade Mountains, the corps encountered Native Americans who had been exposed to the cunning ways of Northwest coast traders. Clark noticed that the Chinooks carried good fusils (flintlock muskets), often used by soldiers called fusiliers, and was chagrined to see that these Native Americans were able to match the sharp trading practices of the sea captains. His observations left him with the impression that it was not a good idea to accept presents from Indians "as they are never satisfied in return."

The passage over four major cataracts, which today are covered by water from dams, took almost two weeks of extraordinary effort. Celilo Falls, the Dalles, the Short Narrows and Long Narrows, and the Cascades taxed the men's courage and endurance. At times portages safe-guarded canoes, supplies, and lives. On other occasions, the captains, eager to reach the ocean, ran the rapids at great risk to equipment and crew.

Leaving the Cascades behind and emerging from the Columbia Gorge, the river broadened steadily: The explorers had reached the beginning of the tidewater. At the river's mouth, the captains looked for a place to build winter quarters. North of the Columbia game was scarce, and the Indians traded high for dried fish and roots. They reported, however, that elk and roots were plentiful on the southern shore. There, in the vicinity of a coastal village of the Clatsop Indians, Fort Clatsop was completed on December 30. Most of the men actually moved in on Christmas Eve, after a frantic race to finish the roof before a heavy downpour.

Hunting elk and deer kept the best hunters busy every day. As they depleted the game nearby, the hunters moved farther afield and packing the meat back to camp became more difficult. Despite the efforts at their salt camp, the explorers rarely had enough salt to cure and preserve the meat properly in the humid weather. Even though they smoked the meat for a long time, some of it began to rot. To vary the monotonous diet, they traded for berries, roots, and dried fish with the Native Americans.

The coastal winter weather was much milder than at Fort Mandan, but the damp and chill and the continual rain, fog, and murky skies depressed the explorers. The men suffered from rheumatism, colds, and influenza. Fleas pestered everyone. And the expedition ran out of tobacco in March. The dampness damaged gunpowder, clothing, bedding, and trade goods. The captains struggled to counter the effects of boredom on men who were accustomed to the strain and danger of the trail.

Even the hope of contacting Northwest trading ships proved to be in vain in the off-season. Most ships usually arrived in April and stayed until October or November, trading with the Indians for pelts, particularly sea otter. During the winter there was no chance to use Jefferson's letter of credit to get new supplies or to arrange travel by ship back to the East Coast. Only one Boston skipper traded along the mouth of the Columbia for a few weeks in November 1805, but he and the explorers were unaware of each other.

The captains worked on their journals and maps during the dreary winter. They were satisfied with the route they had traveled, except for one stretch. They had not taken a shortcut between Great Falls and Travelers Rest, which the Minitari had mentioned and their guide Toby, other Shoshoni, and the Nez Perce had all confirmed later. Since they planned to explore the upper Marias and the Yellowstone on the return voyage, they decided to divide the expedition into two groups at Travelers Rest, the eastern end of the Lolo Trail.

The end of the winter approached, but the soggy weather continued. The men's restlessness mounted, and the captains were anxious to cross the dreaded Lolo Trail as soon as possible. Everyone was eager to move along. Although they had planned to stay at Fort Clatsop until April 1, the explorers were homeward bound on March 23, 1806.

Passing the Falls of the Columbia

CLARK   OCTOBER 23.ᴰ WEDNESDAY 1805
. . . I with the greater part of the men crossed in the canoes to opposit side above the falls and hauled them across the portage of 457 yards which is on the Lar.ᵈ Side and certainly the best side to pass the canoes, I then decended through a narrow chanel of about 150 yards wide forming a kind of half circle in it[s] course of a mile to a pitch of 8 feet in which the chanel is divided by 2 large rocks, at this place we were obliged to let the Canoes down by strong ropes of Elk Skin which we had for the purpose, one Canoe in passing this place got loose by the cords breaking, and was cought by the Indians below. I accomplished this necessary business and landed Safe with all the canoes at our Camp below the falls by 3 oClock P.M.

Thwaites, *Original Journals of the Lewis and Clark Expedition,* 3:150.

Descending the Columbia

CLARK   NOVEMBER 17ᵀᴴ SUNDAY 1805
. . . every tide which rises 8 feet 6 Inches at this place, comes in with high swells which brake on the sand shore with great fury. . . .
      at half past 1 oClock Capᵗ Lewis and his Party returned haveing around

Thwaites, *Original Journals of the Lewis and Clark Expedition,* 3:228–29.

passed Point Disappointment and some distance on the Main Ocian to the N W. several Indians followed him & soon after a canoe with *Wapto* roots, & Liquorice boiled, which they gave as presents, in return for which we gave more than the worth to satisfy them a bad practice to receive a present of Indians, as they are never satisfied in return. . . . The Chief of the nation below us came up to see us the name of the nation is *Chin-nook* and is noumerous live principally on fish roots a fiew Elk and fowls. they are well armed with good Fusees. I directed all the men who wished to see more of the Ocean to Get ready to set out with me on tomorrow day light. the following men expressed a wish to accompany me i.e. Serj. Nat Pryor Serj! J. Ordway, Jo: Fields R. Fields, Jo. Shannon, Jo. Colter, William Bratten, Peter Wiser, Shabono & my servant York. all others being well contented with what part of the Ocean & its curiosities which could be seen from the vicinity of our Camp.

The First View of the Pacific

CLARK   NOVEMBER 18TH MONDAY 1805
. . . at the South of a deep bend in which the nativs inform us the Ships anchor, and from whence they receive their goods in return for their peltries and Elk skins &c. this appears to be a very good harber for large Ships. here I found Cap! Lewis name on a tree. I also engraved my name, & by land the day of the month and year, as also Several of the men.

. . . 2 Miles to the iner extremity of *Cape Disapointment* passing a nitch in which there is a Small rock island. . . . this Cape is an ellivated circlier [circular] point covered with thick timber on the iner Side and open grassey exposur next to the Sea and rises with a Steep assent to the hight of about 150 or 160 feet above the leavel of the water this cape as also the Shore both on the Bay & Sea coast is a dark brown rock. I crossed the neck of Land low and ½ of a mile wide to the main Ocian, at the foot of a high open hill projecting into the ocian, and about one mile in Si[r]cumfrance. I assended this hill which is covered with high corse grass.[1] . . .

---

[1]Clark climbed to the top of Cape Disappointment. [O.D. Wheeler's note.]

Thwaites, *Original Journals of the Lewis and Clark Expedition,* 3:233–34.

... the water appears verry Shole from off the mouth of the river for a great distance, and I cannot assertain the direction of the deepest chanel, the Indians point nearest the opposit Side. the waves appear to brake with tremendious force in every direction quite across a large Sand bar lies within the mouth nearest to point Adams which is nearly covered at high tide. ... men appear much Satisfied with their trip beholding with estonishment the high waves dashing against the rocks & this emence Ocian

Winter Quarters

CLARK   DECEMBER 30ᵀᴴ MONDAY 1805

... The fort was completed this evening and at sun set we let The Indians know that, our custom will be to shut the gates at sun set, at which time they must all go out of the fort.[1] those people who are verry foward and disegreeable, left the huts with reluctiance. This day proved the best we have had since at this place, only 3 Showers of rain to day, cloudy nearly all day, in the evening the wind luled and the fore part of the night fair and clear. . . .

LEWIS   SUNDAY JANUARY 5ᵀᴴ 1806.

... Willard and Wiser . . . informed us that it was not untill the fifth day after leaving the Fort that they could find a convenient place for making salt; that they had at length established themselves on the coast about 15 Miles S.W. from this, near the lodge of some Killamuck families; that the Indians were very friendly and had given them a considerable quantity of the blubber of a whale which perished on the coast some distance S.E. of them; part of this blubber they brought with them, it was white &

[1] The sketch-plan here given of the fort on the Pacific Coast, wherein the Lewis and Clark expedition spent the winter of 1805–06 was traced by Clark upon the rough elk-skin cover of his field-book. In the original it is much faded, and the lines have been pulled out of shape by a fold in the skin; no doubt, when drawn, the walls of the fort were straight. Apparently the stockade was 50 feet square, with a long cabin of three rooms ranged along the upper wall, each with what seems to be a central fire-place; and along the lower wall four cabins, two of them with fire-places and one with an outside chimney; the gates are to the left and the parade ground is 20 × 48 feet. [Thwaites's note.]

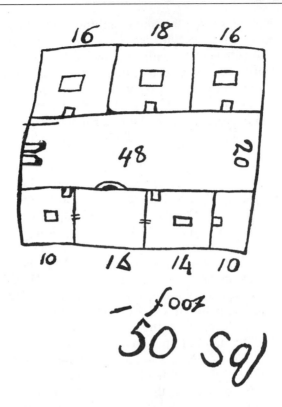

not unlike the fat of Poork, tho' the texture was more spongey and somewhat coarser. I had a part of it cooked and found it very pallitable and ten-
der, it resembled the beaver or the dog in flavour. it may appear somewhat extraordinary tho' it is a fact that the flesh of the beaver and dog
possess a very great affinity in point of flavour. These lads also informed
us that J. Fields, Bratton and Gibson (the Salt Makers) had with their
assistance erected a comfortable camp killed an Elk and several deer and
secured a good stock of meat; they commenced the making of salt and
found that they could obtain from 3 quarts to a gallon a day; they brought
with them a specemine of the salt of about a gallon, we found it excellent,
fine, strong, & white; this was a great treat to myself and most of the party,
having not had any since the 20th Ult[mo].; I say most of the party, for my
friend Cap[t] Clark. declares it to be a mear matter of indifference with him
whether he uses it or not; for myself I must confess I felt a considerable
inconvenience from the want of it; the want of bread I consider as trivial
provided, I get fat meat, for as to the species of meat I am not very par-

ticular, the flesh of the dog the horse and the wolf, having from habit become equally formiliar with any other, and I have learned to think that if the chord be sufficiently strong, which binds the soul and boddy together, it dose not so much matter about the materials which compose it. . . . Cap! Clark determined this evening to set out early tomorrow with two canoes and 12 men in quest of the whale, or at all events to purchase from the Indians a parcel of the blubber, for this purpose he prepared a small assortment of merchandize to take with him.

LEWIS   SATURDAY (FRIDAY) JANUARY 10TH 1806.
Capt Clark returned at 10 P.M. this evening with the majority of the party who accompanyed him; having left some men to assist the saltmakers to bring in the meat of two Elk which they had killed, and sent 2 others through by land to hunt. Capt. Clark found the whale on the Coast about 45 Miles S.E. of Point Adams, and about 35 Miles from Fort Clatsop by the rout he took; The whale was already pillaged of every valuable part by the Killamucks, in the vicinity of one of whose villages it lay on the strand where the waves and tide had driven [it] up and left it. this skelleton measured one hundred and five feet. Cap! C. found the natives busily engaged in boiling the blubber, which they performed in a large wooden trought by means of hot stones; the oil when extracted was secured in bladders and the guts of the whale; the blubber, from which the oil was only partially extracted by this process, was laid by in their lodges in large fliches[1] for uce; this they usually expose to the fire on a wooden spit untill it is pretty well warmed through and then eat it either alone or with the roots of the rush, squawmash, fern wappetoe &c. The natives although they possessed large quantities of this blubber and oil were so penurious that they disposed of it with great reluctance and in small quantities only; insomuch that the utmost exertions of Cap! C. and the whole party aided by the little stock of merchandize he had taken with him and some small articles which the men had, were not able to procure more blubber than about 300 lb. and a few gallons of the oil; this they have brought with them, and small as the store is, we prize it highly, and thank providence for directing the whale to us, and think him much more kind to us than he was [to] jonah, having sent this monster to be *swallowed by us* in stead of *swallowing of us* as jona's did.[2] Cap! C. found the

---

[1]Flich or flitch is the side of a hog salted and cured. The strips of blubber evidently reminded the captains of the familiar way to preserve butchered hog.
[2]According to older translations of the Bible, the prophet Jonah was swallowed by a whale and remained in its belly for three days and three nights. The whale then spit Jonah out again on the dry land. (Jonah, 1:17–2:10.)

road along the coast extreemly difficult of axcess, lying over some high rough and stoney hills, one of which he discribes as being much higher than the others; having it's base washed by the Ocea[n] over which it rares it's towering summit perpendicularly to the hight of 1500 feet; from this summit Cap! C. informed me that there was a delightfull and most extensive view of the ocean, the coast and adjacent country; this Mou! I have taken the liberty of naming *Clark's Mountain and point of view;* it is situated about 30 M. S.E. of Point Adams. *(Disapointment)* and projects about 2½ miles into the Ocean; *Killamucks [Qu. Clatsop]* river falls in a little to the N.W. of this mountain. . . .

The coast in the neighbourhood of Clarks Mountain is sliping off & falling into the Ocean in immence masses; fifty or a hundred acres at a time give way and a great proportion in an instant [is] precipitated into the Ocean. these hills and mountains are principally composed of a yellow clay; there sliping off or spliting assunder at this time is no doubt caused by the incessant rains which have fallen within the last two months. the country in general as about Fort Clatsop is covered with a very heavy growth of several species of pine & furr, also the arbor vita or white cedar and a small proportion of the black Alder which last sometimes grows to the hight of sixty or seventy feet, and from two to four feet in diameter. some species of the pine rise to the immence hight of 210 feet and are from 7 to 12 feet in diameter, and are perfectly sound and solid.

CLARK   MONDAY MARCH 3ᴿᴰ 1806

. . . no movement of the party to day worthey of notice. every thing moves on in the old way and we are counting the days which seperate us from the 1ˢᵗ of April, & which bind us to Fort Clatsop.

HOMEWARD BOUND

During the return trip to the Nez Perce, the captains were required to make several changes in their plans. The fierce currents and rapids of the lower Columbia, fed by the spring runoff, convinced them to shift from canoes to horses as soon as possible. To avoid the major force of the river, the boats hugged the south, instead of the north, bank of the river. On April 2 and 3, 1806, Clark took a side trip with an Indian guide and seven men to scout the Willamette River, known to the explorers as the Multnomah. On the way downstream skirting the north shore of the Columbia they had not seen the river because islands obscured its mouth.

After portaging the Dalles Falls between April 9 and 13, the explorers started using the horses they had obtained in trade with Indians. On April 21 a Nez Perce who knew the way to his nation joined the expedition, and three days later the explorers left the river, broke up the last of the canoes, and moved by foot and horse. The Walla Walla Indians they met recommended a shortcut from the Columbia to the Kooskooske that saved them an eighty-mile upstream canoe voyage on the Snake. On May 3, they were again in Nez Perce country.

The explorers retrieved most of the horses that they had left in the care of the Nez Perce, but they were shocked when the Native Americans told them it would be one month before they could walk the Lolo Trail. The corps waited impatiently at Camp Chopunnish. When the overeager captains broke camp and set out against the warnings of the Nez Perce and without waiting for guides, they found the trail blocked by deep snow. On June 17, the explorers retreated, for the first time on their entire trip, as Clark rather proudly stated.

A few days later the guides joined them, and the explorers crossed the Bitterroot range between June 24 and July 1. The captains marveled at the skill of the Nez Perce guides, who expertly led the explorers to the crest of the range, which wind and sun had freed from snow. On June 29 they had crossed the Continental Divide and were camped at Lolo Hot Springs. On the following day Clark knew that they had left the "tremendous mountains" behind them.

In the Mountains

CLARK   TUESDAY JUNE 17ᵀᴴ 1806
. . . we proceeded down hungary Creek about 7 miles passing it twice; we found it difficuelt and dangerous to pass the creek in consequence of it's debth and rapidity; we avoided two other passes of the creek, by assending a steep rockey and difficuelt hill. beyond this creek the road assends the mountain to the hight of the main leading ridges, which divides the waters of the Kooskooske and Chopunnish Riv's. This mountain we ascended about 3 miles when we found ourselves invelloped in

snow from 8 to 12 feet deep even on the South Side of the mountain. I was in front and could only prosue the derection of the road by the trees which had been peeled by the nativs for the iner bark of which they scraped and eate, as those pealed trees were only to be found scattered promisquisley, I with great difficulty prosued the direction of the road one mile further to the top of the mountain where I found the snow from 12 to 15 feet deep, but fiew trees with the fairest exposure to the Sun; here was Winter with all it's rigors; the air was cold my hands and feet were benumed. we knew that it would require four days to reach the fish weare[1] at thc enterance of Colt Creek, provided we were so fortunate as to be enabled to follow the p[r]oper ridge of the mountains to lead us to that place; of this all of our most expert woodsmen and principal guides were extreemly doubtfull; Short of that point we could not hope for any food for our horses not even under wood itself as the whole was covered many feet deep in snow. if we proceeded and Should git bewildered in those Mountains the certainty was that we Should lose all of our horses and consequently our baggage enstruments perhaps our papers and thus eventially resque the loss of our discoveries which we had already made if we should be so fortunate as to escape with life. the snow bore our horses very well and the traveling was therefore infinately better than the obstruction of rocks and fallen timber which we met with in our passage over last fall when the snow lay on this part of the ridge in detached spop[t]s only. under these circumstances we conceived it madness . . . to proceed without a guide. . . . we therefore come to the resolution to return with our horses while they were yet strong and in good order, and indeaver to keep them so untill we could precure an indian to conduct us over the Snowey Mountains, and again to proceed as soon as we could precure such a guide, knowing from the appearance of the snows that if we remained untill it had disolved sufficiently for us to follow the road that we should not be enabled to return to the United States within this season. having come to this resolution, we ordered the party to make a deposit of all the baggage which we had not imediate use for, and also all the roots and bread of Cows which they had except an allowance for a fiew days to enable them to return to some place at which we could sub-sist by hunting untill we precured a guide. we left our instruments, and I even left the most of my papers believing them safer here than to Wrisk them on horse back over the road, rocks and water which we had passed. our baggage being laid on Scaffolds and well covered, we began our retragrade march at 1 P.M. haveing remain⁴ about three hours on this

[1]Weir, a fence of stakes set in a stream for catching fish.

Snowey mountain. we returned . . . to hungary Creek, which we assended about 2 miles and encamped. we had here more grass for our horses than the proceeding evening, yet it was but scant. the party were a good deel dejected, tho' not as much so as I had apprehended they would have been. this is the first time since we have been on this tour that we have ever been compelled to retreat or make a retragrade march. it rained on us the most of this evening. on the top of the Mountain the Weather was very fluctiating and uncertain snowed cloudy & fair in a few minets.

LEWIS   SATURDAY JUNE 21ˢᵀ 1806
We collected our horses early set out on our return to the flatts. we all felt some mortification in being thus compelled to retrace our steps through this tedious and difficult part of our rout, obstructed with brush and innumerable logs of fallen timber which renders the traveling distressing and even dangerous to our horses. . . . at the pass of Collin's Creek we met two indians who were on their way over the mountain; they had brought with them the three horses and the mule that had left us and returned to the quawmash grounds. these indians returned with us about ½ a mile down the creek where we halted to dine. . . . as well as we could understand the indians they informed us that they had seen Drewyer and Shannon and that they would not return untill the expiration of two days; the cause why Drewyer and Shannon had not returned with these men we are at a loss to account for. we pressed these indians to remain with us and to conduct us over the mountain on the return of Drewyer and Shannon. they consented to remain two nights for us and accordingly deposited their store of roots and bread in the bushes at no great distance and after dinner returned with us, as far as the little prarie about 2 miles distant from the creek, here they halted with their horses and informed us they would remain untill we overtook them or at least two nights. they had four supenumery horses with them. . . . at seven in the evening we found ourselves once more at our old encampment where we shall anxiously await the return of Drewyer and Shannon.

LEWIS   MONDAY JUNE 23ᴿᴰ 1806.
. . . at 3 P.M. Drewyer Shannon and Whitehouse returned. Drewyer brought with him three indians who had consented to accompany us to the falls of the Missouri for the compensation of two guns. one of those men is the brother of the cutnose and the other two are the same who presented Capt. Clark and myself each with a horse on a former occasion

at the Lodgc of the broken arm. these are all young men of good character and much respected by their nation. . . .

Lewis   Wednesday June 25ᵀᴴ 1806.
last evening the indians entertained us with seting the fir trees on fire. they have a great number of dry lims near their bodies which when set on fire creates a very suddon and immence blaze from bottom to top of those tall trees. they are a beatifull object in this situation at night. this exhibition reminded me of a display of fireworks. the natives told us that their objcct in seting those trees on fire was to bring fair weather for our journey. We . . . set out at an early hour this morning. one of our guides complained of being unwell, a symptom which I did not much like as such complaints with an indian is generally the prelude to his abandoning any enterprize with which he is not well pleased. we left them at our encampment and they promised to pursue us in a few hours. at 11. A.M. we arrived at the branch of hungary creek where we found R. & J. Feilds. they had not killed anything. here we halted and dined and our guides overtook us. . . . after dinner we continued our rout to hungary Creek and encamped about one and a half miles below our encampment of the 16ᵗʰ . . . the indians continued with us and I beleive are disposed to be faithfull to their engagement. I gave the si[c]k indian a buffaloe robe he having no other covering except his mockersons and a dressed Elkskin without the hair. . . .

Lewis   Thursday June 26ᵀᴴ 1806.
This morning . . . we passed by the same rout we had travelled on the 17ᵗʰ . . . to our deposit on the top of the snowey mountain to the N. E. of hungary Creek. here we necessarily halted about 2 hours to arrange our baggage and prepare our loads. we cooked and made a haisty meal of boiled venison and mush of cows. the snow has subsided near four feet since the 17ᵗʰ . . . we now measured it accurately and found from a mark which we had made on a tree when we were last here on the 17ᵗʰ that it was then 10 feet 10 inches which appeared to be about the common debth though it is deeper still in some places. it is now generally about 7 feet. . . . the indians haistened to be off, and informed us that it was a considerable distance to the place which they wished to reach this evening where there was grass for our horses. accordingly we set out with our guides who lead us over and along the steep sides of tremendious mountains entirely covered with snow except about the roots of the trees where the snow had sometimes melted and exposed a few square feet of the

earth. we ascended and decended several lofty and steep hights but keeping on the dividing ridge between the Chopunnish and Kooskooske rivers we passed no stream of water.[1] late in the evening much to the satisfaction of ourselves and the comfort of our horses we arrived at the desired spot and encamped on the steep side of a mountain convenient to a good spring *(having passed a few miles our camp of 18 Sepr 1805)*. there we found an abundance of fine grass for our horses. this situation was the side of an untimbered mountain with a fair southern aspect where the snows from appearance had been desolved about 10 days. . . . soon after we had encamped we were overtaken by a Chopunnish man who had pursued us with a view to accompany me to the falls of the Missouri. we were now informed that the two young men whom we met on the 21st and detained several days are going on a party of pleasure mearly to the Oote-lash-shoots or as they call them Sha-lees a band of the Tush-she-pâh nation who reside on Clark's river in the neighbourhood of traveller's rest. . . .

CLARK   FRIDAY JUNE 27TH 1806
. . . the road Still continue[d] on the hights of the Dividing ridge on which we had traveled yesterday for 9 Ms. or to our encampment of the 16th Septr last. about 1 M. short of the encampment we halted by the request of the Guides a fiew minits on an ellevated point and smoked a pipe on this eminance the nativs have raised a conic mound of Stons of 6 or 8 feet high and erected a pine pole of 15 feet long. from hence they informed us that when passing over with their families some of the men were usually sent on foot by the fishery at the enterance of Colt Creek in order to take fish and again meet the party at the quawmash glade on the head of Kóoskoské river. from this place we had an extencive view of these Stupendeous Mountains principally covered with snow like that on which we stood; we were entirely serounded by those mountains from which to one unacquainted with them it would have Seemed impossible ever to have escaped, in short without the assistance of our guides, I doubt much whether we who had once passed them could find our way to Travellers rest in their present situation for the marked trees on which we had placed considerable reliance are much fewer and more difficuelt to find than we had apprehended. those indians are most admireable pilots; we find the road wherever the snow has disappeared tho' it be only for a fiew paces. after haveing smoked the pipe and contemplating this Scene Suf-

[1]The route now coincides essentially with the one of the year before until the camp of Sept. 15, 1805, at the snow bank, is reached. [O. D. Wheeler's note.]

ficient to have dampened the Sperits of any except such hardy travellers as we have become, we continued our march and at the dist[ance] of 3 M. decended a steep Mountain and passed two small branches of the Chopunnish river just above their fo[r]k, and again assend the ridge on which we passed. at the distance of 7 M. arived at our Encampment of 16ᵗʰ Septʳ last passed 3 small branches passed on a dividing ridge rugid and we arived at a Situation very similar to our situation of last night tho' [as] the ridge was somewhat higher and the snow had not been so long disolved of course there was but little grass. here we Encamped for the night haveing traveled 28 Mˢ over these mountains without releiving the horses from their packs or their haveing any food. . . . our Meat being exhosted we issued a point of *Bears Oil* to a mess which with their boiled roots made an agreeable dish. Jo. Potts leg which had been much Swelled and inflaimed for several days is much better this evening and givs him but little pain. we applied the pounded root & leaves of wild ginger from which he found great relief. . . . My head has not pained me so much to day as yesterday and last night.

Lewis   Sunday June 29ᵀᴴ 1806.

We collected our horses early this morning and set out, having previously dispatched Drewyer and R. Fields to the warm springs to hunt. we pursued the hights of the ridge on which we have been passing for several days; it terminated at the distance of 5 mˢ from our encampment. . . . when we decended from this ridge we bid adieu to the snow. near the river we f[o]und a deer which the hunters had killed and left us. this was a fortunate supply as all our oil was now exhausted and we were reduced to our roots alone without salt. the Kooskooske at this place is about 30 yᵈˢ wide and runs with great velocity. . . . beyond the river we ascended a very steep acclivity of a mountain about 2 Miles and arrived at it's summit where we found the old road which we had pased as we went out. . . . after dinner we continued our march seven miles further to the warm springs where we arrived early in the evening and sent out several hunters, who as well as R. Fields and Drewyer returned unsuccessful; late in the evening Colter and J. Fields joined us with the lost horses and brought with them a deer which they had killed, this furnished us with supper. these warm springs are situated at the base of a hill . . . and near the bank of travellers rest creek which at that place is about 10 yards wide. . . . the prinsipal spring is about the temperature of the warmest baths used at the hot springs in Virginia. In this bath which had been prepared by the Indians by stoping the run with stone and gravel, I bathed and remained in 19 minutes, it was with dificulty I could remain thus long and it caused a profuse sweat two other bold springs adjacent to this are much warmer, their heat being so great as to make the hand of a person smart extreemly when immerced. I think the temperature of these springs about the same as the hotest of the hot springs in Virginia. both the men and indians amused themselves with the use of a bath this evening. I observed that the indians after remaining in the hot bath as long as they could bear it ran and plunged themselves into the creek the water of which is now as cold as ice can make it; after remaining here a few minutes they returned again to the warm bath, repeating this transision several times but always ending with the warm bath. . . .

LEWIS   MONDAY JUNE 30TH 1806.
. . . just as we had prepared to set out at an early hour a deer came in to lick at these springs and one of our hunters killed it; this secured us our dinners, and we proceeded down the creek. . . . in decending the creek this morning on the steep side of a high hill my horse sliped with both his hinder feet out of the road and fell, I also fell off backwards and slid near 40 feet down the hill before I could stop myself such was the steepness of the declivity; the horse was near falling on me in the first instance but fortunately recovers and we both escaped unhirt. . . . Deer are very abundant in the neighbourhood of travellers rest of both speceis, also some bighorns and Elk. a little before sunset we arrived at our old encampment on the south side of the creek a little above it's entrance into Clark's river. here we encamped with a view to remain two days in order to rest ourselves and horses & make our final arrangements for seperation. . . . our horses have stood the journey supprisingly well, most of them are yet in fine order, and only want a few days rest to restore them perfectly.

4

Encounters with Native Americans

Given the instructions and aims of the expedition, as well as the size of their contingent, the explorers were almost guaranteed peaceful encounters with Native Americans. Their goal to explore westward to the Pacific committed them not only to avoid conflicts with Indians but also actively to encourage peace among the Indian nations, enticing them to trade with Americans. This multifaceted assignment required the corps to respect the myriad cultures they encountered. A few other white people had set outstanding examples of peaceful relations with Native Americans, but the record of Lewis and Clark stands in sharp contrast to the conflict that so often accompanied previous Anglo-American intruders in North America.

The explorers knew that the success of their endeavor depended on the goodwill of Native Americans. That did not mean, however, that Lewis and Clark consciously tried to question their biases against Native Americans. At that time, almost a century before ideas of cultural relativism gained some acceptability, the explorers regarded Indians as "savages." Even a century later Thwaites, editor of the Lewis and Clark journals, still employed the term. Used as a slur, the word automatically relegated the Indians to an inferior position, characterizing them as squalid and cruel.

In addition to the label "savages," North American officials, traders, missionaries, and explorers had contributed another popular term to the collective subconscious and the common speech of white people. They referred to Indians and addressed them as "children." In common parlance, it was not an endearing term. It certainly was not a word of affection for Native Americans, who were succumbing to the onslaught of new diseases, trade, and forced removal from their lands. It presumed that the conquerors were superior in religion, morals, and intelligence and that they generously condescended to aid lesser people. (See p. 127.) Lewis and Clark used the phrase routinely. In councils and during meetings they addressed Native Americans as "our children," assuming that the words aptly fit the relationship between Indian nations and their "Great Father" in Washington. Use of the term implied a distant, hierarchical relationship, not one of equality.

The common stereotype of Native Americans denigrated their customs and behavior as inherently irrational. To the corps, Indian attitudes seemed illogical sometimes, particularly when they thwarted the logistics of the expedition and interfered with its timetable. In Shoshoni culture, as in almost all Indian cultures, any warrior could express his views on an important matter, such as selling horses to the explorers. The custom of hearing everyone's opinion often prolonged councils or negotiations with the explorers. At times the expedition "appeared . . . to depend in a great measure upon the caprice of a few savages who are ever as fickle as the wind," Lewis complained after negotiations with the Shoshoni on August 16, 1805. (See p. 130.)

During meetings and negotiations with Native Americans, Lewis and Clark sought to elicit as much general information as possible. Part of their task was to assess the political, economic, and social conditions of each nation they encountered. Although they could not follow all the details of what they heard, the explorers came to realize that several centuries of interactions, meticulously recorded in Indian legend and memory, linked these nations in exceedingly intricate and sensitive relations with one another.

Working as peacemakers among Native Americans was one of the explorers' most unsatisfying roles. They could not fathom that both war and peace were accepted ways of life of many Indian nations they met. Since they regarded peace as a prerequisite for trade, they often worked hard to bring representatives of warring nations together in councils to make a lasting peace. Lewis and Clark spoke to the council members as representatives of the new authority of the "Great Father" in Washington and tried to explain the benefits of trading houses the government would establish to expedite trade relations. It did not occur to the captains that promises or agreements the chiefs made at a council might not be binding for an entire nation. Nor did they realize that trade would bring rather uneven benefits to the Indians: Each nation would assume *it* was the favorite trading partner, and nations with existing trade monopolies would resent the introduction of equal trade at the trading houses. Instead of establishing peace, the captains' councils frequently ended up intensifying long-standing trade rivalries among nations. (See p. 146.)

Their search for information, guides, provisions, and horses often propelled Lewis and Clark into situations that forced them to put aside their prejudice and abide by an Indian nation's cultural traditions and roles. During the most critical portion of their journey through the lands unknown to Europeans between the Mandan villages and the lower Columbia River, the explorers depended on Native Americans for descriptions of the land and people along their intended route. The knowledge they gained and the guides they obtained aided their progress decisively. (See p. 154.)

And yet the tendency to categorize Indians as lesser people persisted throughout the entire journey, despite their observations that Indians shared many traits of white people. Sometimes a comment expressed admiration. On December 12, 1805, Clark wrote wryly at the end of a trading session with Indians at Fort Clatsop that they "never close a bargin except they think they have the advantage."

Medical aid was one form of human contact with Indians the captains dispensed as their daily duty. (See p. 158.) Their attempts to cure or alleviate suffering were limited to whatever medical aid was available in the baggage and heads of the explorers. The major share fell to Clark because Indian patients seemed drawn to him. Among the ailments he treated were sore eyes, rheumatism, strained muscles, and abrasions. He relied on sympathy and "commonsense" cures, such as ointments and eyewashes, as well as more severe treatments such as bleeding and sweating. To dull pain, he resorted at times to laudanum (a tincture of opium) from the medicine chest of the expedition.

The two captains realized that successful medical treatment increased the goodwill of the Native Americans. Fortunately, the patients' own stamina and faith also worked in their favor. None of their patients died, and the "physicians" never had to face the ramifications of that blow to their power as healers. At times the attention given, and the cures provided, seemed to vary with the rank of the patients as well as the success of the therapy.

The captains also tried to handle the complexities of a more intimate social relationship than doctoring the sick. Sexual intercourse between the explorers and Indian women extended relations into the realm of personal contact and tribal custom and ritual. In his *Narrative,* Pierre Antoine Tabeau, a fur trader from Montreal, refers to the explorers' participation in a Mandan ritual at the beginning of January 1805.[1] Years before the arrival of the corps, the Mandan had begun admitting white men, mostly traders, to the ceremony. Together with distinguished Native Americans they were believed to be sources of power. During the ritual, young Indians offered their wives as partners for the night to accomplished Mandan hunters, warriors, and orators as well as to traders and soldiers. The custom aimed at acquiring for a future child the best attributes of the father, whether power, wisdom, or expertise in some skill. (See p. 163.)

In general, the captains viewed sexual relations between their men and

---

[1]Anne Heloise Abel, ed., *Tabeau's Narrative of Loisel's Expedition to the Upper Missouri* (Norman: University of Oklahoma Press, 1939), 196–97.

Indian women as a fact of life. Neither Lewis and Clark nor other corps members wrote anything about the captains' sexual relations with Native American women. Other than some vague speculation, Lucius Virgil McWhorter's magistral history of the Nez Perce records an Indian claim that Clark took a Nez Perce wife in 1806 who bore him a son, Halahtookit. In 1877 Halahtookit was captured with his daughter and granddaughter in Montana when at the Bear Paw battlefield Chief Joseph surrendered the surviving Nez Perce who had been driven from their homeland and pursued by soldiers.[2] Assuming that Halatookit was Clark's Nez Perce son, it is clear that his mother retained standing in her nation and that his biracial parentage did not adversely affect his daughter and granddaughter.

Like most men of their times, when Lewis and Clark wrote about sexual intercourse in their journals, they treated the subject with circumspection and circumlocutions. On the rare occasions that they discussed the subject, they dealt with its health consequences, especially syphilis. Venereal disease was a common ailment for the corps during stays in winter quarters at Fort Mandan and Fort Clatsop, where the men had more frequent contact with Indian women. They used mercury as a remedy, although "it is highly unlikely that Lewis cured any syphilis using mercury," a naturalist and historian of the expedition has stressed. He points out that the ointment may have cleared up the first two stages of the disease but not the third one, which shows up many years after the original infection.[3]

The subject of sexual intercourse once led Lewis to speculate about cultural differences between red and white people as well as between Indian nations. In a few instances, the captains admonished the men about the health threats involved in intercourse with Native American women. They also placated warriors who felt the etiquette governing these sexual relations had been violated because the husbands had not been asked for their consent when their wives slept with an explorer. (See p. 165.)

The captains' responsibilities often involved dealing with issues of hostilities with Indian nations. On the outward and return voyages, the expedition's encounters with the Teton Sioux seemed to border on open conflict. (See p. 169.) In July 1806, a chance meeting between Lewis and three companions and a group of Blackfeet Indians, while tracing the

[2]L. V. McWhorter, *Hear Me, My Chiefs! Nez Perce History and Legend* (1952; reprint, Caldwell, Idaho: Caxton, 1980), 498–99.
[3]Paul Russell Cutright, *Lewis and Clark: Pioneering Naturalists* (Urbana: University of Illinois Press, 1969), 255.

course of the Marias River in present-day Montana, led to bloodshed. One of the explorers stabbed and killed an Indian who was trying to run away with two guns he had stolen. Shortly afterward Lewis shot another Blackfeet warrior in an attempt to get his horse back. Despite his fear that the escaping Blackfeet might rally to stage an attack, Lewis kept himself and his men from any more killing. (See p. 178.) His restraint formed a striking contrast with the behavior of many white men before and after him.

Lewis and Clark sprinkled tributes to Native Americans throughout their journals, usually when reflecting on various characteristics of Indian cultures. Their praise was often intertwined with disparaging comments about some aspect of Indian tradition they misunderstood or scorned. But admiration flowed spontaneously when the captains observed the dignity of chiefs, the horsemanship of warriors, the crafts of Indian women, or the Native Americans' apparent indifference to pain. At least one nation, the Nez Perce, treasured the memories of Lewis and Clark and extolled their conduct later when government officials, miners, and settlers began ruthlessly encroaching on the Nez Perce lands.

The captains' long efforts to ensure peace among the Indian nations along their route and to establish trade relations as part of a national Indian policy ultimately proved futile. But the corps did bring back a wealth of dynamic and descriptive detail about Native American cultures just as they reached the point of disintegration.

THE "GREAT FATHER"

During his exploration of the Yellowstone River, Clark had hoped to meet Crow Indians. His speech designed for the occasion is undated. The admonition to Native Americans not to take the horses of white people suggests, however, that the speech may have been written between July 21, when Clark noticed that Indians had driven off half of his horses, and August 3, 1806, when his party reached the Missouri. Clark's systematic listing of the topics, his blunt approach, and his directness would have struck his intended listeners as an attack on their ceremonious way of public speaking. Of course, no interpreter would have rendered his speech verbatim.

Clark's speech relies on Indian images to retain his listeners' attention. Appropriately, he evokes the "Great Spirit" to judge the truth of his words and then introduces the "Great Father," the president of the United States, the "Great Chief" of the multitudes of white people in the East. Clark presents him not only as benevolent, just, and wise but also as rich beyond imagination, ready to build a trading post for his "red children" where they can exchange fur for manufactured goods at low prices. Fatuous statements about the generosity of white people who love their red brethren are followed by the condemnation of Indian horse thieves. Clark mixes veiled threats against unruly Indians with exhortations to be at peace with one another and with the white people, who will come as friends. He concludes his offer of rich rewards for chiefs willing to visit the Great Father with the exaggerated claim that white people always speak the truth and make no empty promises.

Clark's Exploration

Speech Prepared for the Yellowstone (Crow) Indians

CLARK   1806
   Children. The Great Spirit has given a fair and bright day for us to meet together in his View that he may inspect us in this all we say and do.
   Children I take you all by the hand as the children of your Great father the President of the U. States of America who is the great chief of all the white people towards the riseing sun.
   Children This Great Chief who is Benevolent, just, wise & bountifull has sent me and one other of his chiefs (who is at this time in the country of the Blackfoot Indians) to all his read children on the Missourei and its waters quite to the great lake of the West where the land ends and the [sun] sets on the face of the great water, to know their wants and inform him of them on our return.
   Children We have been to the great lake of the west and are now on our return to my country. I have seen all my read children quite to that great lake and talked with them, and taken them by the hand in the name of their great father the Great Chief of all the white people.
   Children We did not see the [blank space in MS.] or the nations to the North. I have [come] across over high mountains and bad road to this river to see the [blank space in MS.] Nat ⁿ I have come down the river from the foot of the great snowey mountain to see you, and have looked in every derection for you, without seeing you untill now
   Children I heard from some of your people [blank space in MS.]

nights past by my horses who complained to me of your people haveing taken 4 [24] of their cummerads.

Children The object of my comeing to see you is not to do you injurey but to do you good the Great Chief of all the white people who has more goods at his command than could be piled up in the circle of your camp, wishing that all his read children should be happy has sent me here to know your wants that he may supply them.

Children Your great father the Chief of the white people intends to build a house and fill it with such things as you may want and exchange with you for your skins & furs at a very low price. & has derected me [to] enquire of you, at what place would be most convenient for to build this house. and what articles you are in want of that he might send them imediately on my return

Children The people in my country is like the grass in your plains noumerous they are also rich and bountifull. and love their read brethren who inhabit the waters of the Missoure

Children I have been out from my country two winters, I am pore necked and nothing to keep of[f] the rain. when I set out from my country I had a plenty but have given it all to my read children whome I have seen on my way to the Great Lake of the West. and have now nothing.

Children Your Great father will be very sorry to here of the [blank space in MS.] stealing the horses of his Chiefs & warrors whome he sent out to do good to his red children on the waters of Missoure.

[Two lines in MS. so worn and torn as to be illegible.] their ears to his good counsels he will shut them and not let any goods & guns be brought to the red people. but to those who open their Ears to his counsels he will send every thing they want into their country. and build a house where they may come to and be supplyed whenever they wish.

Children Your Great father the Chief of all the white people has derected me [to] inform his red children to be at peace with each other, and with the white people who may come into your country under the protection of the Flag of your great father which you. those people who may visit you under the protection of that flag are good people and will do you no harm

Children Your great father has derected me to tell you not to suffer your young and thoughtless men to take the horses or property of your neighbours or the white people, but to trade with them fairly and honestly, as those of his red children below.

Children The red children of your great father who live near him and have opened their ears to his counsels are rich and happy have plenty of horses cows & Hogs fowls bread &c. &c. live in good houses, and sleep sound. . . .

Children   It is the wish of your Great father the Chief of all the white people that some 2 of the principal Chiefs of this [blank space in MS.] Nation should Visit him at his great city and receive from his own mouth. his good counsels, and from his own hands his abundant gifts, Those of his red children who visit him do not return with empty hands, he [will] send them to their nation loaded with presents

Children   If any one two or 3 of your great chiefs wishes to visit your great father and will go with me, he will send you back next Summer loaded with presents and some goods for the nation. You will then see with your own eyes and here with your own years what the white people can do for you. they do not speak with two tongues nor promis what they can't perform

Children   Consult together and give me an answer as soon as possible your great father is anxious to here from (& see his red children who wish to visit him) I cannot stay but must proceed on & inform him &c.

RELATIONS WITH THE SHOSHONI

Native Americans, from their earliest contacts, were appalled or amused by the white men's impetuous behavior and their lack of patience. The way most white men conducted councils and trade negotiations differed from Indian custom; white men's procedures had no provision for the dignity and the opinion of the individual. Every member of an Indian nation who wished to speak in council did so, often at considerable length. For weighty matters, consensus was usually reached only after long discussion.

This Indian custom struck Lewis as needless interference in his negotiations with Native Americans along the route. After reaching the headwaters of the Missouri in August 1805, the explorers needed horses to continue their journey, yet they had not met any Indians since leaving the Mandan villages in the spring. Regardless of whether the Shoshoni were avoiding the expedition, as Lewis feared, the first contact with Cameahwait's Shoshoni was fraught with tension and delay. The Indians who met Lewis's group were ready for combat, having been alerted to the approach of hostile Pah-kee (the Shoshoni name for Blackfeet). Even after the mistaken identity was cleared up, Lewis still had to quell the Indians' suspicions and wait for the Indian council to run its course. Sacagawea, as sister of the chief, was able to dispel the Shoshoni's suspicion (which Lewis perceived as a "capricious disposition") that they were being lured into an ambush. Her presence dissipated that mistrust far more effectively than Lewis's explanation that white men would consider it disgraceful to entrap an enemy with lies or his threat that no white men would ever trade guns with the Indians if they would not trust him.

At an opportune moment, Lewis obtained information about their future route. When the Shoshoni spoke of the difficult mountain trail ahead, Lewis rather blithely assumed that if Indians with women and children could cross those mountains, the corps could pass over them easily.

Lewis incidentally noted, and with some satisfaction, that the Shoshoni did not like Spaniards. Unlike the French, British, and Americans, the Spanish forbade trading guns to Indians. The regulation was a considerable disadvantage for the Shoshoni who had no access to eastern trade routes that furnished their enemies, the Blackfeet and the Minitari, with rifles.

Lewis's interest in the Spanish connection of the Shoshoni seems to have been an expression of his own concern about rumors of earlier Spanish threats against the expedition. His statement that the Shoshoni could reach the Spanish in ten days seems to indicate that he was willing to believe everything he heard about the Spanish. It seems unlikely that Shoshoni traders could get to New Mexico or California so quickly. If they could not obtain guns from the outposts of New Spain, Spanish horses and bridles would also make the long trip worthwhile. Or did Lewis misunderstand his interpreter while the interpreter, in turn, had failed to get Sacagawea's words? Perhaps the Shoshoni thought that the Spanish domain extended to the trade fairs of the Rocky Mountains, or did their travel time merely count the distance to an Indian nation to the South that served as middleman for the Spaniards?

Beaverhead to Great Divide

LEWIS   SUNDAY AUGUST 11ᵀᴴ 1805.—
... the track which we had pursued last evening soon disappeared. I therefore resolved to proceed to the narrow pass on the creek ... in hopes that I should again find the Indian road at the place. ... I now sent Drewyer

to . . . my right and Shields to my left, with orders to surch for the road which if they found they were to notify me by placing a hat in the muzzle of their gun. I kept McNeal with me; after having marched . . . for about five miles I discovered an Indian on horse back about two miles distant coming down the plain towards us. with my glass I discovered from his dress that he was of a different nation from any that we had yet seen, and was satisfyed of his being a Sosone; his arms were a bow and quiver of arrows, and was mounted on an eligant horse without a saddle, and a small string which was attatched to the under jaw of the horse which answered as a bridle. I was overjoyed . . . and had no doubt of obtaining a friendly introduction to his nation provided I could get near enough to him to convince him of our being whitemen. I therefore proceeded towards him at my usual pace. when I had arrived within about a mile he mad[e] a halt which I did also and unloosing my blanket from my pack, I mad[e] him the signal of friendship . . . which is by holding the mantle or robe in your hands at two corners and then th[r]owing [it] up in the air higher than the head bringing it to the earth as if in the act of spreading it, thus repeating three times. . . . this signal had not the desired effect, he still kept his position and seemed to view Drewyer an[d] Shields who were now comiming in sight on either hand with an air of suspicion, I wo[u]ld willingly have made them halt but they were too far distant to hear me and I feared to make any signal to them least it should increase the suspicion in the mind of the Indian. . . . I therefore haistened to take out of my sack . . . a few trinkets which I had brought with me for this purpose and leaving my gun and pouch with McNeal advanced unarmed. . . . he remained in the same stedfast poisture untill I arrived in about 200 paces of him when he turn[ed] his ho[r]se about and began to move off slowly . . . ; I now called to him in as loud a voice as I could . . . repeating the word *tab-ba-bone,* which in their language signifyes *white-man.* but l[o]oking over his sholder he still kept his eye on Drewyer and Sheilds who wer still advancing neither of them haveing segacity enough to recollect the impropriety of advancing when they saw me thus in parley with the Indian. I now made a signal to these men to halt, Drewyer obeyed but Shields who afterwards told me that he did not obse[r]ve the signal still kept on the Indian . . . turned his hor[s]e about as if to wait for me, and I beleive he would have remained untill I came up whith him had it not been for Shields who still pressed forward. whe[n] I arrived within about 150 paces I again repepeated the word tab-ba-bone and held up the trinkits in my hands and striped up my shirt sleve to give him an opportunity of seeing the colour of my skin and advanced leasure[ly] towards him but he did not remain untill I got nearer than about 100 paces when he suddenly turned his ho[r]se about, gave him the whip . . . and disa-peared in the willow brush in an instant and with him vanished all my hopes of obtaining horses for the present. I now felt quite as much mor-tification and disappointment as I had pleasure and expectation at the first sight of this indian. I fe[l]t soarly chargrined at the conduct of the men particularly Sheilds to whom I principally attributed this failure in obtain-ing an introduction to the natives. I now called the men to me and could not forbare abraiding them a little for their want of attention and impru-dence. . . . we now set out on the track of the horse hoping by that means to be lead to an indian camp, the trail of inhabitants of which should they abscond we should probably be enabled to pursue to the body of the nation to which they would most probably fly for safety. . . .

LEWIS   TUESDAY AUGUST 13ᵀᴴ 1805.
. . . we had proceeded about four miles through a wavy plain . . . when at the distance of about a mile we saw two women, a man and some dogs on an eminence immediately before us. they appeared to v[i]ew us with attention and two of them after a few minutes set down as if to wait our arrival we continued our usual pace towards them. when we had arrived within half a mile of them I directed the party to halt and leaving my pack and rifle I took the flag which I unfurled and a[d]vanced singly towards them the women soon disappeared behind the hill, the man continued untill I arrived within a hundred yards of him and then likewise absconded. tho' I frequently repeated the word *tab-ba-bone* sufficiently loud for him to have heard it. I now haistened to the top of the hill where they had stood but could see nothing of them. the dogs were less shye than their masters they came about me pretty close I therefore thought of tying a handkerchief about one of their necks with some beads and other trinkets and then let them loose to surch their fugitive owners thinking by this means to convince them of our pacific disposition towards them but the dogs would not suffer me to take hold of them; they also soon disappeared. I now made a signal fror the men to come on, they joined me and we pursued the back track of these Indians which lead us along the same road which we had been traveling. the road was dusty and appeared to have been much traveled lately both by men and horses. these praries are very poor. . . . we had not continued our rout more than a mile when we were so fortunate as to meet with three female savages. the short and steep ravines which we passed concealed us from each other untill we arrived within 30 paces. a young woman immediately took to flight, an Elderly woman and a girl of about 12 years old remained. I instantly laid by my gun and advanced towards them. they appeared

much allarmed but saw that we were to near for them to escape by flight they therefore seated themselves on the ground, holding down their heads as if reconciled to die which the[y] expected no doubt would be their fate; I took the elderly woman by the hand and raised her up repeated the word *tab-ba-bone* and strip[ped] up my shirt sleve to s[h]ew her my skin; to prove to her the truth of the ascertion that I was a white man for my face and ha[n]ds which have been constantly exposed to the sun were quite as dark as their own. they appeared instantly reconciled, and the men coming up I·gave these women some beads a few mockerson awls some pewter looking-glasses and a little paint. I directed Drewyer to request the old woman to recall the young woman who had run off to some distance by this time fearing she might allarm the camp before we approached and might so exasperate the natives that they would perhaps attack us without enquiring who we were. the old woman did as she was requested and the fugitive soon returned almost out of breath. I bestoed an equ[i]volent portion of trinket on her with the others. I now painted their tawny cheeks with some vermillion which with this nation is emblematic of peace. after they had become composed I enformed them by signs that I wished them to conduct us to their camp that we wer anxious to become acquainted with the chiefs and warriors of their nation. they readily obeyed and we set out, still pursuing the road down the river. we had marched about 2 miles when we met a party of about 60 warriors mounted on excellent horses who came in nearly full speed, when they arrived I advanced towards them with the flag leaving my gun with the party about 50 paces behi[n]d me. the chief and two others who were a little in advance of the main body spoke to the women, and they informed them who we were and exultingly shewed the presents which had been given them these men then . . . embraced me very affectionately in their way which is by puting their left arm over you[r] wright sholder clasping your back, while they apply their left cheek to yours and frequently vociforate the word *âh-hí-e, âh-hí-e* that is, I am much pleased, I am much rejoiced. bothe parties now advanced and we wer all carresed and besmeared with their grease and paint till I was heartily tired of the national hug. I now had the pipe lit and gave them smoke; they seated themselves in a circle around us and pulled of[f] their mockersons before they would receive or smoke the pipe. this is a custom among them as I afterwards learned indicative of a sacred obligation of sincerity in their profession of friendship given by the act of receiving and smoking the pipe of a stranger. or which is as much as to say that they wish they may always go bearfoot if they are not sincere; a pretty heavy penalty if they are to march through the plains of their country. after smoking a few pipes with them I distributed some trifles among them, with which they seemed much pleased particularly with the blue beads and vermillion. I now informed the chief that the object of our visit was a friendly one, that after we should reach his camp I would undertake to explain to him fully those objects, who we wer, from whence we had come and w[h]ither we were going; that in the mean time I did not care how soon we were in motion, as the sun was very warm and no water at hand. they now put on their mockersons, and the principal chief Ca-me-âh-wait made a short speach to the warriors. I gave him the flag which I informed him was an emblem of peace among whitemen and now that it had been received by him it was to be respected as the bond of union between us. I desired him to march on, which [he] did and we followed him; the dragoons moved on in squadron in our rear. after we had marched about a mile in this order he halted them and gave a second harang; after which six or eight of the young men road forward to their encampment and no further regularity was observed in the order of march. I afterwards understood that the Indians we had first seen this morning had returned and allarmed the camp; these men had come out armed . . . for action expecting to meet with their enimies . . . they were armed with b[o]ws arrow and Shields except three whom I observed with small pieces such as the N.W. Company furnish the natives with which they had obtained from the Rocky Mountain Indians on the Yellow stone river with whom they are at peace. on our arrival at their encampmen[t] on the river in a handsome level and fertile bottom . . . they introduced us to a londge made of willow brush and an old leather lodge which had been prepared for our reception by the young men which the chief had dispatched for that purpose. Here we were seated on green boughs and the skins of Antelopes. one of the warriors then pulled up the grass in the center of the lodge forming a smal[l] circle of about 2 feet in diameter the chief next produced his pipe and native tobacco and began a long cerimony of the pipe when we were requested to take of[f] our mockersons, the Chief having previously taken off his as well as all the warriors present. this we complyed with; the Chief then lit his pipe at the fire kindled in this little magic circle, and standing on the oposite side of the circle uttered a speach of several minutes in length at the conclusion of which he pointed the stem to the four cardinal points of the heavens first begining at the East and ending with the North. he now presented the pipe to me as if desirous that I should smoke, but when I reached my hand to receive it, he drew it back and repeated the same c[e]remony three times, after which he pointed the stem first to the heavens then to the center of the magic circle smoked himself with three whifs and held the pipe untill I took as many as I thought proper; he then held it to each of the white persons and then gave it to be consumed by his warriors. . . . I now explained to them the objects of our journey &c. all the women and children of the camp were shortly collected about the lodge to indulge themselves with looking at us, we being the first white persons they had ever seen. after the cerimony of the pipe was over I distributed the remainder of the small articles I had brought with me among the women and children. by this time it was late in the evening and we had not taisted any food since the evening before. the Chief informed us that they had nothing but berries to eat and gave us some cakes of serviceberries and Choke cherries which had been dryed in the sun; of these I made a hearty meal, and then walked to the river, which I found about 40 yards wide very rapid clear and about 3 feet deep. the banks low and abrupt as those of the upper part of the Missouri, and the bed formed of loose stones and gravel. Cameahwait informed me that this stream discharged itself into another doubly as large at the distance of half a days march which came from the S.W. but he added on further enquiry that there was but little more timber below the junction of those rivers than I saw here, and that the river was confined between inacessable mountains, was very rapid and rocky insomuch that it was impossible for us to pass either by land or water down this river to the great lake where the white men lived as he had been informed. this was unwelcome information but I still hoped that this account had been exagerated with a view to detain us among them. . . . these people had been attacked by the Minetares of Fort de prarie this spring and about 20 of them killed and taken prisoners. on this occasion they lost a great part of their horses and all their lodges except that which they had erected for our accomodation; they were now living in lodges of a conic figure made of willow brush. I still observe a great number of horses feeding in every direction around their camp and therefore entertain but little doubt but we shall be enable[d] to furnish ourselves with an adiquate number to transport our stores even if we are compelled to travel by land over these mountains. on my return to my lodge an indian called me in to his bower and gave me a small morsel of the flesh of an antelope boiled, and a peice of a fresh salmon roasted; both which I eat with a very good relish. this was the first salmon I had seen and perfectly convinced me that we were on the waters of the Pacific Ocean. . . .

  This evening the Indians entertained us with their dancing nearly all night. at 12 O'C^k I grew sleepy and retired to rest leaving the men to amuse themselves with the Indians. I observe no essential difference between the music and manner of dancing among this nation and those of the Missouri. I was several times awoke in the course of the night by their yells but was too much fortiegued to be deprived of a tolerable sound night's repose. . . .

LEWIS   WEDNESDAY AUGUST 14TH

In order to give Capt Clark time to reach the forks of Jefferson's river I concluded to spend this day at the Shoshone Camp and obtain what information I could with rispect to the country. as we had nothing but a little flour and parched meal to eat except the berries with which the Indians furnished us I directed Drewyer and Shields to hunt a few hours and try to kill something, the Indians furnished them with horses and most of their young men also turncd out to hunt. the game which they principally hunt is the Antelope which they pursue on horseback and shoot with their arrows. this animal is so extreemly fleet and dureable that a single horse has no possible chance to overtake them or to run them down. . . . about 1.A.M. the hunters returned had not killed a single Antelope, and their horses foaming with sweat. my hunters returned soon after and had been equally unsuccessfull. I now directed MᶜNeal to make me a little paist with the flour and added some berries to it which I found very pallatable.

The means I had of communicating with these people was by way of Drewyer who understood perfectly the common language of jesticulation or signs which seems to be universally understood by all the Nations we have yet seen. . . .

I now told Cameahwait that I wished him to speak to his people and engage them to go with me tomorrow to the forks of Jeffersons river where our baggage was by this time arrived with another Chief and a large party of whitemen who would wait my return at that place. that I wish them to take with them about 30 spare horses to transport our baggage to this place where we would then remain sometime among them and trade with them for horses, and finally concert our future plans for getting on to the ocean and of the traid which would be extended to them after our return to our homes. he complyed with my request and made a lengthey harrangue to his village. he returned in about an hour and a half and informed me that they would be ready to accompany me in the morning. I promised to reward them for their trouble. Drewyer who had had a good view of their horses estimated them at 400. most of them are fine horses. indeed many of them would make a figure on the South side of James River or the land of fine horses. I saw several with spanish brands on them, and some mules which they informed me that they had also obtained from the Spaniards. I also saw a bridle bit of spanish manufactary, and sundry other articles which I have no doubt were obtained from the same source. notwithstanding the extreem poverty of those poor people they are very merry they danced again this evening untill midnight. each warrior keep[s] one or more horses tyed by a cord to a stake near his lodge both day and night and are always prepared for action at a moments warning. they fight on horseback altogether. . . .

LEWIS   THURSDAY AUGUST 15ᵀᴴ 1805.
. . . I hurried the departure of the Indians. the Chief addressed them several times before they would move they seemed very reluctant to accompany me. I at length asked the reason and he told me that some foolish persons among them had suggested the idea that we were in league with the Pahkees and had come on in order to decoy them into an ambuscade where their enimies were waiting to receive them. but that for his part he did not believe it. I readily perceived that our situation was not enterely free from danger as the transicion from suspicion to the confermation of the fact would not be very difficult in the minds of these ignorant people who have been accustomed from their infancy to view every stranger as an enimy. I told Cameahwait that I was sorry to find that they had put so little confidence in us, that I knew they were not acquainted with whitemen and therefore could forgive them. that among whitemen it was considered disgracefull to lye or entrap an enimy by falsehood. I told him if they continued to think thus meanly of us that they might rely on it that no whitemen would ever come to trade with them or bring them arms and amunition and that if the bulk of his nation still entertained this opinion I still hoped that there were some among them that were not affraid to die, that were men and would go with me and convince themselves of the truth of what I had asscerted. that there was a party of whitemen waiting my return either at the forks of Jefferson's river or a little below coming on to that place in canoes loaded with provisions and merchandize. he told me for his own part he was determined to go, that he was not affraid to die. I soon found that I had touched him on the right string; to doubt the bravery of a savage is at once to put him on his metal. he now mounted his horse and haranged his village a third time; the perport of which as he afterwards told me was to inform them that he would go with us and convince himself of the truth or falsity of what we had told him if he was sertain he should be killed, that he hoped there were some of them who heard him were not affraid to die with him and if there was to let him see them mount their horses and prepare to set out. shortly after this harange he was joined by six or eight only and with these I smoked a pipe and directed the men to put on their packs being determined to set out with them while I had them in the humour at half after 12 we set out, several of the old women were crying and imploring the great sperit to protect their warriors as if they were going to inevitable distruction. we had

not proceeded far before our party was augmented by ten or twelve more, and before we reached the Creek which we had passed in the morning of the 13ᵗʰ it appeared to me that we had all the men of the village and a number of women with us. this may serve in some measure to ilustrate the capricious disposition of those people, who never act but from the impulse of the moment. they were now very cheerfull and gay, and two hours ago they looked as sirly as so many imps of satturn. when we arrived at the spring on the side of the mountain where we had encamped on the 12ᵗʰ the Chief insi[s]ted on halting to let the horses graize with which I complyed and gave the Indians smoke. they are excessively fond of the pipe; but have it not much in their power to indulge themselves with even their native tobacco as they do not cultivate it themselves. after remaining about an hour we again set out, and by engaging to make compensation to four of them for their trouble obtained the previlege of riding with an indian myself and a similar situation for each of my party. I soon found it more tiresome riding without [s]tirrups than walking and of course chose the latter making the Indian carry my pack. about sunset we reached the upper part of the level valley of the Cove which [we] now called Shoshone Cove. the grass being birned on the North side of the river we passed over to the south and encamped near some willow brush about 4 miles above the narrow pass between the hills noticed as I came up this cove. the river was here about six yards wide, and frequently damed up by the beaver. I had sent Drewyer forward this evening before we halted to kill some meat but he was unsuccessfull and did not rejoin us untill after dark I now cooked and [divided] among six of us [to] eat the remaining pound of flour stired in a little boiling water. . . .

Among the Shoshoni

Lewis   Saturday August 17ᵗʰ 1805.—

This morning I arrose very early and dispatched Drewyer and the Indian down the river. sent Shields to hunt. I made M͟cNeal cook the remainder of our meat which afforded a slight breakfast for ourselves and the Chief. Drewyer had been gone about 2 hours when an Indian who had straggled some little distance down the river returned and reported that the

Thwaites, *Original Journals of the Lewis and Clark Expedition*, 2:361–64, 375–76, 380, 382–83.

whitemen were coming, that he had seen them just below. they all appeared transported with joy, & the ch[i]ef repeated his fraturnal hug. I felt quite as much gratifyed at this information as the Indians appeared to be. Shortly after Cap.ᵗ Clark arrived with the Interpreter Charbono, and the Indian woman, who proved to be a sister of the Chief Cameahwait. the meeting of those people was really affecting, particularly between Sah-cah-gar-we-ah and an Indian woman, who had been taken prisoner at the same time with her and who, had afterwards escaped from the Min-netares and rejoined her nation. At noon the Canoes arrived, and we had the satisfaction once more to find ourselves all together, with a flattering prospect of being able to obtain as many horses shortly as would enable us to prosicute our voyage by land should that by water be deemed unad-visable.

We now formed our camp . . . in a level smooth bottom covered with a fine terf of greenswoard. here we unloaded our canoes and arranged our baggage on shore; formed a canopy of one of our large sails and planted some willow brush in the ground to form a shade for the Indians to set under while we spoke to them, which we thought it best to do this evening. acordingly about 4.P.M. we called them together and through the medium of Labuish, Charbono and Sah-cah-gar-weah, we communicated to them fully the objects which had brought us into this distant part of the country, in which we took care to make them a conspicuous object of our own good wishes and the care of our government. we made them sensible of their dependance on the will of our government for every species of merchandize as well for their defence & comfort; and apprized them of the strength of our government and it's friendly dispositions towards them. we also gave them as a reason why we wished to pe[ne]trate the country as far as the ocean to the west of them was to examine and find out a more direct way to bring merchandize to them. that as no trade could be carryed on with them before our return to our homes that it was mutually advantageous to them as well as to ourselves that they should render us such aids as they had it in their power to fur-nish in order to haisten our voyage and of course our return home. that such were their horses to transport our baggage without which we could not subsist, and that a pilot to conduct us through the mountains was also necessary if we could not decend the river by water. but that we did not ask either their horses or their services without giving a satisfactory compensation in return. that at present we wished them to collect as many horses as were necessary to transport our baggage to their village on the Columbia where we would then trade with them at our leasure for such horses as they could spare us. They appeared well pleased with what had been said. the chief thanked us for friendship towards himself and nation

& declared his wish to serve us in every rispect. that he was sorry to find that it must yet be some time before they could be furnished with firearms but said they could live as they had done heretofore untill we brought them as we had promised. he said they had not horses enough with them at present to remove our baggage to their village over the mountain, but that he would return tomorrow and encourage his people to come over with their horses and that he would bring his own and assist us. . . . we next enquired who were chiefs among them. Cameahwait pointed out two others whom he said were Chiefs. we gave him a medal of the small size with the likeness of M.ʳ Jefferson the President of the U' States in releif on one side and clasp hands with a pipe and tomahawk on the other, to the other Chiefs we gave each a small medal which were struck in the Presidency of George Washing[ton] Esqʳ we also gave small medals of the last discription to two young men whom the 1ˢᵗ Chief informed us wer good young men and much rispected among them. we gave the 1ˢᵗ Chief an uniform coat shirt a pair of scarlet legings a carrot of tobacco and some small articles to each of the others we gave a shi[r]t leging[s] handker-chief a knife some tobacco and a few small articles we also distributed a good quantity paint mockerson awles knives beads looking-glasses &c among the other Indians and gave them a plentifull meal of lyed *(hull taken off by being boiled in lye)* corn which was the first they had ever eaten in their lives. they were much pleased with it. every article about us appeared to excite astonishment in ther minds; the appearance of the men, their arms, the canoes, our manner of working them, the b[l]ack man york and the sagacity of my dog were equally objects of admiration. I also shot my air-gun which was so perfectly incomprehensible that they immediately denominated it the great medicine. the idea which the indi-ans mean to convey by this appellation is something that eminates from or acts immediately by the influence or power of the great sperit; or that, in which, the power of god is manifest by it's incomprehensible power of action. our hunters killed 4 deer and an Antelope this evening of which we also gave the Indians a good proportion. the cerimony of our council and smoking the pipe was in conformity of the custom of this nation perfo[r]med bearfoot. on those occasions points of etiquet are quite as much attended to by the Indians as among scivilized nations. To keep indians in a good humour you must not fatiegue them with too much business at one time. therefore after the council we gave them to eat and amused them a while by shewing them such articles as we thought would be entertaining to them, and then renewed our enquiries with rispect to the country. the information we derived was only a repetition of that they had given me before and in which they appeared to be so candid that I could not avoid yeal[d]ing confidence to what they had said. Cap.ᵗ Clark and myself now concerted measures for our future operations, and it was mutually agreed that he should set out tomorrow morning with eleven men furnished with axes and other necessary tools for making canoes, their arms accoutrements and as much of their baggage as they could carry. also to take the indians, C[h]arbono and the indian woman with him; that on his arrival at the Shoshone camp he was to leave Charbono and the Indian woman to haisten the return of the Indians with their horses to this place, and to proceede himself with the eleven men down the Columbia in order to examine the river and if he found it navigable and could obtain timber to set about making canoes immediately. In the mean time I was to bring on the party and baggage to the Shoshone Camp, calculating that by the time I should reach that place that he would have sufficiently informed himself with rispect to the state of the river &c. as to determine us whether to prosicute our journey from thence by land or water. in the former case we should want all the horses which we could perchase, and in the latter only to hire the Indians to transport our baggage to the place at which we made the canoes. in order to inform me as early as possible of the state of the river he was to send back one of the men with the necessary information as soon as he should satisfy himself on this subject. this plan being settled we gave orders accordingly and the men prepared for an early march. the nights are very cold and the sun excessively hot in the day. we have no fuel here but a few dry willow brush. and from the appearance of [the] country I am confident we shall not find game here to subsist us many days. these are additional reasons why I conceive it necessary to get under way as soon as possible. . . .

LEWIS   TUESDAY AUGUST 20TH 1805.
. . . I walked down the river . . . and scelected a place near the river bank unperceived by the Indians for a cash, which I set three men to make, and directed the centinel to discharge his gun if he pereceived any of the Indians going down in that direction which was to be the signal for the men at work on the cash to desist and seperate, least these people should discover our deposit and rob us of the baggage we intend leaving here. by evening the cash was completed unperceived by the Indians, and all our packages made up. the Pack-saddles and harnes is not yet complete. in this operation we find ourselves at a loss for nails and boards; for the first we substitute throngs of raw hide which answer verry well, and for the last [had] to cut off the blades of our oars and use the plank of some boxes which have heretofore held other articles and put those articles into sacks of raw hide which I have had made for the purpose. by this means I have obtained as many boards as will make 20 saddles which I suppose will be sufficient for our present exegencies. The Indians with

us behave themselves extreemly well; the women have been busily engaged all day making and mending the mockersons of our party. . . .

I . . . prevailed on the Chief to instruct me with rispect to the geography of his country. this he undertook very cheerfully, by delienating the rivers on the ground. but I soon found that his information fell far short of my expectation or wishes. he drew the river on which we now are [*i.e.,* Lemhi] to which he placed two branches just above us, which he shewed me from the openings of the mountains were in view; he next made it discharge itself into a large river which flowed from the S.W. about ten miles below us, then continued this joint stream in the same direction of this valley or N.W. for one days march and then enclined it to the West for 2 more days march. here he placed a number of heaps of sand on each side which he informed me represented the vast mountains of rock eternally covered with snow through which the river passed. that the perpendicular and even juting rocks so closely hemned in the river that there was no possibil[it]y of passing along the shore; that the bed of the river was obstructed by sharp pointed rocks and the rapidity of the stream such that the whole surface of the river was beat into perfect foam as far as the eye could reach. that the mountains were also inaccessible to man or horse. he said that this being the state of the country in that direction that himself nor none of his nation had ever been further down the river than these mountains. I then enquired the state of the country on either side of the river but he could not inform me. . . . the Chief further informed me that he had understood from the persed nosed[1] Indians who inhabit this river below the rocky mountains that it ran a great way toward the seting sun and finally lost itself in a great lake of water which was illy taisted, and where the white men lived. . . . I now asked Cameahwait by what rout the Pierced nosed indians, who he informed me inhabited this river below the mountains, came over to the Missouri; this he informed me was to the north, but added that the road was a very bad one as he had been informed by them and that they had suffered excessively with hunger on the rout being obliged to subsist for many days on berries alone as there was no game in that part of the mountains which were broken rockey and so thickly covered with timber that they could scarcely pass. however knowing that Indians had passed, and did pass, at this season on that side of this river to the same below the mountains, my rout was instantly settled in my own mind, p[r]ovided the account of this river should prove true on an investigation of it, which I was

---

[1]Some of the Chopunnish, as Lewis and Clark called the Nez Perce, wore pieces of shells as ornaments in their noses. French-speaking trappers who came into contact with the Chopunnish called them Nez Percé. That term, without the accent and with an English pronunciation, or its English translation, "pierced noses," most Americans use to designate the Chopunnish.

determined should be made before we would undertake the rout by land in any direction. I felt perfectly satisfyed, that if the Indians could pass these mountains with their women and Children, that we could also pass them; and that if the nations on this river below the mountains were as numerous as they were stated to be that they must have some means of subsistence which it would be equally in our power to procure in the same country. they informed me that there was no buffaloe on the West side of these mountains; that the game consisted of a few Elk deer and Antelopes, and that the natives subsisted on fish and roots principally. in this manner I spent the day smoking with them and acquiring what information I could with respect to their country. they informed me that they could pass to the Spaniards by the way of the yellowstone river in 10 days. . . . these people are by no means friendly to the Spaniards. their complaint is, that the Spaniards will not let them have fire arms and amunition, that they put them off by telling them that if they suffer them to have guns they will kill each other, thus leaving them defenceless and an easy prey to their bloodthirsty neighbours to the East of them, who being in possession of fire arms hunt them up and murder them without rispect to sex or age and plunder them of their horses on all occasions. they told me that to avoid their enemies . . . they were obliged to remain in the interior of these mountains at least two thirds of the year where the[y] suffered as we then saw great heardships . . . sometimes living for weeks without meat and only a little fish roots and berries. but this added Câmeahwait, with his ferce eyes and lank jaws grown meager for the want of food, would not be the case if we had guns, we could then live in the country of buffaloe and eat as our enimies do and not be compelled to hide ourselves in these mountains and live on roots and berries as the bear do. we do not fear our enimies when placed on an equal footing with them. . . .

Seeking Western Waters

LEWIS   MONDAY AUGUST 26TH 1805.
. . . one of the women who had been assisting in the transportation of the baggage halted at a little run about a mile behind us, and sent on the two pack horses which she had been conducting by one of her female friends.

Thwaites, *Original Journals of the Lewis and Clark Expedition*, 3:40–43.

I enquired of Cameahwait the cause of her detention, and was informed by him in an unconcerned manner that she had halted to bring fourth a child and would soon overtake us; in about an hour the woman arrived with her newborn babe and passed us on her way to the camp apparently as well as she ever was. . . . the tops of the high and irregular mountains which present themselves to our view on the opposite side of this branch of the Columbia are yet perfectly covered with snow; the air which proceeds from those mountains has an agreeable coolness and renders these parched and South hillsides much more supportable at this time of the day it being now about noon. I observe the indian women collecting the root of a speceis of fennel which grows in the moist grounds and feeding their poor starved children; it is really distressing to witness the situation of those poor wretches. . . . Cameahwait requested that we would discharge our guns when we arrived in sight of the Village, accordingly when I arrived on an eminence above the village in the plain I drew up the party at open order in a single rank and gave them a runing fire discharging two rounds. they appeared much gratifyed with this exhibition. we then proceeded to the village or encampment of brush lodges 32 in number. we were conducted to a large lodge which had been prepared for me in the center of their encampment which was situated in a beautifull . . . bottom near the river about 3 miles above the place I had first found them encamped. here we arrived at 6 in the evening. . . . I found Colter here who had just arrived with a letter from Cap! Clark in which Cap! C. had given me an account of his perigrination and the description of the river and country as before detailed [*advised the purchase of horses and the pursute of a rout he had learned from his guide who had promised to pilot ous to a road. to the North &c.*] from this view of the subject I found it a folly to think of attemp[t]ing to decend this river in canoes and therefore determined to commence the purchase of horses in the morning from the indians in order to carry into execution the design we had formed of [*Capt C had recomended in*] passing the rocky Mountains. I now informed Cameahwait . . . that I wished to purchase 20 horses of himself and his people to convey our baggage. . . . I also asked a *(another)* guide, he observed that he had no doubt but the old man who was with Cap! C. would accompany us if we wished him and that he was better informed of the country than any of them. matters being thus far arranged I directed the fiddle to be played and the party danced very merily much to the amusement and gratification of the natives, though I must confess that the state of my own mind at this moment did not well accord with the prevailing mirth as I somewhat feared that the caprice of the indians might suddenly induce them to withhold their horses from us without which my hopes of prosicuting my voyage to advantage was lost; however I determined to keep the indians in a good humour if possible, and to loose no time in obtaining the necessary number of horses. . . .

COUNCILS AND FAILED ATTEMPTS
AT PEACEKEEPING

"Peace and Friendship," proclaimed the words on the verso of the presidential medal. These three words, horizontally separated by a battle-ax crossed with a peace pipe and by two clasped hands, aptly illustrated one of the most difficult tasks of the expedition: to work for peace and friendship with each Indian nation and then between all Indian nations and the United States.

The explorers pursued this goal as best they could with their limited knowledge of the intricate relations among the many Indian nations and in the face of white people relentlessly encroaching on Indian land. They did not realize that the notion of a lasting peace was alien to Indian traditions and beliefs or that war was often an individual decision in societies that placed the highest regard on bravery and individual dignity. Despite the obstacles, Lewis and Clark stuck to their task of making peace while struggling to talk to or trade with Native Americans.

The major channel for the expedition's Indian diplomacy was the Indian council. Unlike councils during the colonial period in the East, the councils on the expedition's route were rather impromptu affairs. In most cases, the time and place of a meeting were uncertain. On the lower Missouri, whenever possible, the captains used white traders as messengers to alert the Native Americans to the arrival of the expedition and to invite them to a council. Only when they reached villages or stayed longer with an Indian nation could the captains attempt to set a date and a location.

The explorers were the hosts of the Indian councils because an audience was needed to convey messages of the "Great Father" to the Native Americans, explain to them his views on trade, peace, and war, and impress them with a display of his power and his presents. Initially, a bit of ceremony struck Lewis and Clark as the appropriate way to establish the significance of the meeting. In many cases, however, they simply put a flag on a pole and organized a parade of the soldiers because they quickly realized that their guests outclassed them in ceremonies.

The Native Americans brought to the council a decorum that had developed over centuries of intertribal contacts. Political rank and social standing were reflected in every guest's attire and bearing. The resources to stage a dramatic setting came naturally to the fore: Dances, speeches, and a ceremonial temperament sustained the rituals with which Indian nations celebrated and remembered important events. Despite the plain setting, the Native Americans came because their curiosity was aroused by white men who talked trade but had no goods and proclaimed peace but were soldiers.

Lewis and Clark noted in particular the demeanor of the warriors. On August 30, 1804, the corps met the Yankton Sioux in present-day South Dakota. Clark admired the bold warriors and the daring young men. At this time Clark first became aware of the existence of warrior societies within Indian nations. Each nation had between four and twelve warrior societies of varying prominence, ranging from untried warriors to veterans. At councils, on hunts, and in wars, the individual societies performed dances in their ceremonial attire or policed the behavior of the entire nation. The so-called Dog Soldiers of the Cheyenne became so well known for their bravery and leadership that the name has often been attached to all Indian military societies.

After the expedition left the Mandan villages, diplomacy lost much of the small formalities the captains had employed. There were no longer American traders around to serve as intermediaries, to bring about peace, and to urge chiefs to visit Washington. Now Lewis and Clark depended on sign language or Sacagawea's translations. While the explorers were on the move, they had to approach the Native Americans themselves, and the proceedings followed Indian custom. Along the lower Columbia, the captains did not even need to improvise a ceremonial atmosphere. They were short on trade goods and medals, and the Indians measured the expedition strictly by the gifts they received.

Peace and trade were the central subjects of the councils. They also yielded, however, a great deal of information on Native Americans. The captains were particularly interested in the origin stories of the Indian nations, their present numbers and political, economic, and social structure, as well as in the vocabulary of their languages. Despite misunderstandings and confusion, the newly acquired knowledge enabled Lewis and Clark to gain a sense of the complex tasks of peace and trade before them. They continued to hope that they could bring permanent peace among the many groups of Sioux and all Plains Indians.

At several councils, the captains' attempts to initiate discussions were stymied because they could not distinguish the ranks of the various chiefs or decipher protocols for addressing them. One-on-one conversations were more fruitful. On February 8, 1805, after a visit from the Mandan chief Black Cat, Lewis emphatically favored him above all Indians and considered him as a potential government representative.

Ultimately, the captains had to accept the fact that neither councils nor one-on-one conversations guaranteed a lasting peace. They had spoken with conviction and enthusiasm about peace and the establishment of trading posts, but their efforts were to no avail. When the expedition arrived at the Mandan villages on October 4, 1804, Lewis and Clark were greeted with the news that the Minitari were on the warpath against the Shoshoni. The captains' peace speech on October 29, 1804, seemed quite inappropriate under these circumstances, but undaunted they urged the Mandan to make peace with an Arikara chief whom they had brought along for that purpose. The Mandan obliged, and the captains thought peace between the two nations had been achieved. On December 2, 1804, among the Mandan visiting the fort were four Cheyenne Indians who had come to smoke the peace pipe with the Mandan. The captains jumped at the opportunity to urge an extensive peace and blithely assumed it could be accomplished. They wrote a letter about the Cheyenne to the white Arikara traders asking them to stop the fighting between Arikara and Sioux and warning that, if the Indians were disobedient, both nations would not receive the promised trade benefits.

In August 1806, on the return trip, Lewis and Clark learned that immediately after their departure the Mandan had killed several Shoshoni who traveled with the captains' promise of safety. Furthermore, the Mandan had gone to war against the Sioux and ran into Arikara planning to attack the Mandan who killed two Arikara. In several councils beginning on August 14, 1806, the captains started working once more to restore peace, but again to no avail. Their attempts to induce various chiefs to accompany the corps to see the Americans' "Great Father" also was not successful because the captains' determination shamed the chiefs into admitting that they feared being killed by the Sioux on the trip downriver.

With peace talks still going on, Minitari warriors started another of the apparently spontaneous forays that made it seem impossible to bring peace to the Plains Indians. While their neighbors the Mandan were at war downriver with the Arikara and Sioux, a Minitari war party went upriver, setting into motion another round of attack and retaliation. They killed two Shoshoni and lost two of their warriors, one of them the son of a head chief, in the engagement.

Vermilion to Teton

CLARK   30TH OF AUGUST THURSDAY 1804.

... after Prepareing Some presents for the Cheifs which we intended [to] make by giving Meadels, and finishing a Speech which we intended to give them, we sent M.ʳ Dorion in a Perogue for the Cheifs and Warriers to a Council under an Oak Tree near where we had a flag flying on a high flagstaff at 12 oClock we met and Cap. L. Delivered the Speach & then made one great Chiff by giving him a Meadel & Some Cloathes, one 2.ᵈ Chief & three Third Chiefs in the same way, they rec.ᵈ those things with the goods and tobacco with pleasure To the Grand Chief we gave a Flag and the parole *(certificate)* & Wampom with a hat & Chief.ˢ Coat,[1] We Smoked out of the pipe of peace, & the Chiefs retired to a Bourey [*Bowray*] made of bushes by their young men to Divide their presents and Smoke eate and Council Capt. Lewis & My self retired to dinner and consult about other measures. ... The Souex is a Stout bold looking people, (the young men handsom) & well made, the greater part of them make use of Bows & arrows, Some fiew fusees[2] I observe among them, notwith standing they live by the Bow and arrow, they do not Shoot So Well as the Nothern Indians the Warriers are Verry much deckerated with Paint Porcupine quils & feathers, large leagins and mockersons, all with buffalow roabs of Different Colours. the Squars wore Peticoats & a White Buffalow roabe with the black hare turned back over their necks and Sholders.

I will here remark a SOCIETY[3] which I had never before this day heard was in any nation of Indians, four of which is at this time present and all who remain of this Band. Those who become Members of this Society must be brave active young men who take a *Vow* never to give back let the danger be what it may, in War Parties they always go forward without screening themselves behind trees or anything else to this Vow they Strictly adhier dureing their Lives. ... Those men are likely fellows the[y] Set together Camp & Dance together. This Society is in imitation of the Societies of the de Curbo or Crow *(De Corbeau, Kite)* Indians, whom they imitate.

[1]Described by Biddle as "a richly laced uniform of the United States artillery corps, with a cocked hat and red feather." [Thwaites's note.]

[2]Muskets.

[3]Ethnographers have frequently described the existing warrior societies among the Indian nations of the Great Plains, particularly among the Sioux, Cheyenne, Arapaho, Kiowa, Crow, and Blackfeet.

Thwaites, *Original Journals of the Lewis and Clark Expedition,* 1:129–30, 131–32.

CLARK   31ˢᵀ OF AUGUST, 1804—

after the Indians got their Brackfast the Chiefs met and arranged themselves in a row with elligent pipes of peace all pointing to our Seets, we
Came foward and took our Seets, the Great Cheif *The Shake hand* rose
and Spoke to some length aproving what we had said and promissing to
pursue the advice. . . .

last night the Indians Danced untill late in their Dances we *gave them
[throw into them as is usual]* Som Knives Tobacco & bells & tape & Binding with which they wer Satisfied.

We gave a Certificate to two Men of War, attendants on the Chief. gave
to all the Chiefs a Carrot of Tobacco. had a talk with Mr. Dorion,[1] who
agreed to Stay and Collect the Chiefs from as Many Bands of Soux as he
coud this fall & bring about a peace between the suoex and their neighbours &c. &c. &c.

After Dinner we gave Mr. Peter Dorion, a Commission to act with a
flag and some Cloathes & Provisions & instructions to bring about a
peace with the Seioux, Mahars, Panies, Poncaries, . . . Ottoes & Missouries, and to employ any trader to take Some of the Cheifs of each or
as many of those nations as he Could Perticularly the Seuouex *(down to
Washⁿ)* I took a Vocabulary of the Suoux Language, and the Answer to a
fiew quaries such a[s] refured to their Situation, Trade, Number, War,
&c. &c. This Nation is Divided into 20 Tribes, possessing Seperate interests. Collectively they are noumerous say from 2 to 3000 men, their interests are so unconnected that Some bands are at war with Nations [with]
which other bands are on the most friendly terms. Thiś Great Nation who
the French has given the Nickname of Suouex, Call themselves *Dar co
tar*. . . . Those *Dar ca ter's* or Suoux . . . are only at peace with 8 nations,
& agreeable to their Calculation at War with twenty odd. Their trade coms
from the British, except this Band and one on Demoin who trade with
the Traders of Sᵗ Louis. The[y] furnish *Beaver,* Martain, Loups, *(Wolfs)*
Pekon, *(pichou)* Bear & Deer Skins, and have about 40 Traders among
them. The *Dar co tar* or Suouez rove & follow the Buffalow raise no corn
or any thing else the woods & praries affording a suff[i]cency, the[y] eat
Meat, and Substitute the Ground potato which grow in the Plains for
bread. . . .

---

[1]Pierre Dorion, a trader and an interpreter. See page 169.

With the Mandan

... after Brackfast we were visited by the old Cheaf of the *Big bellies* or [blank space in MS.] this man was old and had transfired his power to his Sun, who was then out at War against the Snake Indians[1] who inhabit the Rockey Mountains. at 10 oClock ... we Collected the Chiefs and Commenced a Councel ounder a orning, and our Sales Stretched around to keep out as much wind as possible, we delivered a long Speech the Substance of which [was] Similer to what we had Delivered to the nations below. the old Chief of the Grosvanters was verry restless before the Speech was half ended observed that he Could not wait long that his Camp was exposed to the hostile Indians, &c. &c. he was rebuked by one of the Chiefs for his uneasiness at Such a time as the present, we at the end of the Speech mentioned the *Recare*[2] who accompanied us to make a firm Peace, they all Smoked with him (I gave this Cheaf a Dollar of the American Coin as a Meadel with which he was much pleased) In Councel we prosented him with a certificate of his sin[c]errity and good Conduct &c. ... after the Council we gave the presents with much serimoney, and put the Meadels on the Chiefs we intended to make viz. one for each Town to whome we gave coats hats & flags, one Grand Chief to each nation to whome we gave meadels with the presidents likeness in Council we requested them to give us an answer tomorrow or as Soon as possible to Some Points which required their Deliberation. after the Council was over we Shot the air gun which appeared to astonish the nativs much, the greater part then retired Soon after.

The *Recare* Cheaf *Ar-ke-tar-na-shar* came to me this evening and tells me that he wishes to return to his Village & nation, I put him off Saying tomorrow we would have an answer to our talk to the Satisfaction & send by him a String of Wompom informing what had passed here. a Iron or Steel Corn Mill which we gave to the Mandins, was verry thankfully receved. ...

... visited by the *black-Cat* the principal chief of the Roop-tar-he, or upper mandane village. this man possesses more integrety, firmness,

---

[1] The Shoshoni.
[2] Recare, Rickeres, Rickores, and Ree are variants of Arikara.

Thwaites, *Original Journals of the Lewis and Clark Expedition*, 1:210–11, 256.

inteligence and perspicuety of mind than any indian I have met with in this quarter, and I think with a little management he may be made a usefull agent in furthering the views of our government. The black Cat presented me with a bow and apologized for not having completed the shield he had promised alledging that the weather had been too could to permit his making it, I gave him som small shot 6 fishing-hooks and 2 yards of ribbon his squaw also presented me with 2 pair of mockersons for which in return I gave a small lookingglass and a couple of nedles. the chief dined with me and left me in the evening. he informed me that his people suffered very much for the article of meat, and that he had not himself tasted any for several days.

Mandan Revisited

CLARK   THURSDAY (SATURDAY) 14.TH AUGUST 1806
. . . I spoke to the chief of the Village informing them that we spoke to them as we had done when we were with them last and we now repeeted our invitation to the principal Chiefs of all the Villages to accompany us to the U States &.[c] &.[c] the Black Cat Chief of the Mandans, spoke and informed me that he wished to Visit the United States and his Great Father but was afraid of the *Sioux* who were yet at war with them and had killed several of their men since we had left them, and were on the river below and would certainly kill him if he attempted to go down. I indeavered to do away [with] his objections by informing him that we would not suffer those indians to hurt any of our red children who should think proper to accompany us, and on their return they would be equally protected, and their presents which would be very liberal, with themselves, conveyed to their own Country at the expence of the U. States &.[c] &.[c] . . . The Great Chief of all the Menitarras the one eye came to camp also Several other Chiefs of the different Villages. I assembled all the Chiefs on a leavel Spot on the band[k] and spoke to them.

CLARK   THURSDAY AUGUST 15ᵀᴴ 1806 (CONTINUED)
                                                            MANDANS VILG.

after assembling the Chiefs and Smokeing one pipe, I informed them that I still Spoke the Same words which we had Spoken to them when we first arived in their Country in the fall of 1804. we then envited them to visit their great father the president of the U. States and to hear his own Councils and recieve his Gifts from his own hands as also See the population of a government which can at their pleasure protect and Secure you from all your enimies, and chastize all those who will shut their years to his Councils. we now offer to take you at the expense of our Government and Send you back to your Country again with a considerable present in Merchendize which you will receive of your great Father. I urged the necessity of their going on with us as it would be the means of hastening those Suppl[i]es of Merchindize which would be Sent to their Country and exchanged as before mentioned for a moderate price in Pelteries and furs &c. the great chief of the Menetaras Spoke, he Said he wished to go down and see his great father very much, but that the Scioux were in the road and would most certainly kill him or any others who should go down they were bad people and would not listen to any thing which was told them. when he Saw us last we told him that we had made peace with all the nations below, Since that time the Seioux had killed 8 of their people and Stole a number of their horses. he Said that he had opened his ears and followed our Councils, he had made peace with the Chyennes and rocky Mountains indians, and repieted the same objecctions as mentioned. that he went to war against none and was willing to recieve all nations as friends. he Said that the Ricaras had Stolen from his people a number of horses at different times and his people had killed 2 Ricaras. if the Sieoux were at peace with them and could be depended on he as also other Chiefs of the villages would be glad to go and See their great father, but as they were all afraid of the Sieoux they should not go down &c.

    The Black Cat Chief of the Mandans Village on the North Side of the Missouri . . . informed me that as the Scioux were very troublesom and the road to his great father dangerous none of this village would go down with us. I told the Cheifs and wariers of the village who were then present that we were anxious that some of the village Should go and See their great father and hear his good words & receve his *bountifull gifts* &c. and told them to pitch on Some Man on which they could rely on and Send him to see their Great father, they made the same objections which the Chief had done before. a young man offered to go down, and they all agreed for him to go down the charactor of this young man I knew as a bad one and made an objection as to his age and Chareckter at this time Gibson who was with me informed me that this young man had Stole his knife and had it then in his possession, this I informed the Chief and directed him to give up the knife he delivered the knife with a very faint apology for his haveing it in his possession. I then reproached those people for wishing to send such a man to See and hear the words of so great a man as their great father, they hung their heads and said nothing for some time when the Cheif spoke and Said that they were afraid to Send any one for fear of their being killed by the Sieux. . . . being informed by one of our enterpreters that the 2^{d} Chief of the Mandans comonly called the little crow intended to accompany us down, I . . . walked to the Village to . . . talk with him on the subject he told me he had deturmined to go down, but wished to have a council first with his people which would be in the after part of the day. . . . This evening Charbono informed me that our back was scercely turned before a war party from the two menetarry villages followed on and attacked and killed the Snake Indians whome we had seen and in the engagement between them and the Snake indians they had lost two men one of which was the Son of the principal Chief of the little village of the Menitarras. that they had also went to war from the Menetarras and killed two Ricaras. he further informed me that a missunderstanding had taken place between the Mandans & Minetarras and had very nearly come to blows about a woman, the Menitarres at length presented a pipe and a reconsilliation took place between them.

SEEKING KNOWLEDGE AND GUIDES

Without the knowledge and help of Native Americans, the accuracy of the captains' North American landform map could not have been so comprehensive, a fact that the explorers gratefully acknowledged. The Mandan's geographical knowledge enabled the captains to travel and map the Missouri to its headwaters and to find the Shoshoni. When they finally reached the Columbia, it was the Indians who explained that the Columbia was not the short coastal feeder Lewis and Clark had imagined, but a powerful river like the lower Missouri. The captains owed the concept of a huge, high plateau or a basin surrounded by mountains to the coastal Indians, Chinook, Clatsop, and Multnomah. They realized there were two gigantic north-south chains of mountains: the Rockies and the Cascades.

Almost none of the indispensable Indian guides were referred to by name in the journals. A few, like the Shoshoni whom the captains called Old Toby, were the exception. Sacagawea, of course, was unique. Early commentators on the journals idealized and overemphasized her role, making her out to be the expedition's primary guide. She is now recognized as a native of the Missouri's headwaters, as Shoshoni interpreter, and as a sister of Cameahwait.

At Fort Mandan

CLARK   7 ™ OF JANUARY MONDAY 1805—
... the Big White Chief of the Lower Mandan Village, Dined with us, and gave me a Scetch of the Countrey as far as the high Mountains, & on the South Side of the River Rejone,[1] he Says that the river rejone recvees *(receives)* 6 Small rivers on the S. Side, & that the Countrey is verry hilley and the greater part Covered with timber Great numbers of *beaver* &c. . . . I continue to Draw a connected plott from the information of Traders, Indians & my own observation & ideas. from the best information, the Great falls is about *(800)* miles nearly West.

[1] An imperfect phonetic rendering of the French name Roche-Jaune, meaning "Yellowstone," still applied to the river here described. [Thwaites's note.]

Thwaites, *Original Journals of the Lewis and Clark Expedition,* 1:245–46.

At Fort Clatsop

LEWIS   FRIDAY FEBRUARY 14™ 1806.
... Cap⁺ Clark completed a map of the country through which we have been passing from Fort Mandan to this place. in this map the Missouri Jefferson's river the S. E. branch of the Columbia, Kooskooske and Columbia from the entrance of the S. E. fork to the pacific Ocean as well as a part of Flathead *(Clarks)* river and our tract [track] across the Rocky Mountains are laid down by celestial observation and survey. the rivers are also connected at their sources with other rivers agreeably to the

Thwaites, *Original Journals of the Lewis and Clark Expedition,* 4:68–69.

information of the natives and the most probable conjecture arrising from their capacities and the relative positions of their rispective entrances which last have with but few exceptions been established by celestial observation. we now discover that we have found the most practicable and navigable passage across the Continent of North America; it is that which we traveled with the exception of that part of our rout from the neighbourhood of the entrance of Dearborn's River untill we arrived on the Flat-head . . . river at the entrance of Travelers rest creek; the distance between those two points would be traveled more advantageously by land as the navigation of the Missouri above the river Dearborn is laborious and 420 miles distant by which no advantage is gained as the rout which we are compelled to travel by land from the source of Jefferson's river to the entrance of Travelers rest Creek is 220 miles being further by 500 miles than that from the entrance of Dearborn's river to the last mentioned point and a much worse rout if Indian information is to be relyed on; from the same information the Flathead river like that of the S.E. fork of the Columbia which heads with Jefferson's and Madison's Rivers can not be navigated through the Rocky Mountains in consequence of falls & rappids and as a confermation of this fact, we discovered that there were no salmon in the Flathead river, which is the case in the S.E. branch of the Columbia although it is not navigable. added to this, the Indians further inform us, that the Flathead river runs in the direction of the Rocky Mountains for a great distance to the North before it discharges itself into the Columbia river, which last from the same information from the entrance of the S.E. fork to that of Flathead . . . river is obstructed with a great number of difficult and dangerous rappids. considering therefore the danger and difficulties attending the navigation of the Columbia in this part, as well as the circuitous and distant rout formed by itself and the Flathead . . . river we conceive that even admitting the Flathead . . . river contrary to information to be as navigable as the Columbia river below it's entrance, that the tract by land over the Rocky Mountains usually traveled by the natives from the Entrance of Traveller's rest Creek to the forks of the Kooskooske is preferable; the same being a distance of 184 Miles. The inferrence therefore deduced from those premices are that the best and most Practicable rout across the Continent is by way of the Missouri *(falls of Missouri)* to the entrance of Dearborn's river or near that place; from thence to flathead . . . river *(by land to)* at the entrance of Traveller's rest Creek, from thence up Traveller's rest creek to the forks, from whence you pursue a range of mounttains which divides the waters of the two forks of this creek, and which still continuing it's Westwardly course divides the waters of the two forks of the

Kooskooske river to their junction; from thence to decend this river by water to the S.E. branch of the Columbia, thence down that river to the Columbia and with the latter to the Pacific Ocean.

In the Mountains

LEWIS   FRIDAY JUNE 27TH 1806.
. . . on an elivated point we halted by the request of the Indians a few minutes and smoked the pipe. . . . from this place we had an extensive view of these stupendous mountains principally covered with snow like that on which we stood; we were entirely surrounded by those mountains from which to one unacquainted with them it would have seemed impossible ever to have escaped; in short without the assistance of our guides I doubt much whether we who had once passed them could find our way to Travellers rest in their present situation for the marked trees on which we had placed considerable reliance are much fewer and more difficult to find than we had apprehended. these fellows are most admireable pilots; we find the road wherever the snow has disappeared though it be only for a few hundred paces. after smoking the pipe and contemplating this seene sufficient to have damp[ened] the sperits of any except such hardy travellers as we have become, we continued our march. . . .

CLARK   TUESDAY JULY 1ST 1806
                                                       ON CLARKS RIVER
. . . one of the Indians who accompanied us swam Clarks river and examined the country around, on his return he informed us that he had discovered where a Band of the *Tushepaws*[1] had encamped this Spring passed of 64 Lodges, & that they had passed Down Clarks river. . . . those guides expressed a desire to return to their nation and not accompany us further, we informed them that if they was deturmined to return we would kill some meat for them, but wished that they would accompy Capt Lewis on the rout to the falls of Missouri only 2 nights and show him the right road to cross the Mountains. this they agreed to do. we gave a medal

[1]Tushepas, or Flatheads.

Thwaites, *Original Journals of the Lewis and Clark Expedition*, 5:164–65, 179–80.

of the small size to the young man son to the late Great Chief of the Chopunnish Nation who had been remarkably kind to us in every instance, to
all the others we tied a bunch of blue ribon about the hair, which pleased
them very much. the Indian man who overtook us in the Mountain, presented Cap[t] Lewis with a horse and said that he opened his ears to what
we had said, and hoped that Cap[t] Lewis would see the Crovanters [Gros
Ventres][2] of Fort de Prarie and make a good peace that it was their desire
to be at peace.

TREATING SICK INDIANS

Jefferson's initial instructions to Lewis (see p. 18) stressed the need not
only to gather information about Native Americans but also to treat them
humanely. The impact of epidemics on Indian nations, in particular the
smallpox death toll among the Oto, the Omaha, the Arikara, the Shoshoni,
and the Chinook, drew the captains' attention to their other medical problems. Generally they included the ague (an attack of fever with recurrent
chills or fits of shivering), frostbites, rheumatism, sore eyes, aching
backs, abscesses and boils, sprained muscles and broken bones, and
stomach disorders.

The captains alleviated symptoms as best as they could. In the spirit
of frontier medicine, Lewis and Clark placed a premium on their patients'
sturdy constitution and stoicism about pain. Patients with stomach trouble sometimes received Rushes's pills, which Dr. Benjamin Rush, the
most famous American physician of his day, had provided for Lewis. On
May 23, 1806, among the Nez Perce, Lewis wished that they were able
to help "these poor afflicted wretches." The captains' reputation had
spread, and Clark's "eye water" was in great demand. Although their success as physicians and the usefulness of their medicine enhanced their
reputation as healers among Indian nations, both captains remained skep-
tical about the extent of their skills and took care that their treatments
would not harm Native Americans.

Along the trail, treatment could take place only on the day the expedition passed an encampment, which left the patient with the feeling of
receiving exceptional medical attention. The sudden appearance of a
white man who briefly took on the traditional role of the medicine man
may also have had a powerful placebo effect and provided some improvement in the patient.

The captains carefully avoided approaching their patients with any sort

---

[2]Atsinas, enemies of the Tushepas.

of magic cure that would, for example, promise to thwart the malign influence of a sorcerer, spirit, or mythic animal. They never employed prayers, songs, or ceremonies used by medicine men or medicine women. If the expedition stayed for some time with an Indian nation, the captains could also adjust their diagnoses and care to suit the response of the patients to treatment.

In most cases the captains treated the sick Native Americans even-handedly. In special circumstances, however, they did not hesitate to use the power their remedies gave them in a somewhat diplomatic way to obtain canoes, horses, or food. At times a chief or his wife received more attention when it seemed that the rewards for the expedition would be greater. On several occasions during the return trip, Clark directly linked providing medical treatment to obtaining food for the starving explorers.

At Fort Mandan

CLARK   21ST DECEMBER FRIDAY 1804—
... a Womon brought a Child with an abcess on the lower part of the back, and offered as much Corn as she Could Carry for some Medison, Capt Lewis administered &c. ...

CLARK   10TH OF JANUARY THURSDAY 1805
last night was excessively Cold the Murkery this morning Stood at 40° below 0 which is 72° below the freesing point.... The Indians of the lower Villege turned out to hunt for a man & a boy who had not returnd from the hunt . . . and borrow'd a Slay to bring them in expecting to find them frosed to death about 10 oClock the boy about . . . 13 years of age Came to the fort with his feet frosed and had layed out last night without fire with only a Buffalow Robe to Cover him, the Dress which he wore was a pr. of Cabra *(antelope)* Legins, which is verry thin and mockersons we had his feet put in cold water and they are Comeing too. Soon after the arrival of the Boy, a Man Came in who had also Stayed out without fire, and verry thinly Clothed, this man was not the least injured. Customs & the habits of those people has anured [them] to bare more Cold than I thought it possible for man to endure. ...

CLARK   27ᵀᴴ OF JANUARY SUNDAY 1805
. . . Cap! Lewis took off the Toes of one foot of the Boy who got frost bit
Some time ago

Dalles to Walla Walla

CLARK   FRIDAY 18ᵀᴴ APRIL 1806
. . . Collected the 4 horses purchased yesterday and sent Frazier and
Shabono with them to the bason where I expected they would meet Cap
L——s and commence the portage of the baggage. . . . I dressed the sores
of the principal Chief gave some small things to his children and
promised the chief some Medicine for to cure his sores. his wife who I
found to be a sulky Bitch and was somewhat efflicted with pains in her
back. this I thought a good oppertunity to get her on my side giveing her
something for her back. I rubed a little camphere on her temples and
back, and applyed worm flannel to her back which she thought had
nearly restored her to her former feelings. this I thought a favourable time
to trade with the chief who had more horses than all the nation besides.
I accordingly made him an offer which he excepted and sold me two
horses.

CLARK   MONDAY, APRIL 28ᵀᴴ 1806
. . . I saw a man who had his knee contracted who had previously applyed
to me for some medisene, that if he would fournish another canoe I would
give him some medisene. he readily consented and went himself with his
canoe by means of which we passed our horses over the river safely and
hobbled them as usial. . . . they brought several disordered persons to
us for whome they requested some medical aid. . . . to all of whome we
administered much to the gratification of those pore wretches, we gave
them some eye water which I believe will render them more essential sir-
vice than any other article in the medical way which we had it in our power
to bestow on them sore eyes seam to be a universal complaint among
those people; I have no doubt but the fine sands of those plains and the

river contribute much to the disorder. The man who had his arm broken had it loosely bound in a piece of leather without any thing to surport it. I dressed the arm which was broken short above the wrist & supported it with broad sticks to keep it in place, put [it] in a sling and furnished him with some lint bandages & c to Dress it in future.

Walla Walla to Lawyers

CLARK   MONDAY MAY 5TH 1806
. . . we continued our march 12 miles to a large lodge of 10 families have-ing passed two other large Mat Lodges the one at 5 and the other at 8 miles from the Mouth of the Kosskooske, but not being able to obtain provisions at either of those Lodges continued our march to the 3rd where we arived at 1 P.M. and with much dificuelty obtained 2 dogs and a small quantity of bread and dryed roots. at the second Lodge of Eight families Capt L. & myself both entered smoked with a man who appeared to be a principal man. as we were about to . . . proceed on our journey, he brought forward a very eligant Gray mare and gave her to me, requesting some eye water. I gave him a phial of Eye water a handker-chief and some small articles of which he appeared much pleased. while we were encamped last fall at the enterance of Chopunnish river, I gave an Indian man some Volitile liniment to rub his knee and thye for a pain of which he complained, the fellow soon after recovered and have never seased to extol the virtue of our medicines. near the enterance of the Kooskooske, as we decended last fall I met with a man, who could not walk with a tumure on his thye, this had been very bad and recovering fast. I gave this man a jentle pirge cleaned & dressed his sore and left him some casteel soap to wash the sore which soon got well. this man also assigned the restoration of his leg to me. those two cures has raised my reputation and given those nativs an exolted oppinion of my skill as a phi[si]cian. I have already received maney applications. in our present situation I think it pardonable to continue this deception for they will not give us any provisions without compensation in merchendize, and our stock is now reduced to a mear handfull. We take care to give them no

article which can possibly injure them, and in maney cases can administer & give such medicine & sirgical aid as will effectually restore in simple cases &ᶜ . . . We encamped . . . a little distance from two Lodges. . . . we arrived here extreemly hungary and much fatigued, but no articles of merchindize in our possession would induce them to let us have any . . . Provisions except a small quantity of bread of *Cows* and some . . . roots dryed. We had several applications to assist their sick which we refused unless they would let us have some dogs or horses to eat. a man whose wife had an abcess formed on the small of her back promised a horse in the morning provided we would administer to her, I examined the abcess and found it was too far advanced to be cured. I told them her case was desperate. agreeably to their request I opened the abcess. I then introduced a tent and dressed it with bisilican; and prepared some dozes of the flour of sulpher and creem of tarter which were given with directions to be taken on each morning. a little girl and sundery other patients were brought to me for cure but we posponed our opperations untill the morning; they produced us several dogs but they were so pore that they were unfit to eat.

LEWIS   TUESDAY MAY 6ᵀᴴ 1806.
This morning the husband of the sick woman was as good as his word, he produced us a young horse in tolerable order which we immediately killed and butchered. the inhabitants seemed more accomodating this morning; they sold us some bread. we received a second horse for medicine and prescription for a little girl with the rheumatism. Capt. C. dressed the woman again this morning who declared that she had rested better last night than she had since she had been sick. . . . Capt. C. was busily engaged for several hours this morning in administering eye-water to a croud of applicants. we once more obtained a plentifull meal, much to the comfort of all the party.

CLARK   MONDAY 12ᵀᴴ MAY 1806
. . . after brackfast I began to administer eye water and in a fiew minits had near 40 applicants with sore eyes, and maney others with other complaints most common Rhumatic disorders & weaknesses in the back and loins perticularly the womin. the Indians had a grand Council this morning . . . as a great number of men women & children were wateing and requesting medical assistance maney of them with the most simple complaints which could be easily releived, independent of maney with disorders intirely out of the power of Medison all requesting something, we agreed that I should administer and Capᵗ L to here and answer

the Indians. I was closely employed untill 2 P.M. administering eye water to about 40 grown persons. some simple cooling medicenes . . . to several women with rhumatic effections & a man who had a swelled hip. &ᶜ &ᶜ

On the Upper Kooskooske

LEWIS   FRIDAY MAY 23ᴿᴰ 1806.
. . . we were visited by 4 indians who . . . had come from their village . . . at the distance of two days ride in order to . . . obtain a little eyewater, Capt. C. washed their eyes and they set out on their return to their village. our skill as phisicians and the virtue of our medicines have been spread it seems to a great distance. I sincerely wish it was in our power to give releif to these poor aff[l]icted wretches.

THE BUFFALO DANCE

On January 5, 1805, Clark described the Mandan Buffalo Dance, which was performed to bring game close to the villages when food was scarce. It included a ritual to transfer the virtues of Indians and white traders to the next generation through intercourse with Mandan women. Members of the corps were invited to participate. The captains' cultural distance from the meaning of the ritual may have kept them from realizing that any soldier's presence reflected the warriors' appreciation of the explorers' strength. In the context of the ritual the invited explorer bestowed honors on both husbands and wives.

Clark's references to sexual intercourse are couched in euphemisms. In parenthesis he adds: "We Sent a man to this Medisan Dance last night, they gave him 4 Girls." When Biddle in his *History* of the expedition deals with these events, he uses sixteen lines of Latin to explain the young Indian husbands' efforts to preserve their honor by getting old men "to embrace their wives" and to pass on to the women's children their noble qualities. Clark's aside about the soldier who had been

Thwaites, *Original Journals of the Lewis and Clark Expedition,* 5:58.

given four women is adjusted in Biddle's Latin to stress the *husbands'* role: "One of our men . . . saved the honor of four husbands."[1]

Biddle, the man of letters, was able to analyze the power aspects of the ritual better than Clark was. For without the advantages to the husbands, the wives would not have been there. Pierre-Antoine Tabeau, a fur trader, was the only outsider who related the soldier's role in the ritual.[2]

[1] Nicholas Biddle, *History of the Expedition under the Command of Captains Lewis and Clark to the Source of the Missouri, Thence across the Rocky Mountains and down the River Columbia to the Pacific Ocean. Performed during the Years 1804–5–6. By Order of the Government of the United States. Prepared for the Press by Paul Allen, Esquire,* 2 vols. (Philadelphia: Bradford and Inskeep, 1814), 1:150–51.

[2] Anne Heloise Abel, ed., *Tabeau's Narrative of Loisel's Expedition to the Upper Missouri* (Norman: University of Oklahoma Press, 1939), 196–97.

At Fort Mandan

CLARK   5ᵀᴴ OF JANUARY SATTURDAY 1805—

. . . a Buffalow Dance (or Medeson) *(Medecine)* for 3 nights passed in the 1ˢᵗ Village, a curious Custom the old men arrange themselves in a circle & after Smoke[ing] a pipe which is handed them by a young man, Dress[ed] up for the purpose, the young men who have their wives back of the Circle go [each] to one of the old men with a whining tone and request the old man to take his wife (who presents [herself] necked except a robe) and—(or Sleep with her) the Girl then takes the Old Man (who verry often can scarcely walk) and leades him to a convenient place for the business, after which they return to the lodge; if the old man (or a white man) returns to the lodge without gratifying the Man & his wife, he offers her again and again; it is often the Case that after the 2ᵈ time without Kissing the Husband throws a new robe over the old man &c. and begs him not to dispise him & his wife (We Sent a man to this Medisan Dance last night, they gave him 4 Girls) all this is to cause the buffalow to Come near So that they may Kill them.

Thwaites, *Original Journals of the Lewis and Clark Expedition,* 1:245.

SEXUAL RELATIONS WITH NATIVE AMERICAN WOMEN

Indian customs about sexual relations at first baffled the explorers. The Indian practice combined hospitality with diplomacy by providing a guest with a woman's company. The captains considered it a "curious custom," which the men took advantage of when given the chance. After an irate Mandan warrior confronted an alarmed captain about a sergeant's affair with his wife, it became clear that the consent of a husband was required. The captains were, however, astonished when a Mandan woman with her husband's help tried to join the voyage.

The Mandan experience provided some knowledge about sex with other Indian women. Lewis pondered the problems again when with the Shoshoni. Later, at Fort Clatsop the explorers met Indians whose customs had been eroded by Northwest traders, and contacts were simply promiscuous. As a growing number of men caught syphilis, the captains pressured their men into a vow of abstinence and hoped that they would stay away from Chinook women. A few men may have thought twice about sex with infected women. After it became a major problem at Fort Clatsop, Lewis tried in vain to discover if the Indians had any effective "simples"—that is, medicine such as an herb having only one constituent, to treat the disease.

Clark dealt with syphilis outbreaks at Fort Mandan with a mercury ointment, and from then on there are references to men sick with "the pox," sometimes painfully so. While with the Shoshoni, Lewis speculated on the origin of the illness (a question that scientists still debate) but did not reach a conclusion.

Teton to Mandans

CLARK   12ᵀᴴ OCTOBER FRIDAY 1804—
a curious custom with the Souix as well as the rickeres[1] is to give hand-som squars[2] to those whome they wish to Show some acknowledgements to. The Seauex we got clare of without taking their squars,[2] they

[1] Arikara.
[2] Squaws.

Thwaites, *Original Journals of the Lewis and Clark Expedition,* 1:189, 194.

followed us with Squars two days. The Rickores we put off dureing the time we were at the Towns but 2 [*handsom young*] Squars were Sent by a man to follow us, they came up this evening, and pursisted in their civilities.

CLARK   15ᵀᴴ OF OCTOBER MONDAY 1804—

... at Sunset we arrived at a Camp of Recares of 10 Lodges ... Capᵗ Lewis and my self went with the Chief who accompanis us, to the Huts of Several of the men all of whome Smoked & gave us something to eate also Some meat to take away, those people were kind and appeared to be much plsᵈ at the attentioned paid them. . . . Their womin verry fond of carressing our men &c.

At Fort Mandan

CLARK   22ᴺᴰ OF NOVEMBER THURSDAY 1804—

... I was allarmed about 10 oClock by the Sentinal, who informed that an Indian was about to kill his wife in the interpeters fire about 60 yards below the works, I went down and Spoke to the fellow about the rash act which he was like to commit and forbid any act of the kind near the fort. Some misunderstanding took place between this man & his fife [wife] about 8 days ago, and she came to this place, & continued with the Squars of the interpeters, *(he might lawfully have killed her for running away)* 2 days ago She returned to the vill'ge. in the evening of the Same day She came to the interpeters fire appearently much beat, & Stabed in 3 places. We Derected that no man of this party have any intercourse with this woman under the penalty of Punishment. he the Husband observed that one of our Serjeants Slept with his wife & if he wanted her he would give her to him, We derected the Serjeant (Odway) to give the man Some articles, at which time I told the Indian that I believed not one man of the party had touched his wife except the one he had given the use of her for a nite, in his own bed, no man of the party Should touch his squar, or the wife of any Indian, nor did I believe they touch a woman if they knew her to be the wife of another man, and advised him to take his squar home and live hapily together in future, at this time the Grand Chief of the nation arrived, & lectured him, and they both went off apparently dis *(dissatisfied)*

CLARK   21ˢ™ DECEMBER FRIDAY 1804—
... the Indian whome I stoped from Commiting Murder on his wife, 'thro jellosy of one of our interpeters, Came & brought his two wives and Shewed great anxiety to make up with the man with whome his joulussey Sprung.

CLARK   31ˢ™ (30ᵗʰ) SATURDAY. OF MARCH MONDAY (SATURDAY) (SUNDAY) 1805— all the party in high sperits they pass but fiew nights without amuseing themselves danceing possessing perfect harmony and good understanding towards each other, Generally helthy except Venerials Complaints which is very Common amongst the natives ... and the men Catch it from them

Crossing the Divide

LEWIS   MONDAY AUGUST 19ᵀᴴ 1805
... I have requested the men to give them[1] no cause of jealousy by having connection with their women without their knowledge, which with them, strange as it may seem is considered as disgracefull to the husband, as clandestine connections of a similar kind are among civilized nations. to prevent this mutual exchange of good officies altogether I know it impossible to effect, particularly on the part of our young men whom some months abstanence have made very polite to those tawney damsels. no evil has yet resulted and I hope will not from these connections. . . .

... I was anxious to learn whether these people had the venerial, and made the enquiry through the intrepreter and his wife; the information was that they sometimes had it but I could not learn their remedy; they most usually die with it's effects. this seems a strong proof that these disorders bothe ganaraehah [gonorrhea] and Louis Venerae are native disorders of America. tho' these people have suffered much by the small pox

[1]The Shoshoni.

which is known to be imported and perhaps those other disorders might have been contracted from other indian tribes who by a round of communications might have obtained from the Europeans since it was introduced into that quarter of the globe. but so much detached on the other ha[n]d from all communication with the whites that I think it most probable that those disorders are original with them.

At Fort Clatsop

LEWIS   TUESDAY (MONDAY) JANUARY 27TH 1806.
. . . Goodrich has recovered from the Louis Veneri [*lues veneris*] which he contracted from an amorous contact with a Chinnook damsel. I cured him as I did Gibson last winter by the uce of murcury. I cannot learn that the Indians have any simples which are sovereign specifics in the cure of this disease; and indeed I doubt very much whet[h]er any of them have any means of effecting a perfect cure. when once this disorder is contracted by them it continues with them during life; but always ends in dec[r]ipitude, death, or premature old age; tho' from the uce of certain simples together with their diet, they support this disorder with but little inconvenience for many years, and even enjoy a tolerable share of health; particularly so among the Chippeways who I believe to be better skilled in the uce of those simples than any nation of Savages in North America. The Chippeways use a decoction of the [*root of the*] Lobelia, and that of a species of sumac common to the Atlantic states and to this country near and on the Western side of the Rocky Mountains. this is the smallest species of the sumac, readily distinguished by it's winged rib, or common footstalk, which supports it's oppositely pinnate leaves. these decoctions are drank freely and without limitation. the same decoctions are used in cases of the gonnaerea and are effecatious and sovereign. notwithstanding that this disorder dose exist among the Indians on the Columbia yet it is witnessed in but few individuals, at least the males who are always sufficiently exposed to the observations or inspection of the phisician. in my whole rout down this river I did not see more than two or three with the gonnaerea and about double that number with the pox. . . .

Thwaites, *Original Journals of the Lewis and Clark Expedition*, 4:15–16, 170, 176.

LEWIS   SATURDAY MARCH 15ᵀᴴ 1806.
. . . we were visited this afternoon by Delashshelwilt a Chinnook Chief
his wife and six women of his nation which the old baud his wife had
brought for market. this was the same party that had communicated the
venerial to so many of our party in November last, and of which they have
finally recovered. I therefore gave the men a particular charge with rispect
to them which they promised me to observe.

LEWIS   MONDAY MARCH 17ᵀᴴ 1806.
. . . Old Delashelwilt and his women still remain they have formed a
ca[m]p near the fort and seem to be determined to lay close s[i]ege to
us but I beleive notwithstanding every effort of their wining graces, the
men have preserved their constancy to the vow of celibacy which they
made on this occasion to Capᵗ C. and myself. . . .

In the Mountains

LEWIS   WEDNESDAY JULY 2ᴺᴰ 1806.
. . . Goodrich and MᶜNeal are both very unwell with the pox which they
contracted last winter with the Chinnook women this forms my inducement principally for taking them to the falls of the Missouri where during an interval of rest they can use the murcury freely.

TROUBLE WITH THE TETON SIOUX

The bravery of the Dakota, known commonly as the Sioux, has rarely
been questioned. They conquered or drove every rival out of their way.
The captains had only a vague concept of the many Indian nations con-
stituting the Sioux, but they expected trouble with at least some of them.
Pierre Dorion, who had lived for twenty years with the Sioux on the Des
Moines River, accompanied the explorers as a knowledgeable interpreter.
He was very helpful at a meeting with the Yankton Sioux in late August
1804 near the present-day South Dakota city of Yankton. The captains felt
that success bode well for contact with the Teton Sioux upstream, and
they did not bring Dorion farther.

Thwaites, *Original Journals of the Lewis and Clark Expedition,* 5:180.

From September 24 to September 28, the explorers spent time among the Teton Sioux along the Teton River. The Sioux made two attempts to block the progress of the expedition, but the captains had taken precautions against surprise attacks and were not detained. They were able to gather a wealth of information from and about the Teton, a fact contradicting some later interpretations that suggest that during the explorers' stay their fate hung in the balance.

Clark was wary of the Teton Sioux's "rascally intentions" to test the explorers' courage and remained suspicious of "their devious nature." He seemed quite unaware that the powerful Sioux had far more than other Indian nations to lose if the corps actually carried out its goal of establishing peace and new U.S. trading houses. Both measures would strip the Sioux of their constantly guarded dominance of lower Missouri trade and power.

Teton to Mandans

CLARK   25ᵀᴴ SEPT. [1804]—

... raised a Flag Staff & made a orning or Shade on a Sand bar in the mouth of Teton River, for the purpose of Speeking with the Indians under, ... about 11 OClock the 1ˢᵗ & 2ᵈ Chief Came we gave them Some of our Provisions to eat, they gave us great Quantitis of Meet Some of which was Spoiled we feel much at a loss for the want of an interpeter the one we have can Speek but little.

Met in Council at 12 oClock and after Smokeing, agreeable to the useal Custom, Cap. Lewis proceeded to Deliver a Speech which we [were] oblige[d] to Curtail for want of a good interpeter all our party paraded. gave a Medal to the Grand Chief Callᵈ in Indian *Un ton gar Sar bar* in French *Beeffe nure* [Beuffle noir] Black Buffalow. Said to be a good Man, 2nd Chief *Torto hon gar* or the *Parti sin* or Partizan *bad* the 3ʳᵈ is the Beffe De Medison [Beuffe de Medecine] his name is *Tar ton gar Wa ker* 1st Considerable Man, *War zing go.* 2nd Considerable Man *Second Bear—Mato co que par.*

Envited those Cheifs on board to Show them our boat and such Curiossities as was Strange to them, we gave them ¼ a glass of whiskey which they appeared to be verry fond of, Sucked the bottle after it was out & Soon began to be troublesom, one the 2ᵈ Cheif assumeing Drunkness, as a Cloake for his rascally intentions I went with those Cheifs . . . to Shore with a view of reconsileing those men to us, as Soon as I landed the Perogue three of their young Men Seased the Cable of the Perogue, *(in which we had pressents &c)* the Chiefs Sold! *[each Chief has a soldier]* Huged the mast, and the 2ᵈ Chief was verry insolent both in words & justures *(pretended Drunkenness & staggered up against me)* declareing I should not go on, Stateing he had not receved presents sufficent from us, his justures were of Such a personal nature I felt My self Compeled to Draw my Sword *(and Made a Signal to the boat to prepare for action)* at this Motion Cap! Lewis ordered all under arms in the boat, those with me also Showed a Disposition to Defend themselves and me, the grand Chief then took hold of the roap & ordered the young Warrers away, I felt My Self warm & Spoke in verry positive terms.

Most of the Warriers appeared to have ther Bows strung and took out their arrows from the quiver. as I *(being surrounded)* was not permited *(by them)* to return, I Sent all the men except 2 Inpˢ [Interpreters] to the boat, the perogue Soon returned with about 12 of our determined men ready for any event. this movement caused a no: of the Indians to withdraw at a distance, *(leaving their chiefs & soldiers alone with me)*. Their treatment to me was verry rough & I think justified roughness on my part, they all lift my Perogue, and Councilᵈ with themselves the result I could not lern and nearly all went off after remaining in this Situation Some time I offered my hand to the 1. & 2. Chiefs who refusᵈ to receve it. I turned off & went with my men on board the perogue, I had not prosᵈ more the [than] 10 paces before the 1ˢᵗ Cheif 3ʳᵈ & 2 Brave Men Waded in after me. I took them in & went on board

We proceeded on about 1 Mile & anchored out off a Willow Island placed a guard on Shore to protect the Cooks & a guard in the boat, fastened the Perogues to the boat, I call this Island bad humered Island as we were in a bad humer.

CLARK   26ᵀᴴ OF SEPTEMBER WEDNESDAY 1804—

. . . proceeded on and Came to by the Wish of the Chiefs for to let their Squars [squaws] & boys see the Boat and Suffer them to treat us well great numbers of men womin & children on the banks viewing us, these people Shew great anxiety. . . . after Comeing too Cap! Lewis & 5 men went on Shore with the Cheifs, who appeared disposed to make up & be friendly, after Captain Lewis had been on Shore about 3 hours I became uneasy for fear of Deception & Sent a Serjeant to See him and know his treatment which he reported was friendly, & they were prepareing for a Dance this evening The[y] made frequent Selicitiations for us to remain one night only and let them Show their good disposition towards us, we deturmined to remain, after the return of Cap! Lewis, I went on Shore on landing . . . I was met . . . by about 10 Well Dress.d young Men who took me up in a roabe Highly adecrated and Set me Down by the Side of their Chief on a Dressed Robe in a large Council House, this house formed a ¾ Circle of Skins Well Dressed and Sown together under this Shelter about 70 Men Set forming a Circle in front of the Cheifs a plac of 6 feet Diameter was Clear and the pipe of peace raised on *(forked)* Sticks *(about 6 or 8 inches from the ground)* under which there was swans down scattered, on each Side of this Circle two Pipes, the *(two)* flags of Spain 2 & the Flag we gave them in front of the Grand Chief a large fire was near in which provisions were Cooking, in the Center about 400lbs of excellent Buffalo Beef as a present for us. Soon after they Set me Down, the Men went for Cap! Lewis brought him in the same way and placed him also by the Chief in a fiew minits an old man rose & Spoke aproveing what we had done & informing us of their situation requesting us to take pity on them & which was answered. The great Chief then rose with great State [speaking] to the Same purpote as far as we Could learn & then with Great Solemnity took up the pipe of Peace & after pointing it to the heavins the 4 quarters of the Globe & the earth, he made Some disertation, *(then made a Speech)* lit it and presented the Stem to us to Smoke, when the Principal Chief Spoke with the Pipe of Peace he took in one hand some of the most Delicate parts of the Dog which was prepared for the fiest & made a Sacrefise to the flag. . . . after A Smoke had taken place, & a Short Harange to his people, we were requested to take the Meal . . . We Smoked for an hour *(till)* Dark & all was Cleared away a large fire made in the Center, about 10 Musitions playing on tambereens *(made of hoops & Skin stretched)*, long Sticks with Deer & Goats Hoofs tied so as to make a gingling noise, and many others of a Similer Kind, those Men began to Sing, & Beet on the Tamboren, the Women Came foward highly Deckerated in their Way, with the Scalps and Tropies of War of their fathers Husbands Brothers or near Connections & proceeded to Dance the War Dance . . . which they done with great Chearfullness untill about 12 oClock when we informed the Cheifs that they were [*must be*] fatigued [*amusing us*] &c. they then retired & we Accomp.d by 4 Cheifs returned to our boat, they Stayed with us all night. Those people have Some brave men which they make use of as Soldiers those men attend to the police of the Village Correct all errors I saw one of them to day whip 2 Squars, who appeared to have fallen out, when he approachᵈ all about appeared to flee with great turrow [terror]. at night they keep two 3, 4 5 men at different Distances walking around Camp Singing the accurrunces of the night

All the Men on board 100 paces from Shore . . . All in Spirits this evening.

In this Tribe I saw 25 Squars and Boys taken 13 days ago in a battle with the Mahars in this battle they Destroyᵈ 40 Lodges, Killed 75 Men, & som boys & Children, & took 48 Prisoners Womin & boys which they promis both Capᵗ Lewis and my self Shall be Delivered up to Mr. Durion at the Bous rulie *(Bois brulé)* Tribe,[1] those are a retched and Dejected looking people the Squars appear low & Corse but this is an unfavourable time to judge of them

We gave our Mahar inteptʳ some fiew articles to give those Squars in his name Such as Alls, needles &c. &c. . . .

CLARK   27ᵀᴴ OF SEPT. THURSDAY 1804—

I rose early after a bad nights Sleep found the Chief[s] all up, and the bank as useal lined with Spectators we gave the 2 great Cheifs a Blanket a peace, or rether they took off agreeable to their Custom the one they lay on and each one Peck of corn. after Brackfast Capᵗ Lewis & the Cheifs went on Shore, as a verry large part of their nation was comeing in, the Disposition of whome I did not know one of us being sufficent on Shore, I wrote a letter to Mr. P. Durion & prepared a meadel & Some Comsⁿˢ *(Certificates)* & Sent to Cap Lewis at 2 oClock Capᵗ Lewis Returned with 4 Chiefs & a Brave Man *(Considᵉ Man)* named *War tha pa* or on his Guard . . .

. . . after Staying about half an hour, I went with them on Shore, Those men left the boat with reluctience, I went first to the 2ᵈ Cheifs Lodge, where a croud came around after Speeking on various Subjects I went to a princpal mans lodge from them to the grand Chiefs lodge, after a fiew minits he invited me to a Lodge within the Circle in which I Stayed with all their principal Men untill the Dance began, which was Similer to the one of last night performed by their women with poles *(in their hands)* on which Scalps of their enemies were hung, Some with the Guns Spears & War empliments of *(taken by)* their husbands [*&c.*] in their hands.

Capᵗ Lewis Came on Shore and we Continued untill we were Sleepy & returned to our boat, the 2ⁿᵈ Chief & one principal Man accompanied

---

[1] One of the bands of the Teton Sioux. [Thwaites's note.]

us, Those two Indians accompanied me on board in the Small Perogue; Cap! Lewis with a guard Still on Shore the man who Steered not being much acustomed to Steer, passed the bow of the boat & the peroge Came broad Side against the Cable & broke it which obliged me to order in a loud voice all hands up & at their ores, my preemptry order to the men and the bustle of their getting to their ores allarm͏d the Cheifs, together with the appearance of the Men on Shore, as the boat turn͏d The Cheif hollowaed & allarmed the Camp or Town informing them that the Mahars was about attacking us *(them)*. In about 10 minits the bank was lined with men armed the 1ˢͭ Cheif at their head, about 200 men appeared and after about ½ hour returned all but about 60 men who continued on the bank all night, the Cheifs Cont͏d all night with us. This allarm I as well as Cap! Lewis Considered as the Signal of their intentions (which was to Stop our proceeding on our journey and if Possible rob us) we were on our Guard all night, the misfortune of the loss of our Anchor obliged us to Lay under a falling bank much expos͏d to the accomplishment of their hostile intentions. P. C. our Bowman who c͏d Speek Mahar informed us in the night that the Maha Prisoners informed him we were to be Stoped. we Shew as little Sighns of a Knowledge of their intentions as possible all prepared on board for any thing which might hapen, we kept a Strong guard all night in the boat, no Sleep . . .

Little Missouri to White

Clark   Saturday 30ᵀᴴ of August 1806.
. . . I saw Several men on horseback which with the help of a spie glass I found to be Indians on the high hills to the N. E. we landed on the S. W. side . . . imedeatily after landing about 20 indians was discovered on an eminance a little above us on the opposite Side. one of those men I took to be a french man from his [having] a blanket capo[t]e & a handkerchief around his head. imediately after 80 or 90 Indian men all armed with fusees[1] & Bows & arrows came out of a wood on the opposite bank about ¼ of a mile below us. they fired of[f] their guns as a Salute we returned the Salute with 2 rounds. we were at a loss to deturmin of what nation

[1]Muskets.

those indians were. from their hostile appearance we were apprehensive they were Tetons, but from the country through which they roved we were willing to believe them either the Yanktons, Pon[c]ars or Mahars either of which nations are well disposed towards the white people. I deturmined to find out who they were without running any risque of the party and indians, and therefore took three french men who could Speak the Mahar Pania and some Seeoux and in a Small canoe I went over to a Sand bar which extended Sufficiently near the opposite shore to converse. imedeately after I set out 3 young men set out from the opposite Side and swam next me on the Sand bar. I derected the men to Speak to them in the Pania and Mahar Languages first neither of which they could understand I then derected the man who could speak a fiew words of Seioux to inquire what nation or tribe they belong to they informed me that they were Tetons and their chief was *Tar-tack-kah-sab-bar* or the black buffalow this chief I knew very well to be the one we had seen with his band at Teton river which band had attempted to detain us in the fall of 1804 as we assended this river and with whome we wer near comeing to blows. I told those Indians that they had . . . ill treated us as we assended this river two years past, that they had abused all the whites who had visited them since. I believed them to be bad people & should not suffer them to cross to the Side on which the party lay, and directed them to return with their band to their camp, that if any of them come near our camp we Should kill them certainly. I lef[t] them on the bear [bar] and returned to th[e] party and examined the arms &ᶜ those indians seeing some corn in the canoe requested some of it which I refused being deturmined to have nothing to do with those people. Several others swam across one of which understood pania, and as our pania interpreter was a very good one we had it in our power to inform what we wished. I told this man to inform his nation that we had not forgot their treatment to us as we passed up this river &ᶜ that they had treated all the white people who had visited them very badly; robed them of their goods, and had wounded one man whom I had Seen. we viewed them as bad people and no more traders would be Suffered to come to them, and whenever the white people wished to visit the nations above they would come sufficiently Strong to whip any vilenous party who dare to oppose them and words to the same purpote. I also told them that I was informed that a part of all their bands were going to war against the Mandans &c, and that they would be well whiped as the Mandans & Minitarres &[c] had a plenty of Guns Powder and ball, and we had given them a cannon to defend themselves. and derected them to return from the Sand bar and inform their chiefs what we had said to them, and to keep away from the river or we Should kill every one of them &c. &c. those fellows requested to be allowed to come across and make cumerads which we positively refused and I directed them to return imediately which they did and after they had informed the Chiefs &c. as I suppose what we had said to them, they all set out on their return to their camps back of a high hill. 7 of them halted on the top of the hill and blackguarded us, told us to come across and they would kill us all &ᶜ of which we took no notice. we all this time were extreamly anxious for the arival of the 2 fields & Shannon whome we had left behind, and were some what consᵈ as to their Safty. to our great joy those men hove in Sight at 6 P.M. . . . we then Set out, as I wished to see what those Indians on the hill would act, we steared across near the opposit Shore, this notion put them [in] some agitation as to our intentions, some set out on the direction towards their Camps others walked about on the top of the hill and one man walked down the hill to meet us and invited us to land to which invitation I paid no kind of attention. this man I knew to be the one who had in the fall 1804 accompanied us 2 days and is said to be the friend to the white people. after we passᵈ him he returned on the top of the hill and gave 3 strokes with the gun *(on the earth — this is swearing by the earth)* he had in his hand this I am informed is a great oath among the indians. we proceeded on down about 6 miles and encamped on a large Sand bar in the middle of the river about 2 miles above our encampment on Mud Island on the 10ᵗʰ Septᵣ 1804 haveing made 22 miles only to Day. Saw Several indians on the hills at a distance this evening viewing us. our encampment of this evening was a very disagreeable one, bleak exposed to the winds, and the sand wet. I pitched on this Situation to prevent being disturbed by those Scioux in the course of the night as well as to avoid the musquetors.

The Home Stretch

CLARK   MONDAY 1ˢᵀ OF SEPTEMBER 1806
. . . 9 Indians ran down the bank and beckened to us to land, they appeared to be a war party, and I took them to be Tetons and paid no kind of attention to them further than an enquirey to what tribe they

belonged, they did not give me any answer, I prosume they did not understand the man who Spoke to them as he Spoke but little of their language. as one canoe was yet behind we landed in an open commanding Situation out of sight of the indians deturmined to delay untill they came up. about 15 minits after we had landed Several guns were fired by the indians, which we expected was at the three men behind. I call^d out 15 men and ran up with a full deturmination to cover them if possible let the number of the indians be what they might. Cap! Lewis hobled up on the bank and formed the remainder of the party in a Situation well calculated to defend themselves and the Canoes &c. when I had proceeded to the point about 250 yards I discovered the Canoe about 1 mile above & the indians where we had left them. I then walked on the Sand beech and the indians came down to meet me I gave them my hand and enquired of them what they were Shooting at, they informed me that they were Shooting off their guns at an old Keg which we had thrown out of one of the Canoes and was floating down. those indians informed me they were Yanktons, one of the men with me knew one of the Indians to be the brother of young Durion's wife. finding those indians to be Yanktons I invited them down to the boats to Smoke. when we arived at the Canoes they all eagerly Saluted the Mandan Chief, and we all set and smoked Several pipes. I told them that we took them to be a party of Tetons and the fireing I expected was at the three men in the rear Canoe and I had went up with a full intention to kill them all if they had been tetons & fired on the canoe as we first expected, but finding them Yanktons and good men we were glad to see them and take them by the hand as faithfull Children who had opened their ears to our Councils. one of them Spoke and Said that their nation had opened their years & done as we had directed them ever since we gave the Meadel to their great Chief, and should continue to do as we had told them we enquired if any of their chiefs had gone down with M! Durion, the[y] answered that their great Chief and many of their brave men had gone down, that the white people had built a house near the Mahar village where they traded. we tied a piece of ribon to each mans hair and gave them some corn of which they appeared much pleased. The Mandan chief gave a par of elegant Legins to the principal man of the indian party, which is an indian fashion *(to make presents)* the Canoe & 3 men haveing joined us we took our leave of this party telling them to return to their band and listen to our councils which we had before given to them. . . . those nine men had five fusees and 4 bows & quivers of arrows. . . . after we all came together we again proceeded on down to a large Sand bar imediately opposit to the place where we met the Yanktons in council at the Calumet Bluffs and which place we left on the 1ˢ of Sept.ᵣ 1804. I observed our old flag Staff or pole Standing as we left it. . . .

FIGHTING A GROUP OF PIEGAN

The language barrier and the necessity to use sign language added to Lewis's anxiety when he and three men met a group of Piegan, a Blackfeet division, on July 26, 1806. The explorers were on their way back to the Missouri after exploring the headwaters of the Marias River in present-day Montana. They had waited several days for a clear sky to determine longitude and latitude, so Lewis could be sure that the Marias was not an important waterway for them. Irritated about the delay, he was surprised by the sudden appearance of the Blackfeet, whom he called the "Minnetares of Fort de Prarie" or the "Minnetares of the North." Lewis saw no choice but to camp with them to demonstrate the peaceful nature of his party. He dreaded the fierce Blackfeet, who dominated the upper Missouri, just as the Sioux controlled the lower. Convinced that the Piegan would rob him and his men, he was ready to defend the party's property with his life. He also tried to forestall any anticipated theft by giving a speech urging the Piegan to make peace with their neighbors and to trade at a soon-to-be-established post on the Missouri. The Piegan expressed hope for peace with the Tushepas (Flatheads), who they said had just killed some of their people. The next morning, in a fight to recover guns and horses stolen by the Blackfeet, one of the explorers killed an Indian, and Lewis shot another whose fate remained uncertain. A rapid flight united Lewis with another party of men left behind on the Missouri, and the combined group remained on the alert against possible Blackfeet retaliation.

Lewis's Exploration

LEWIS   SATURDAY JULY 26ᵀᴴ 1806

I . . . posponed seting out untill 9 A.M. in the hope that it would clear off but finding the contrary result I had the horses caught and we set out biding a lasting adieu to this place which I now call camp *disappointment.* I took my rout through the open plains . . . and struck a principal branch of Maria's river 65 y^{ds} wide, not very deep, I . . . continued down it 2 M^s . . . when another branch of nearly the same dignity formed a junction with it, coming from the S. W. this last is shallow and rappid; has the appearance of overflowing it's banks frequently and discharging vast torrants of water at certain seasons of the year. . . . I passed the S. branch just above it's junction and continued down the river which runs a little to the N. of E. 1 m^s and halted to dine and graize our horses. here I found some indian lodges which appeared to have been inhabited last winter in a large and fertile bottom well stocked with cottonwood timber. . . . after dinner I continued my rout down the river to the North of Ea[s]t about 3 M^s when . . . I determined to ascend . . . the high plain which I did accordingly, keeping the Fieldes with me; Drewyer passed the river and kept down the vally of the river. . . . I had scarcely ascended the hills before I discovered to my left at the distance of a mile an assembleage of about 30 horses, I halted and used my spye glass by the help of which I discovered several indians on the top of an eminence just above them who appeared to be looking down towards the river I presumed at Drewyer. about half the horses were saddled. this was a very unpleasant sight, however I resolved to make the best of our situation and to approach them in a friendly manner. I directed J. Fields to display the flag which I had brought for that purpose and advanced slowly toward them. about this time they discovered us and appeared to run about in a very confused manner as if much allarmed, their attention had been previously so fixed on Drewyer that they did not discover us untill we had began to advance upon them. . . . I calculated on their number being nearly or quite equal to that of their horses, that our runing would invite pursuit as it would convince them that we were their enimies and our horses were so indifferent that we could not hope to make our escape by flight; added to this Drewyer was seperated from us and I feared that his not being apprized of the indians in the event of our attempting to escape he would most probably fall a sacrefice. under these considerations I still advanced towards them; when we had arrived within a quarter of a mile of them, one of them mounted his horse and rode full speed towards us, which when I discovered I halted and alighted from my horse; he came within a hundred paces halted looked at us and . . . returned as briskly to his party . . . while he halted near us I held out my hand and becconed to him to approach but he paid no attention . . . on his return to his party they all decended the hill and mounted their horses and advanced towards us leaving their horses behind them, we also advanced to meet them. I counted eight of them but still supposed that there were others concealed as there were several other horses saddled. I told the two men with me that I apprehended that these were the Minnetares of Fort de Prarie and from their known character I expected that we were to have some difficulty with them; that if they thought themselves sufficiently strong I was convinced they would attempt to rob us in which case be their numbers what they would I should resist to the last extremity prefering death to that of being deprived of my papers instruments and gun and desired that they would form the same resolution and be allert and on their guard. when we arrived within a hundred yards of each other the indians except one halted I directed the two men with me to do the same and advanced singly to meet the indian with whom I shook hands and passed on to those in his rear, as he did also to the two men in my rear; we now all assembled and alighted from our horses; the Indians soon asked to smoke with us, but I told them that the man whom they had seen pass down the river had my pipe and we could not smoke untill he joined us. I requested as they had seen which way he went that they would one of them go with one of my men in surch of him, this they readily concented to and a young man set out with R. Fields in surch of Drewyer. I now asked them by sighns if they were the Minnetares of the North which they answered in the affermative; I asked if there was any cheif among them and they pointed out 3 I did not believe them however I thought it best to please them and gave to one a medal to a second a flag and to the third a handkerchief, with which they appeared well satisfyed. they appeared much agitated with our first interview from which they had scarcely yet recovered, in fact I beleive they were more allarmed at this accedental interview than we were. from no more of them appearing I now concluded they were only eight in number and became much better satisfyed with our situation as I was convinced that we could mannage that number should they attempt any hostile measures. as it was growing late . . . I proposed that we should remove to the nearest part of the river and encamp together, I told them that I was glad to see them and had a great deel to say to them. we mounted our horses and rode towards the river which was at but a short distance, on our way we were joined by Drewyer Fields and the indian. we decended a very steep bluff . . . to the river where there was a small bottom of nearly ½ a mile in length and about 250 yards wide in the widest part, the river washed the bluffs both above and below us and through it's course in this part is very deep; . . . in this bottom there stand t[h]ree solitary trees near one of which the indians formed a large simicircular camp of dressed buffaloe skins and invited us to partake of their shelter which Drewyer and myself accepted and the Fieldses lay near the fire in front of the she[l]ter. with the assistance of Drewyer I had much conversation with these people in the course of the evening. I

learned from them that they were a part of a large band which lay
encamped at present near the foot of the rocky mountains on the main
branch of Maria's river one ½ days march from our present encampment;
that there was a whiteman with their band; that there was another large
band of their nation hunting buffaloe near the broken mountains and were
on there way to the mouth of Maria's river where they would probably
be in the course of a few days. they also informed us that from hence to
the establishment where they trade on the Suskasawan river is only 6
days easy march or such as they usually travel with their women and chil-
dred[n] which may be estimated at about 150 m.ˢ that from these traders
they obtain arm[s] amunition sperituous liquor blankets &c. in exchange
for wolves and some beaver skins. I told these people that I had come a
great way from the East up the large river which runs towards the rising
sun, that I had been to the great waters where the sun sets and had seen
a great many nations all of whom I had invited to come and trade with
me on the rivers on this side of the mountains, that I had found most of
them at war with their neighbours and had succeeded in restoring peace
among them, that I was now on my way home and had left my party at
the falls of the missouri with orders to decend that river to the entrance
of Maria's river and there wait my arrival and that I had come in surch of
them in order to prevail on them to be at peace with their neighbours particularly those on the West side of the mountains and to engage them to
come and trade with me when the establishment is made at the entrance
of this river to all which they readily gave their assent and declared it to
be their wish to be at peace with the Tushepahs whom they said had killed
a number of their relations lately and pointed to several of those present
who had cut their hair[1] as an evidince of the truth of what they had
asserted. I found them extreemly fond of smoking and plyed them with
the pipe untill late at night. I told them that if they intended to do as I
wished them they would send some of their young men to their band with
an invitation to their chiefs and warriors to bring the whiteman with them
and come down and council with me at the entrance of Maria's river and
that the ballance of them would accompany me to that place, where I was
anxious now to meet my men as I had been absent from them some time
and knew that they would be uneasy untill they saw me. that if they
would go with me I would give them 10 horses and some tobacco. to this
proposition they made no reply, I took the first watch tonight and set up
untill half after eleven; the indians by this time were all asleep, I roused
up R. Fields and laid down myself; I directed Fields to watch the move-

[1]As a sign of mourning. [Biddle's note.]

ments of the indians and if any of them left the camp to awake us all as I apprehended they would attampt to s[t]eal our horses. this being done I feel into a profound sleep and did not wake untill the noise of the men and indians awoke me a little after light in the morning.

LEWIS   JULY 27ᵀᴴ 1806. SUNDAY.

This morning at daylight the indians got up and crouded around the fire, J. Fields who was on post had carelessly laid his gun down behi[n]d him near where his brother was sleeping, one of the indians the fellow to whom I had given the medal last evening sliped behind him and took his gun and that of his brother unperceived by him, at the same instant two others advanced and seized the guns of Drewyer and myself, J. Fields seeing this turned about to look for his gun and saw the fellow just runing off with her and his brother's he called to his brother who instantly jumped up and pursued the indian with him whom they overtook at the distance of 50 or 60 paces from the camp s[e]ized their guns and rested them from him and R. Fields as he seized his gun stabed the indian to the heart with his knife the fellow ran about 15 steps and fell dead; of this I did not know untill afterwards,[1] having recovered their guns they ran back instantly to the camp; Drewyer who was awake saw the indian take hold of his gun and instantly jumped up and s[e]ized her and rested her from him but the indian still retained his pouch, his jumping up and crying damn you let go my gun awakened me I jumped up and asked what was the matter which I quickly learned when I saw drewyer in a scuffle with the indian for his gun. I reached to seize my gun but found her gone, I then drew a pistol from my holster and terning myself about saw the indian making off with my gun I ran at him with my pistol and bid him lay down my gun which he was in the act of doing when the Fieldses returned and drew up their guns to shoot him which I forbid as he did not appear to be about to make any resistance or commit any offensive act, he droped the gun and walked slowly off, I picked her up instantly, Drewyer having about this time recovered his gun and pouch asked me if he might not kill the fellow which I also forbid as the indian did not appear to wish to kill us, as soon as they found us all in possession of our

---

[1] . . . The long-continued hostility of the Blackfeet to the whites has often been attributed to this incident. But Chittenden (*History of American Fur Trade*, p. 714) [Hiram Martin Chittenden *The American Fur Trade of the Far West*, 3 vols. (New York: Francis P. Harper, 1902), 2:714)—ED.] declares that Manuel Lisa found that the Indians of that tribe justified the action of Lewis, and were inclined to be friendly to the whites. The real cause of the Blackfeet enmity was the appearance of white trappers in the ranks of their enemies, the Crows. . . . [Thwaites's note.] In later years, two members of the expedition were killed by Blackfeet, Potts and Drouillard; Colter narrowly escaped that fate.

arms they ran and indeavored to drive off all the horses I now hollowed to the men and told them to fire on them if they attempted to drive off our horses, they accordingly pursued the main party who were dr[i]ving the horses up the river and I pursued the man who had taken my gun who with another was driving off a part of the horses which were to the left of the camp. I pursued them so closely that they could not take twelve of their own horses but continued to drive one of mine with some others; at the distance of three hundred paces they entered one of those steep nitches in the bluff with the horses before them being nearly out of breath I could pursue no further, I called to them as I had done several times before that I would shoot them if they did not give me my horse and raised my gun, one of them jumped behind a rock and spoke to the other who turned arround and stoped at the distance of 30 steps from me and I shot him through the belly, he fell to his knees and on his wright elbow from which position he partly raised himself up and fired at me, and turning himself about crawled in behind a rock which was a few feet from him. he overshot me, being bearheaded I felt the wind of his bullet very distinctly. not having my shotpouch I could not reload my peice and as there were two of them behind good shelters from me I did not think it prudent to rush on them with my pistol which had I discharged I had not the means of reloading untill I reached camp; I therefore returned leasurely towards camp, on my way I met with Drewyer who having heared the report of the guns had returned in surch of me and left the Fieldes to pursue the indians, I desired him to haisten to the camp with me and assist in catching as many of the indian horses as were necessary and to call to the Fieldes if he could make them hear to come back that we still had a sufficient number of horses, this he did but they were too far to hear him. we reached the camp and began to catch the horses and saddle them and put on the packs. the reason I had not my pouch with me was that I had not time to return about 50 yards to camp after geting my gun before I was obliged to pursue the indians or suffer them to collect and drive off all the horses. we had caught and saddled the horses and began to arrange the packs when the Fieldses returned with four of our horses; we left one of our horses and took four of the best of those of the indian's; while the men were preparing the horses I put four sheilds and two bows and quivers of arrows which had been left on the fire, with sundry other articles; they left all their baggage at our mercy. they had but 2 guns and one of them they left the others were armed with bows and arrows and eyedaggs. the gun we took with us. I also retook the flagg but left the medal about the neck of the dead man that they might be informed who we were. we took some of their buffaloe meat and set out ascending the

bluffs by the same rout we had decended last evening leaving the ballance
of nine of their horses which we did not want. the Fieldses told me that
three of the indians whom they pursued swam the river one of them on
my horse. and that two others ascended the hill and escaped from them
with a part of their horses, two I had pursued into the nitch one lay dead
near the camp and the eighth we could not account for but suppose that
he ran off early in the contest. having ascended the hill we took our
course through a beatifull level plain a little to the S. of East. my design
was to hasten to the entrance of Maria's river as quick as possible in the
hope of meeting with the canoes and party at that place having no doubt
but that they [the Indians] would pursue us with a large party and as there
was a band near the broken mountains or probably between them and
the mouth of that river we might expect them to receive inteligence from
us and arrive at that place nearly as soon as we could, no time was therefore to be lost and we pushed our horses as hard as they would bear. at
8 miles we passed a large branch 40 y^{ds} wide which I called battle river.
at 3 P.M. we arrived at rose river . . . having traveled by my estimate compared with our former distances and cou[r]ses about 63 m^s here we
halted an hour and a half took some refreshment and suffered our horses
to graize; . . . by dark we had traveled about 17 miles further, we now
halted to rest ourselves and horses about 2 hours, we killed a buffaloe
cow and took a small quantity of the meat. after refreshing ourselves we
again set out by moonlight and traveled . . . untill 2 OCk in the morning
having come by my estimate after dark about 20 m^s we now turned out
our horses and laid ourselves down to rest in the plain very much
fatiegued as may be readily conceived. my indian horse carried me very
well in short much better than my own would have done and leaves me
with but little reason to complain of the robery.

LEWIS   JULY 28TH 1806. MONDAY.
. . . I slept sound but fortunately awoke as day appeared, I awaked the
men and directed the horses to be saddled, I was so soar from my ride
yesterday that I could scarcely stand, and the men complained of being
in a similar situation however I encouraged them by telling them that our
own lives as well as those of our friends and fellow travellers depended
on our exertions at this moment; they were allert soon prepared the
horses and we again resumed our march. . . . we had proceeded about
12 miles on an East course when we found ourselves near the missouri;
we heard a report which we took to be that of a gun but were not certain;
still continuing down the N. E. bank of the missouri about 8 miles further, . . . then . . . we heared the report of several rifles very distinctly on

the river to our right, we quickly repared to this joyfull sound and on arriving at the bank of the river had the unspeakable satisfaction to see our canoes coming down. we hurried down from the bluff on which we were and joined them striped our horses and gave them a final discharge imbarking without loss of time with our baggage. I now learned that they had brought all things safe having sustaned no loss nor met with any accident of importance. . . . we decended the river opposite to our principal cash which we proceeded to open after reconnoitering the adjacent country. we found that the cash had caved in and most of the articles burried therin were injured. . . . the gunpowder corn flour poark and salt had sustained but little injury the parched meal was spoiled or nearly so. . . . we droped down to the point to take in the several articles which had been buried at that place in several small cashes; these we found in good order, and recovered every article except 3 traps belonging to Drewyer which could not be found. here as good fortune would have it Serg^t Gass and Willard who brought the horses from the falls joined us at 1 P.M. . . . having now nothing to detain us we passed over immediately to the island in the entrance of Maria's river to launch the red perogue, but found her so much decayed that it was impossible . . . to repare her. . . . we now reimbarked on board the white perog[u]e and five small canoes and decended the river about 15 m^s and encamped on the S. W. side near a few cottonwood trees, one of them being of the narrow leafed speceis and was the first of that kind which we had remarked on our passage up the river. . . . we encamped late.

5

Flora, Fauna, and Natural Wonders along the Trail

During the years Lewis served as Jefferson's private secretary, he had been imbued with the idea of an expedition committed to scientific investigation. He shared not only the president's political and economic objectives for western exploration but also his enthusiasm for scientific discovery. Before leaving the East Coast for his journey across the continent, Lewis read and studied the sciences intensively, sometimes with the help of the president's friends who were members of the American Philosophical Society. He made a great effort to become familiar with astronomy, natural history, geography, meteorology, ethnology, and medicine. Clark shared the commitment to scientific observation and collecting, even though he lacked the extent of Lewis's knowledge.

The detailed descriptions in their journals of the fauna and flora of the Missouri and the Pacific Northwest are evidence of the captains' dedication. They instilled their own devotion to scientific inquiry into the Corps of Discovery. No corps member was a trained scientist who had systematically studied in any distinct field. Yet some members were skillful and accurate observers, with much practical experience of living off the land. Although they did not understand taxonomy, the classification of animals and plants according to their natural relationships, they relied on comparing a specimen to something they were familiar with on the East Coast or in the Ohio Valley. In that sense they continued to practice the "unlike or like approach" of previous, nonscientific explorers of America.

The explorers' observations of animals and plants never before described in scholarly publications were quite accurate. Unfortunately for Lewis and Clark, and much to Jefferson's disappointment, they never received scientific credit for their pioneering work in the natural sciences because the scientific sections of their journals were not published in the nineteenth century. The Biddle edition of their journals, published in 1814, was supposed to be accompanied by a volume of the explorers' scientific findings. But its ailing editor, Dr. Benjamin Smith Barton, died in 1815, and no one completed the task. Decades later the naturalist Elliott Coues, who had served as an army surgeon in the Far West, drew attention to the wealth of the explorers' natural history writings. The Thwaites edition of the journals (1904–05) finally included the expedition's long-neglected contribution on natural history. But by that time, other explorers not aware of the Lewis and Clark descriptions had already published an account of them and had received the credit.

Animals and plants which they had never seen before were often of particular interest to Lewis and Clark. The buffalo was the first large animal they described. (See p. 190.) This seems appropriate because it later became an emblem of the nineteenth-century American West, and the "buffalo nickel" became part of United States currency. Of course, "buffalo" was not the animal's proper scientific name, but few people cared. James Fenimore Cooper was one who did; in 1827, America's world-famous man of letters criticized Americans for not calling the buffalo by its proper name. "It is scarcely necessary to tell the reader," Cooper explained in a footnote, "that the animal so often alluded to in this book, and which is vulgarly called the buffalo, is in truth the bison."[1]

Despite the buffalo's later prestige as a national emblem, most journal entries about large animals refer to the grizzly bear. (See p. 193.) As the largest and most ferocious predator they had ever seen, the bear captured the explorers' attention, imagination, and respect. In fact, the grizzly received far more attention than the animal that shaped the early economic life and the Indian trade of the upper Missouri and the Pacific Northwest: the beaver.

The captains used several names for the bear because they did not realize that the species had a range of colors. The amazing size of the grizzly challenged the hunting skills of the explorers, who were eager to kill the powerful animal. They were quite familiar with eastern bears, but totally astonished when they had to shoot repeatedly to stop these huge animals. Since they approached the bears as hunters, not as scientific observers, they saw only disturbed and provoked bears, cornered or wounded, maddened by fear or pain. They considered the grizzly a ferocious beast and gruesome monster.

The grizzly made a lasting impression on Lewis's imagination. The brute power of raging nature so evident in the bear's fierce struggle led him to write on May 11, 1805, that the bear "being so hard to die rather intimidates us all." His tribute to the bear's stamina—"so hard to die"—

---

[1] James Fenimore Cooper, *The Prairie* (1827; reprint, New York: New American Library 1980), 105, chap. 9.

stayed with the thirty-one-year-old Lewis for his few remaining years. Four years later, when he lay dying in a tavern on the Natchez Trail in Tennessee, he "often said, 'I am no coward, but I am *so* strong, *so* hard to die.'"[2] So the innkeeper's wife told Alexander Wilson when the ornithologist, on a field trip in Tennessee, inquired about his friend's death.

Unlike the grizzly, most of the birds the explorers shot were killed for observation. Before the age of binoculars and photography it was almost the only way to observe and study the birds up close enough for accurate description and identification. The California condor was an especially tempting target because it was so large and unusual. Before its extinction on the open range, the huge vulture soared over much of the Far West. On November 18, 1805, after the party had reached the Pacific Ocean, one man shot a "Buzzard of the large Kind," which was feeding on a dead whale on the beach. Clark carefully recorded its measurements. Eventually the explorers took the condor's head back to St. Louis, and it reportedly found its way into Peale's Museum in Philadelphia, one of that period's most notable American collections of the arts and sciences. (See p. 199.)

By the time they reached the lower Columbia River and the Pacific Coast, the explorers had plenty of experience to recognize the role of fish in the diet of Native Americans. At Fort Clatsop, salmon was the most important food for Chinook, Clatsop, and Cathlamet Indians. They ate five different species of salmon, which swam up the Columbia River and its tributaries on their way to the spawning grounds. (See p. 202.)

Some small animals affected the corps far more than they wished. Throughout much of the journey countless mosquitoes plagued the explorers. At the Kansas River, mosquito nets were issued to the party, and they quickly became valued equipment. On July 21, 1805, Lewis described them as "made of duck or gauze, like a trunk to get under," adding that it would be impossible for the expedition to continue without them. References to lice, fleas, and other insects run throughout the journals. (See p. 203.)

The shipment of hundreds of botanical specimens from Fort Mandan back to Jefferson included cuttings, seeds, roots, and pressed plants. (See p. 205.) The returning expedition brought back to St. Louis a second lot of specimens which, along with the daily entries of the journals, testify to the explorers' careful examination of the flora along their trail. (See p. 208.)

[2]Alexander Wilson, "Particulars of the Death of Capt. Lewis," *The Port Folio* n.s., 7 (January 1812): 38.

Startling sights during the voyage often roused the captains' zoological and botanical interests. They observed and provided meticulous descriptions and explanations in as scientific a style as possible. Sometimes they weighed the Indians' explanation or identification of a phenomenon; if it seemed improbable or too far-fetched, they investigated for themselves. One incident involved a conical mound in present-day Clay County, South Dakota. On August 25, 1804, a stifling, hot day, the captains probed the mystery of the Hill of Little Devils, as Lewis's map of 1806 called it. The neighboring Indians considered it the home of small monsters, forever armed with tiny, sharp arrows to kill anyone entering their world.

After inspecting the mound, Clark noted that the strong wind driving over the plains against the hill swirled swarms of insects to the leeward side where huge numbers of brown martins (swallows) caught the insects. The Indians had told the captains that the large assembly of birds was a sign of the special status of the hill. Rationality and science as understood by the explorers, based on careful observation and accurate description, gave Clark an explanation for the Indian belief. The pointed beaks of the martins could have been the "sharp arrows" of the Indians' "little monsters."

Despite the awesome, novel, and amazing sights frequently noted by the expedition, the journals often do not deal with concepts of the sublime, the picturesque, and the beautiful, or with the romantic sentiments of later travelers who experienced the wondrous sights and sounds of the continent. The explorers usually curbed their emotional reactions with a deliberate dedication to utility and necessity. David McKeehan, a western Virginia schoolmaster who in 1807 edited and published the first book of the expedition, Sergeant Gass's journal, explained the choice of spare language: "Mr. Gass having declared that the beauties and deformities of the grandest scenes are equally beyond the power of description, no attention has been made either by him or the publisher to give adequate representations to them."[3]

The course of their long journey presented so many challenges and obstacles that the explorers sometimes seemed oblivious to the wonders of nature. Instead they recorded features that boded well for their continuing advance — or presaged some danger. They rarely enjoyed enough of a sense of security to allow themselves to view a mountain

[3]David M. McKeehan, Preface to Patrick Gass, *A Journal of the Voyages and Travels of a Corps of Discovery, under the Command of Capt. Lewis and Capt. Clarke of the Army of the United States, by Patrick Gass* (Pittsburgh, 1807), viii.

ridge or an Indian ritual as a majestic scene or a moving spectacle. "There appears to have been very little romance or sentiment about any of the party," the biographer of the last survivor of the expedition emphasized in his book about Gass in 1859, "all such insubstantial ideas having been starved out by hard, practical experience."[4] It is Lewis who rose occasionally above the practical. Examples are his description of the White Rocks of the Missouri or its Great Falls in words that have often been quoted, testifying to their rarity as well as their vitality. (See p. 209.)

BUFFALO AND ANTELOPE

On August 23, 1804, in the vicinity of present-day Vermillion, South Dakota, Joseph Fields killed the expedition's first buffalo. Lewis went out with twelve men to butcher it and bring the meat to the boats. Two days later Clark first saw large herds of buffalo feeding in several directions.

On May 29, 1805, while the corps camped near the juncture of the Missouri and the Marias, a solitary buffalo startled the sleeping party. Buffalo were so abundant that Indians could afford to use traditional hunting methods: Lewis described an Indian way of killing buffalo by driving them over a cliff.

Estimates indicate that about sixty or seventy million buffalo lived on the Great Plains in the seventeenth century. The figure held steady until the 1830s when advancing settlers began killing the animals to make room for cattle. By the closing decades of the nineteenth century, the large herds had disappeared forever. Between 1866 and 1891, during the final war against the Plains Indians, white buffalo hunters destroyed the remaining herds to break the Indians' resistance to white encroachment on their lands. Only about a thousand buffalo survived the slaughter.

On September 14, 1804, the explorers saw a graceful, fleet animal—a striking contrast to the buffalo—when Clark killed his first antelope in present-day Lyman County, South Dakota. Three days later, Lewis described stalking a herd. Since the swift animal taxonomically is not an antelope, scientists put it in a new, unique family: the pronghorn.

[4]John G. Jacob, *The Life and Times of Patrick Gass, Now Sole Survivor of the Overland Expedition to the Pacific, under Lewis and Clarke* (Wellsburg, Virginia, 1859), 93–94.

Musselshell to Marias

WEDNESDAY MAY 29ᵀᴴ 1805

Last night we were all allarmed by a large buffaloe Bull, which swam over from the opposite shore and coming along side of the white perogue, climbed over it to land, he then allarmed ran up the bank in full speed directly towards the fires, and was within 18 inches of the heads of some of the men who lay sleeping before the centinel could allarm him or make him change his course, still more alarmed, he now took his direction immediately towards our lodge, passing between 4 fires and within a few inches of the heads of one range of the men as they yet lay sleeping, when he came near the tent, my dog saved us by causing him to change his course a second time, which he did by turning a little to the right, and was quickly out of sight, leaving us by this time all in an uproar with our guns in o[u]r hands, enquiring of each other the ca[u]se of the alarm, which after a few moments was explained by the centinel: we were happy to find no one hirt. The next morning we found that the buffaloe in passing the perogue had trodden on a rifle, which belonged to Capt. Clark's black man, who had negligently left her in the perogue, the rifle was much bent, he had also broken the spindle; pivit, and shattered the stock of one of the blunderbushes on board, with this damage I felt well content, happey indeed, that we had sustained no further injury, it appears that the white perogue, which contains our most valuable stores is attended by some evil gennii.

. . . today we passed . . . the remains of a vast many mangled carcases of Buffalow which had been driven over a precipice of 120 feet by the Indians and perished; the water appeared to have washed away a part of this immence pile of slaughter and still their remained the fragments of at least a hundred carcases they created a most horrid stench. in this manner the Indians of the Missouri distroy vast herds of buffaloe at a stroke; for this purpose one of the most active and fleet young men is scelected and disguised in a robe of buffaloe skin, having also the skin of the buffaloe's head with the years and horns fastened on his head in form of a cap, thus caparisoned he places himself at a convenient distance between a herd of buffaloe and a precipice proper for the purpose, which happens in many places on this river for miles together; the other indians now surround the herd on the back and flanks and at a signal agreed on all shew themselves at the same time moving forward towards the buffaloe; the disguised indian or decoy has taken care to place himself sufficiently nigh

Thwaites, *Original Journals of the Lewis and Clark Expedition*, 2:91–94.

the buffaloe to be noticed by them when they take to flight and runing before them they follow him in full speede to the precipice, the cattle behind driving those in front over and seeing them go do not look or hesitate about following untill the whole are precipitated down the precepice forming one common mass of dead an[d] mangled carcases: the decoy in the mean time has taken care to secure himself in some cranney or crivice of the clift which he had previously prepared for that purpose. the part of the decoy I am informed is extreamly dangerous, if they are not very fleet runers the buffaloe tread them under foot and crush them to death, and sometimes drive them over the precipice also, where they perish in common with the buffaloe. we saw a great many wolves in the neighbourhood of these mangled carcases they were fat and extreemly gentle, Capt. C. who was on shore killed one of them with his espontoon.

Vermilion to Teton

LEWIS   MONDAY SEPTEMBER 17TH. 1804.
. . . we had now after various windings in pursuit of several herds of antelopes which we had seen on our way made the distance of about eight miles from our camp. we found the Antelope extreemly shye and watchfull insomuch that we had been unable to get a shot at them; when at rest they generally seelect the most elivated point in the neighbourhood, and as they are watchfull and extreemly quick of sight and their sense of smelling very accute it is almost impossible to approach them within gunshot; in short they will frequently discover and flee from you at the distance of three miles. I had this day an opportunity of witnessing the agility and the superior fleetness of this anamal which was to me really astonishing. I had pursued and twice surprised a small herd of seven, in the first instance they did not discover me distinctly and therefore did not run at full speed, tho' they took care before they rested to gain an elivated point where it was impossible to approach them under cover, except in one direction and that happened to be in the direction from which the wind blew towards them; bad as the chance to approch them was, I made the best of my way towards them, freqeuntly peeping over the ridge with which I took care to conceal myself from their view the male, of which

there was but one, frequently incircled the summit of the hill on which the females stood in a group, as if to look out for the approach of danger. I got within about 200 paces of them when they smelt me and fled; I gained the top of the eminence on which they stood, as soon as possible from whence I had an extensive view of the country the antilopes which had disappeared in a steep reveene now appeared at the distance of about three miles on the side of a ridge which passed obliquely across me and extended about four miles. so soon had these antelopes gained the distance at which they had again appeared to my view I doubted at ferst that they were the same that I had just surprised, but my doubts soon vanishcd when I beheld the rapidity of their flight along the ridge before me it appeared reather the rappid flight of birds than the motion of quadrupeds. I think I can safely venture the asscertion that the speed of this anamal is equal if not superior to that of the finest blooded courser.

GRIZZLY BEARS

The poor firepower and the inaccuracy of their rifles turned the explorers' hunts of the grizzly into terrifying adventures. Even when a ball pierced its heart, the grizzly often lived on. Only several well-placed bullets could bring it down. At times only their wits and agility helped the men get away from a wounded bear. Yet they pursued grizzlies whenever possible since the giant bear constantly challenged the explorers' hunter mentality.

Lewis and another man killed the expedition's first grizzly on April 29, 1805, on the stretch of the Missouri between the Yellowstone and the Marias. The badly wounded bear had chased them eighty yards before their repeated firing killed it. Despite this experience, Lewis treated lightly the Mandan's warnings about the ferocity of an enraged bear. But three weeks of more attempts to kill grizzlies changed his mind; Lewis admitted fearing one grizzly more than two Indians.

The explorers had many chances to observe the bears during repeated encounters at the Great Falls. Yet they remained baffled by the bears' various colors, ranging from dark brown to white—the latter inspiring Lewis to refer to the grizzly as the white bear. Not until the return voyage, on May 15 and May 31, 1806, when the expedition stayed with the Nez Perce in present-day central Idaho, could Lewis resolve the puzzle of the color variations and separate the grizzly from the black bear and the cinnamon bear.

Stories about the hunters' adventures may have contributed to the scientific term for the grizzly, *Ursus horribilis,* "horrible bear," which the naturalist and philologist George Ord chose in his formal description of 1815. Theodore Roosevelt, the big-game hunter among the presidents of the United States, did not like "grizzly" because it means "grizzled" or "gray." He argued that "grisly," signifying "ghastly" or "horrifying," suited the animal better.[1]

The Native Americans worshiped and respected the grizzly. In ceremonies and rituals designed to ask forgiveness of the spirit of the powerful animal, a hunter prepared himself for the encounter. In his meditations he promised to show the dead animal the greatest reverence. A fortunate hunter would wear the claws of the grizzly as a necklace signifying his courage.

[1]Paul Russell Cutright, *Lewis and Clark: Pioneering Naturalists* (Urbana: University of Illinois Press, 1969), 141–42.

Yellowstone to Musselshell

LEWIS   MONDAY APRIL 29TH 1805.
. . . I walked on shore with one man. . . . we fell in with two brown or yellow [*white*] bear; both of which we wounded; one of them made his escape, the other after my firing on him pursued me seventy or eighty yards, but fortunately had been so badly wounded that he was unable to pursue so closely as to prevent my charging my gun; we again repeated our fir[e] and killed him. it was a male not fully grown, we estimated his weight at 300 lb: not having the means of ascertaining it precisely. The legs of this bear are somewhat longer than those of the black, as are it's tallons and tusks incomparably larger and longer. the testicles, which in the black bear are placed pretty well back between the thyes and contained in one pouch like those of the dog and most quadrupeds, are in the yellow or brown bear placed much further forward, and are suspended in separate pouches from two to four inches asunder; it's colour is yellowish brown, the eyes small, black, and piercing; the front of the fore legs near the feet is usually black; the fur is finer thicker and deeper than that of the black bear. these are all the particulars in which this ana-

mal appeared to me to differ from the black bear; it is a much more furious and formidable anamal, and will frequently pursue the hunter when wounded. it is asstonishing to see the wounds they will bear before they can be put to death. the Indians may well fear this anamal equiped as they generally are with their bows and arrows or indifferent fuzees, but in the hands of skillful riflemen they are by no means as formidable or dangerous as they have been represented.

LEWIS   SUNDAY MAY 5TH 1805

. . . Cap! Clark and Drewyer killed the largest brown bear this evening which we have yet seen. it was a most tremendious looking anamal, and extreemly hard to kill notwithstanding he had five balls through his lungs and five others in various parts he swam more than half the distance across the river to a sandbar, & it was at least twenty minutes before he died; he did not attempt to attack, but fled and made the most tremendous roaring from the moment he was shot. We had no means of weighing this monster; Capt. Clark thought he would weigh 500 lbs for my own part I think the estimate too small by 100 lbs he measured 8. Feet 7½ Inches from the nose to the extremety of the hind feet, 5 F. 10½ Ins arround the breast, 1 F. 11. I. arround the middle of the arm, & 3.F. 11.I. arround the neck; his tallons which were five in number on each foot were 4⅜ Inches in length. he was in good order, we therefore divided him among the party and made them boil the oil and put it in a cask for future uce; the oil is as hard as hogs lard when cool, much more so than that of the black bear. this bear differs from the common black bear in several respects; it's tallons are much longer and more blont, it's tale shorter, it's hair which is of a redish or bey brown, is longer thicker and finer than that of the black bear; his liver lungs and heart are much larger even in proportion with his size; the heart particularly was as large as that of a large Ox. his maw was also ten times the size of black bear, and was filled with flesh and fish. his testicles were pendant from the belly and placed four inches assunder in seperate bags or pouches. this animal also feeds on roots and almost every species of wild fruit.

LEWIS   SATURDAY MAY 11ᵀᴴ 1805.

. . . About 5.P.M. my attention was struck by one of the Party runing at a distance towards us and making signs and hollowing as if in distress, I ordered the perogues to put too, and waited untill he arrived; I now found that it was Bratton the man with the soar hand whom I had permitted to walk on shore, he arrived so much out of breath that it was several minutes before he could tell what had happened; at length he informed me that in the woody bottom . . . about 1½ [miles] below us he had shot a brown bear which immediately turned on him and pursued him a considerable distance but he had wounded it so badly that it could not overtake him; I immediately turned out with seven of the party in quest of this monster, we at length found his trale and persued him about a mile by the blood through very thick brush . . . ; we finally found him concealed in some very thick brush and shot him through the skull with two balls; we proceeded [to] dress him as soon as possible, we found him in good order; it was a monstrous beast, not quite so large as that we killed a few days past but in all other rispects much the same the hair is remarkably long fine and rich tho' he appears parshally to have discharged his winter coat; we now found that Bratton had shot him through the center of the lungs, notwithstanding which he had pursued him near half a mile and had returned more than double that distance and with his tallons had prepared himself a bed in the earth of about 2 feet deep and five long and was perfectly alive when we found him which could not have been less than 2 hours after he received the wound; these bear being so hard to die reather intimedates us all; I must confess that I do not like the gentlemen and had reather fight two Indians than one bear; there is no other chance to conquer them by a single shot but by shooting them through the brains, and this becomes difficult in consequence of two large muscles which cover the sides of the forehead and the sharp projection of the center of the frontal bone, which is also of a pretty good thickness. the flece and skin were as much as two men could possibly carry. by the time we returned the sun had set and I determined to remain here all night, and directed the cooks to render the bear's oil and put it in the kegs which was done. there was about eight gallons of it.

Marias to Great Falls

LEWIS   FRIDAY JUNE 14TH 1805.
. . . I decended the hill and directed my course to the bend of the Missouri near which there was a herd of at least a thousand buffaloe; here I thought it would be well to kill a buffaloe and leave him untill my return from the

river . . . I scelected a fat buffaloe and shot him very well, through the lungs; while I was gazeing attentively on the poor anamal discharging blood in streams from his mouth and nostrils, expecting him to fall every instant, and having entirely forgotten to reload my rifle, a large white, or reather brown bear, had perceived and crept on me within 20 steps before I discovered him; in the first moment I drew up my gun to shoot, but at the same instant recolected that she was not loaded and that he was too near for me to hope to perform this opperation before he reached me, as he was then briskly advancing on me; it was an open level plain, not a bush within miles nor a tree within less than three hundred yards of me; the river bank was sloping and not more than three feet above the level of the water; in short there was no place by means of which I could conceal myself from this monster untill I could charge my rifle; in this situation I thought of retreating in a brisk walk as fast as he was advancing untill I could reach a tree about 300 yards below me, but I had no sooner terned myself about but he pitched at me, open mouthed and full speed, I ran about 80 yards and found he gained on me fast, I then run into the water the idea struk me to get into the water to such debth that I could stand and he would be obliged to swim, and that I could in that situation defend myself with my espontoon; accordingly I ran haistily into the water about waist deep, and faced about and presented the point of my espontoon, at this instant he arrived at the edge of the water within about 20 feet of me; the moment I put myself in this attitude of defence he sudonly wheeled about as if frightened, declined the combat on such unequal grounds, and retreated with quite as great precipitation as he had just before pursued me. as soon as I saw him run of[f] in that manner I returned to the shore and charged my gun, which I had still retained in my hand throughout this curious adventure. I saw him run through the level open plain about three miles, till he disappeared in the woods . . . ; during the whole of this distance he ran at full speed, sometimes appearing to look behind him as if he expected pursuit. I now began to reflect on this novil occurrence and indeavoured to account for this sudden retreat of the bear. I at first thought that perhaps he had not smelt me bofore he arrived at the waters edge so near me, but I then reflected that he had pursued me for about 80 or 90 yards before I took [to] the water and on examination saw the grownd toarn with his tallons immediately on the imp[r]ession of my steps; and the cause of his allarm still remains with me misterious and unaccountable. so it was and I felt myself not a little gratifyed that he had declined the combat. my gun reloaded I felt confidence once more in my strength; . . . determined never again to suffer my peice to be longer empty than the time she necessarily required to charge her.

On the Upper Kooskooske

LEWIS   SATURDAY MAY 31ST 1806.

Goodrich and Willard visited the indian Villages. . . . Willard brought with him the dressed skin of a bear which he had purchased for Cap! C. this skin was an uniform pale redish brown colour, the indians informed us that it was not the *Hoh-host* or white bear. that it was the Yâck-kâh. this distinction of the indians induced us to make further enquiry relative to their opinions of the several speceis of bear in this country. we produced the several skins of the bear which we had killed at this place and one very nearly white which I had purchased. The white, the deep and pale red grizzle, the dark bro[w]n grizzle, and all those which had the extremities of the hair of a white or frosty colour without regard to the colour of the ground of the poil,[1] they designated Hoh-host and assured us that they were the same with the white bear, that they ascosiated together, were very vicisious, never climbed the trees, and had much longer nails than the others. the black skins, those which were black with a number of intire white hairs intermixed, the black with a white breast, the uniform bey, brown and light redish brown, they designated the *Yâck-kâh;* said that they climbed the trees, had short nails and were not vicious, that they could pursue them and kill them with safety, they also affirmed that they were much smaller than the white bear. I am disposed to adopt the Indian distinction with respect to these bear and consider them two distinct speceis. the white and the Grizzly of this neighbourhood are the same of those found on the upper portion of the Missouri where the other speceis are not, and that the uniform redish brown black &c. of this neighbourhood are a speceis distinct from our black bear and from the black bear of the Pacific coast which I believe to be the same with those of the Atlantic coast, and that the common black bear do not exist here. I had previously observed that the claws of some of the bear which we had killed here had much shorter tallons than the variagated or white bear usually have but supposed that they had woarn them out by scratching up roots, and these were those which the indians called Yâk-kâh. on enquiry I found also that a cub of an uniform redish brown colour, pup to a female black bear intermixed with entire white hair had climbed a tree. I think this a distinct speceis from the common black bear, because we never find the latter of any other colour than an uniform black, and

[1] French for "hair."

Thwaites, *Original Journals of the Lewis and Clark Expedition,* 5:90–91.

also that the poil of this bear is much finer thicker and longer with a greater proportion of fur mixed with the hair, in other [r]ispects they are much the same. . . .

CALIFORNIA CONDOR AND WESTERN TANAGER

If the captains wanted to get a close look at a bird, they shot it and then described it carefully. On October 30, 1805, in the vicinity of the Cascades of the Columbia, the explorers saw several California condors. On November 18, near the mouth of the Columbia, Reuben Fields shot one, lured by its unusual size, to bring it down. Clark measured and described it, but too hastily, he thought three months later when George Shannon and François Labiche brought in another condor that they had wounded and taken alive. This time Clark took the opportunity to describe it fully.

Before leaving Camp Chopunnish, on the Kooskooske River, Lewis found time to describe and identify some of the birds the explorers had collected. He had the first opportunity to examine Clark's nutcracker and Lewis's woodpecker, which were named for the captains by the ornithologist Alexander Wilson in 1811. On June 6, 1806, Lewis came across one of the most brilliantly colored songbirds of the West Coast, the western tanager. He wrote the bird's first description, which Elliott Coues praised for its clarity.

At Fort Clatsop

CLARK   FEBRUARY 16TH 1806.
. . . Shannon an[d] Labiesh brought in to us today a Buzzard or *Vulture* of the Columbia which they had wounded and taken alive. I believe this to be the largest Bird of North America. it was not in good order and yet it wayed 25lbs had it have been so it might very well have weighed 10lb more or 35lbs. between the extremities of the wings it measured 9 feet 2

Thwaites, *Original Journals of the Lewis and Clark Expedition*, 4:79–81.

Inches; from the extremity of the beak to that of the toe 3 feet 9 inches and a half. from hip to toe 2 feet, girth of the head 9 inches ¾. Girth of the neck 7½ inches; Girth of the body exclusive of the wings 2 feet 3 inches; girth of the leg 3 inches. the diameter of the eye 4½/10[ths] of an inch, the iris of a pale scarlet red, the puple of a deep sea green or black and occupies about one third of the diameter of the eye the head and part of the neck as low as the figures 1.2. is uncovered with feathers except that portion of it represented by dots forward and under the eye. the tail is composed of twelve feathers of equal length, each 14 inches. the legs are 4¾ inches in length and of a whitish colour uncovered with feathers, they are not entirely smooth but not imbricated; the toes are four in number three of which are forward and that in the center much the longest; the fourth is short and is inserted near the inner of the three other toes and reather projecting foward. the thye is covered with feathers as low as the knee. the top or upper part of the toes are imbricated with broad scales lying transversly, the nails are black and in proportion to the size of the bird comparitively with those of the Hawk or Eagle, short and bluntly pointed. the under side of the wing is covered with white down and feathers. a white stripe of about 2 inches in width, also marks the outer part of the wing, imbraceing the lower points of the feathers, which [c]over the joints of the wing through their whole length or width of that part of the wing. all the other feathers of whatever part are of a Glossy shineing black except the down, which is not glossy, but equally black. the skin of the beak and head to the joining of the neck is of a pale orrange Yellow, the other part uncovered with feathers is of a light flesh colour. the skin is thin and wrinkled except on the beak where it is smooth. This bird fly's very clumsily, nor do I know whether it ever seizes it's prey alive, but am induced to believe it does not. we have seen it feeding on the remains of the whale and other fish which have been thrown up by the waves on the sea coast. these I believe constitute their principal food, but I have no doubt but that they also feed on flesh. we did not meet with this bird un[t]ill we had decended the Columbia below the great falls, and have found them more abundant below tide water than above. . . . then I thought this of the Buzzard speces. I now believe that this bird is reather of the Vulture genus than any other, tho' it wants some of their characteristics particularly the hair on the neck, and the feathers on the legs. this is a handsom bird at a little distance. it's neck is proportionably longer than those of the Hawks or Eagle. . . . Shannon and Labiesh informed us that when he approached this Vulture after wounding it, that it made a loud noise very much like the barking of a Dog. the tongue is long firm and broad, filling the under Chap and partakeing of its transvirs curvature, or its sides forming a longitudinal Groove; obtuse at the point, the Margin armed with firm cartelagenous prickkles pointed and bending inwards.

On the Upper Kooskooske

LEWIS   FRIDAY JUNE 6ᵀᴴ 1806

... we meet with a beautifull little bird in this neighbourhood about the size and somewhat the shape of the large sparrow. it is reather longer in proportion to it's bulk than the sparrow. it measures 7 inches from the extremity of the beek to that of the tail, the latter occupying 2-½ inches. the beak is reather more than half an inch in length, and is formed much like the virginia nitingale; it is thick and large for a bird of it's size; wide at the base, both chaps convex, and pointed, the uper exceeds the under chap a little is somewhat curved and of a brown colour; the lower chap of a greenish yellow. the eye full reather large and of a black colour both puple and iris. the plumage is remarkably delicate; that of the neck and head is of a fine orrange yellow and red, the latter predominates on the top of the head and arround the base of the beak from whence it graduly deminishes & towards the lower part of the neck, the orrange yellow prevails most; the red has the appearance of being laid over a ground of yellow. the breast, the sides, rump and some long feathers which lie between the legs and extend underneath the tail are of a fine orrange yellow. the tail, back and wings are black, e[x]cept a small stripe of yellow on the outer part of the middle joint of the wing, ¼ of an inch wide and an inch in length. the tail is composed of twelve feathers of which those in the center are reather shortest, and the plumage of all the feathers of the tail is longest on that side of the quill next the center of the tail. the legs and feet are black, nails long and sharp; it has four toes on each foot, of which three are forward and one behind; that behind is as long as the two outer of the three toes in front.

Thwaites, *Original Journals of the Lewis and Clark Expedition,* 5:111–12.

SALMON AND RED CHAR

In the late fall of 1805, when the explorers struggled with the Celilo Falls of the Columbia, they noted that all Indian life was centered around the river. The Indians' economy depended on the salmon, and their many baskets filled with fish reflected the large amount caught and dried since early spring when the spawning runs began. The explorers' food supply was also affected by the river. On both banks of the Columbia, dense forests prevented using horses for hunting. Even those explorers who disliked fish soon learned to eat salmon. Whenever chance permitted, however, they tried to trade for dogs with the Indians. Lewis described two species of Pacific coast salmon, remarking on their importance for Native Americans.

At Fort Clatsop

LEWIS   THURSDAY MARCH 13TH 1806.
. . . the common Salmon and red Charr are the inhabitants of both the sea and rivers. the former is usually largest and weighs from 5 to 15 lb.ˢ it is this speceis that extends itself into all the rivers and little creeks on this side of the Continent, and to which the natives are so much indebted for their subsistence. the body of this fish is from 2½ to 3 feet long and proportionably broad. it is covered with imbricated scales of a moderate size and is variagated with irregular black spots on it's sides and gills. the eye is large and the iris of a silvery colour the pupil black. the nostrum [rostrum] or nose extends beyond the under jaw, and both the upper and lower jaws are armed with a single series of long teeth which are subulate and infle[c]ted near the extremities of the jaws where they are also more closely arranged. they have some sharp teeth of smaller size and same shape placed on the tongue which is thick and fleshey. the fins of the back are two; the first is plaised nearer the head than the ventral fins and has rays, the second is placed far back near the tail is small and has no rays. the flesh of this fish is when in order of a deep flesh coloured red and every shade from that to an orrange yellow, and when very meager almost white. the roes of this fish are much esteemed by the natives who dry them in the sun and preserve them for a great length of time. they are about the size of a small pea nearly transparent and of a redish

Thwaites, *Original Journals of the Lewis and Clark Expedition,* 4:163–64.

yellow colour. they resemble very much at a little distance the common currants of our gardens but are more yellow. this fish is sometimes red along the sides and belley near the gills; particularly the male. The red Charr are reather broader in proportion to their length than the common salmon, the skales are also imbricated but reather large. . . .

LEWIS'S TRIO OF PESTS

Fleas and lice plagued the explorers throughout their voyage. They were the regular members of a "trio of pests," as Lewis called them. The third member changed from time to time and from place to place. Frequently mosquitoes made up the entire third part of the trio, but at the Great Falls the prickly pears claimed their share, too.

Great Falls to Three Forks

LEWIS   WEDNESDAY JULY 24TH 1805.
. . . our trio of pests still invade and obstruct us on all occasions, these are the Musquetoes eye knats and prickley pears, equal to any three curses that ever poor Egypt laiboured under, except the *Mahometant yoke.*[1]

[1]Muhammad (Mahomet) and Islam, which Lewis considered a greater burden than any of the curses Egypt suffered in Exodus 7–12.

Thwaites, *Original Journals of the Lewis and Clark Expedition,* 2:266.

Descending the Columbia

CLARK   OCTOBER 23D WEDNESDAY 1805
. . . nearly covered with flees which were so thick amongst the Straw and fish Skins at the upper part of the portage at which place the nativs had been Camped not long since; that every man of the party was obliged to

Thwaites, *Original Journals of the Lewis and Clark Expedition,* 3:150.

Strip naked dureing the time of takeing over the canoes, that they might have an oppertunity of brushing the flees of[f] their legs and bodies. . . .

At Fort Clatsop

LEWIS   THURSDAY, JANUARY 2ND 1806

. . . we are infested with swarms of flees already in our new habitations; the presumption is therefore strong that we shall not devest ourselves of this intolerably troublesome vermin during our residence here. . . .

Thwaites, *Original Journals of the Lewis and Clark Expedition,* 3:307.

Clark's Exploration

CLARK   WEDNESDAY 4TH AUGUST 1806

Musquetors excessively troublesom so much so that the men complained that they could not work . . . for those troublesom insects. and I find it entirely impossible to hunt in the bottoms, those insects being so noumerous and tormenting as to render it imposseable for a man to continue in the timbered lands and our best retreat from those insects is on the Sand bars in the river and even those Situations are only clear of them when the Wind Should happen to blow which it did to day for a fiew hours in the middle of the day. the evenings nights and mornings they are almost [un]indureable perticularly by the party with me who have no Bears [biers] to keep them off at night, and nothing to Screen them but their blankets which are worn and have maney holes. . . . The child of Shabono has been so much bitten by the Musquetors that his face is much puffed up & Swelled. . . .

Thwaites, *Original Journals of the Lewis and Clark Expedition,* 5:322–23.

A SHIPMENT OF SPECIMENS

The return party to St. Louis under the command of Corporal Richard Warfington brought back objects collected during the ascent of the Missouri and at Fort Mandan. The specimens were shipped via New Orleans to Washington, where Jefferson directed their distribution. The two animals that survived the four-thousand-mile, seven-month trip alive, a prairie dog and a magpie, went to Peale's Museum in Philadelphia, together with skins, skeletons, and Indian relics. Jefferson kept a few of the ethnographic specimens; he sent the botanical material to the American Philosophical Society. In the subsequent decades, many of the rare Indian relics disappeared. The loss deprived Americans of a part of a priceless heritage representing the culture of the Plains Indian society just before its destruction.[1]

[1]For details see "The Fate of the Lewis and Clark Booty" in Paul Russell Cutright, *Lewis and Clark: Pioneering Naturalists* (Urbana: University of Illinois Press, 1969), 349–92.

Lewis to Jefferson

FORT MANDAN, APRIL 7ᵀᴴ 1805.

DEAR SIR: Herewith inclosed you will receive an invoice of certain articles, which I have forwarded to you from this place. among other articles . . . 67. specimens of earths, salts and minerals; and 60 specimens of plants: these are accompanyed by their rispective labels expressing the days on which obtained, places where found, and also their virtues and properties when known. by means of these labels, reference may be made to the Chart of the Missouri forwarded to the Secretary at War, on which, the encampment of each day has been carefully marked; thus the places at which these specimens have been obtained may be easily pointed out, or again found, should any of them prove valuable to the community on further investegation. (these have been forwarded with a view of their being presented to the Philosophical society of Philadelphia, in order that they may under their direction be examined or analyzed. after examin-

From original manuscript in Bureau of Rolls, *Jefferson Papers,* ser. 2, vol. 51, doc. 107, reprinted in Thwaites, *Original Journals of the Lewis and Clark Expedition,* 7:318, 321.

ing these specimens yourself, I would thank you to have a copy of their labels made out, and retained untill my return. the other articles are intended particularly for yourself, to be retained, or disposed off as you may think proper.) . . .

Your most Ob! Serv!

MERIWETHER LEWIS

Capt. 1ˢᵗ U' S. Reg! Infty.

Thomas Jefferson, President of the U' States.

Invoice of Articles Forwarded to Jefferson from Fort Mandan
April 7, 1805

Invoice of articles forwarded from Fort Mandan to the President of the United States through Capt!. Stoddard at S! Louis and M! H. B. Trist, the Collector of the Port of New Orleans.

Nᴼ	PACKAGE	COMMENT
1	Box	Skins of the Male and female Antelope, with their Skeletons. [*came. P.*]¹
"	do	2 Horns and ears, of the Blacktail, or Mule Deer. [*came*]
"	"	A Martin Skin [*came*] containing the Skin of a weasel [*came. P.*] and three Small squirels of the Rocky Mountains & the tail of a Mule deer fully grown. [*came.*]
"	"	Skeletons of the Small, or burrowing wolf of the Praries, the Skin haveing been lost by accident. [*some skeletons came, not distinguishable. sent to P.*]

(CONTINUED)

¹Italics in brackets are comments by the person who received the items. *P* indicates Peale's Museum in Philadelphia. Mineralogical specimens were sent to the American Philosophical Society, also in Philadelphia.

From original manuscript by Clark, in Bureau of Rolls, *Jefferson Papers,* L, ser. 2, vol. 51, doc. 105a, reprinted in Thwaites, *Original Journals of the Lewis and Clark Expedition,* 7:322–23.

N°	PACKAGE	COMMENT
"	"	2 Skeletons of the White Hair. [*as above. P.*]
"	"	A Mandan bow with a quiver of Arrows [*came*] the quiver containing Some Seed of the Mandan tobacco. [*came*]
"	"	A carrot of Ricara tobacco. [*came*].
2	Box	4 Buffalow Robes [*came*] and an *ear* of Mandan corn.
3	Box	Skins of the Male and female Antelope, with their Skeletons [*undistinguishable*] and the Skin of a brown, or Yellow Bear.
4	Box	Specimens of earths, Salts, and minerals, numbered from 1 to 67. [*came A. Ph. Society.*]
"	"	Specimens of plants numbered from 1 to 60. [*came*]
"	"	1 earthen pot, Such as the Mandans manufacture, and use for culinary purposes. [*came*]
4	Box	1 tin box containing insects, mice &c
"	"	a Specimen of the fur of the Antilope.
"	"	a Specimen of a plant, and a parsel of its roots, highly prized by the natives as an efficatious remidy in the cure of the bite of the rattle snake, or Mad dog.
"	{ Large Trunk }	Skins of a Male and female Braro, or burrowing Dog of the Praries, with the Skeleton of the female. [*came. P.*]
"	in a large Trunk	1 Skin of a red fox containing a Magpie. [*came*]
"	"	2 Cased Skins of the white hare. [*came. P.*]
"	"	1 Minitarre Buffalow robe, [*came*] containing Some articles of Indian dress. [*came*]
"	"	1 Mandan Buffalow robe, [*came*] containing a dressed Skin of the Lousiv[ir]e [*came*] and two cased Skins of the burrowing Squirels of the praries [*came*]
"	"	13 red fox skins [*came*]
"	"	4 horns of the mountain ram, or *big horn* [*came*]
"	"	1 Buffalow robe painted by a Mandan man representing a battle which was fought 8 years since, by the Sioux & Ricaras, against the Mandans, Minitarras & Ahwahharways [*came*]
6	Cage	Containing four liveing Magpies. [*1. came P.*]
7	do.	Containing a liveing burrowing Squirel of the praries. [*came. P*].
9	do.	Containing one liveing hen of the Prarie.
10	—	1 large par of Elk's horns connected by the frontal bone.

CLARKIA PULCHELLA

On June 1, 1806, in present-day central Idaho, Lewis found a primrose variety along the banks of the Kooskooske River, a few weeks before the expedition started its return trip on the Lolo Trail. Today the plant is best known as the ragged robin; *Clarkia pulchella* is its botanical name honoring Clark. Lewis's description of the beautiful clarkia, as it is sometimes called, stands out among his many accounts of plants and animals.

On the Upper Kooskooske

LEWIS   SUNDAY JUNE 1ST 1806.
. . . I met with a singular plant today in blume of which I preserved a specemine; it grows on the steep sides of the fertile hills near this place, the radix is fibrous, not much branched, annual, woody, white and nearly smooth. the stem is simple branching ascending, [2-½ *feet high.*] celindric, villose and of a pale red colour. the branches are but few and those near it's upper extremity. the extremities of the branches are flexable and are bent downward near their extremities with the weight of the flowers. the leaf is sessile, scattered thinly, nearly linear tho' somewhat widest in the middle, two inches in length, absolutely entire, villose, obtusely pointed and of an ordinary green. above each leaf a small short branch protrudes, supporting a tissue of four or five smaller leaves of the same appearance with those discribed. a leaf is placed underneath ea[c]h branch, and each flower. the calyx is a one flowered spathe. the corolla superior consists of four pale perple petals which are tripartite, the central lobe largest and all terminate obtusely; they are inserted with a long and narrow claw on the top of the germ, are long, smooth, & deciduous. there are two distinct sets of stamens the 1st or principal consists of four, the filaments of which are capillary, erect, inserted on the top of the germ alternately with the petals, equal, short, membranous; the anthers are also four each being elivated with it's fillament, they are linear and reather flat, erect, sessile, cohering at the base, membranous, longitudinally furrowed, twice as long as the fillament naked, and of a pale perple colour. the second set of stamens are very minute are also

Thwaites, *Original Journals of the Lewis and Clark Expedition,* 5:95–97.

four and placed within and opposite to the petals, these are scarcely persceptable while the 1st are large and conspicuous; the filaments are capillary equal, very short, white and smooth. the anthers are four, oblong, beaked, erect, cohering at the base, membranous, shorter than the fillaments, white naked and appear not to form pollen, there is one pistillum; the germ of which is also one, cilindric, villous, inferior, sessile, as long as the 1st stamens & marked with 8 longitudinal furrows. the single style and stigma form a perfict monapetallous corolla only with this difference, that the style which elivates the stigma or limb is not a tube but solid tho' it's outer appearance is that of the tube of a monopetallous corolla swelling as it ascends and gliding in such manner into the limb that it cannot be said where the style ends, or the stigma begins; jointly they are as long as the corolla, white, the limb is four cleft, sauser shaped, and the margins of the lobes entire and rounded. this has the appearance of a monopetallous flower growing from the center of a four petalled corollar, which is rendered more conspicuous in consequence of the 1st being white and the latter of a pale perple. I regret very much that the seed of this plant are not yet ripe and it is pro[ba]ble will not be so during my residence in this neighbourhood.

THE WHITE CLIFFS AND GREAT FALLS

On May 31, 1805, the explorers passed through the most spectacular section of the White Cliffs area of the Missouri River Breaks, in present-day Chouteau County, Montana. Wind, sand, and water had sculpted the light sandstone into castles, citadels, and cathedrals. Today it is the only large stretch of the Missouri that still looks almost as the explorers saw it. Karl Bodmer, the Swiss artist who accompanied Prince Maximilian zu Wied to the upper Missouri in 1833, added a painter's version to the vivid words Lewis had found for nature's carvings.

When Lewis saw the Great Falls of the Missouri on June 13, 1805, he was overwhelmed by the series of five spectacular falls within such a short distance. His amazement flowed from his pen as he described the stunning views. He relied on the conventional words of educated men of his time to describe the scenery. Regretting that the corps had no draftsman, he wished for the pencil of Salvator Rosa or the pen of James Thomson to evoke the majesty of nature as only the seventeenth-century Italian painter and the eighteenth-century British nature poet could. Lewis's attempt to compare two of the falls interrupted his splendid description. Groping for words, he resorted to common eighteenth-century phrases:

"At length I determined," he wrote underlining his verdicts emphatically, that one "was *pleasingly beautifull,* while the other was *sublimely grand.*"

Musselshell to Marias

LEWIS   FRIDAY MAY 31ST 1805.—
The hills and river Clifts which we passed today exhibit a most romantic appearance. The bluffs of the river rise to the hight of from 2 to 300 feet and in most places nearly perpendicular; they are formed of remarkable white sandstone which is sufficiently soft to give way readily to the impression of water; two or thre thin horizontal stratas of white free-stone, on which the rains or water make no impression, lie imbeded in these clifts of soft stone near the upper part of them; the earth on the top of these Clifts is a dark rich loam, which forming a graduly ascending plain extends back from ½ a mile to a mile where the hills commence and rise abruptly to a hight of about 300 feet more. The water in the course of time in decending from those hills and plains on either side of the river has trickled down the soft sand clifts and woarn it into a thousand grotesque figures, which with the help of a little immagination and an oblique view, at a distance are made to represent eligant ranges of lofty freestone buildings, having their parapets well stocked with statuary; collumns of various sculpture both grooved and plain, are also seen sup-porting long galleries in front of those buildings; in other places on a much nearer approach and with the help of less immagination we see the remains or ruins of eligant buildings; some collumns standing and almost entire with their pedestals and capitals; others retaining their pedestals but deprived by time or accident of their capitals, some lying prostrate an broken othe[r]s in the form of vast pyramids of connic structure bear-ing a serees of other pyramids on their tops becoming less as they ascend and finally terminating in a sharp point. nitches and alcoves of various forms and sizes are seen at different hights as we pass. a number of the small martin which build their nests with clay in a globular form attatched to the wall within those nitches, and which were seen hovering about the tops of the collumns did not the less remind us of some of those large stone buildings in the U. States. the thin stratas of hard freestone inter-

mixed with the soft sandstone seems to have aided the water in forming this curious scenery. As we passed on it seemed as if those seens of visionary inchantment would never have and [an] end; for here it is too that nature presents to the view of the traveler vast ranges of walls of tolerable workmanship, so perfect indeed are those walls that I should have thought that nature had attempted here to rival the human art of masonry had I not recollected that she had first began her work. These walls rise to the hight in many places of 100 feet, are perpendicular, with two regular faces and are from one to 12 feet thick, each wall retains the same thickness at top which it possesses at bottom. The stone of which these walls are formed is black, dence and durcable, and appears to be composed of a large portion of earth intermixed or cemented with a small quantity of sand and a considerable portion of talk or quarts. these stones are almost invariably regular parallelepipeds, of unequal sizes in the walls, but equal in their horizontal ranges, at least as to debth. these are laid regularly in ranges on each other like bricks, each breaking or covering the interstice of the two on which it rests. thus the purpendicular interstices are broken, and the horizontal ones extend entire throughout the whole extent of the walls. These stones seem to bear some proportion to the thickness of the walls in which they are employed, being larger in the thicker walls; the greatest length of the parallelepiped appears to form the thickness of the thinner walls, while two or more are employed to form that of the thicker walls. These walls pass the river in several places, rising from the water's edge much above the sandstone bluffs, which they seem to penetrate; thence continuing their course on a streight line on either side of the river through the gradually ascending plains, over which they tower to the hight of from ten to seventy feet untill they reach the hills, which they finally enter and conceal themselves. these walls sometimes run parallel to each other, with several ranges near each other, and at other times interscecting each other at right angles, having the appearance of the walls of ancient houses or gardens. I walked on shore this evening and examined these walls minutely and preserved a specimine of the stone. I found the face of many of the river hills formed of Clifts of very excellent free stone of a light yellowish brown colour . . .

Marias to Great Falls

THURSDAY JUNE 13ᵀᴴ 1805.

... I hurryed down the hill ... to gaze on this sublimely grand specticle. I took my position on the top of some rocks about 20 feet high opposite the center of the falls. this chain of rocks appear once to have formed a part of those over which the waters tumbled, but in the course of time has been seperated from it to the distance of 150 yards lying prarrallel to it and a butment against which the water after falling over the precipice beats with great fury; this barrier extends on the right to the perpendicular clift which forms that board [border] of the river, but to the distance of 120 yards next to the clift it is but a few feet above the level of the water, and here the water in very high tides appears to pass in a channel of 40 y^{ds} next to the higher part of the ledg of rocks; on the left it extends within 80 or ninty yards of the lar^d Clift which is also perpendicular; between this abrupt extremity of the ledge of rocks and the perpendicular bluff the whole body of water passes with incredible swiftness. immediately at the cascade the river is about 300 y^{ds} wide; about ninty or a hundred yards of this next the Lar^d bluff is a smoth even sheet of water falling over a precipice of at least eighty feet, the remaining part of about 200 yards on my right formes the grandest sight I ever beheld, the hight of the fall is the same of the other but the irregular and somewhat projecting rocks below receives the water in it's passage down and brakes it into a perfect white foam which assumes a thousand forms in a moment sometimes flying up in jets of sparkling foam to the hight of fifteen or twenty feet and are scarcely formed before large roling bodies of the same beaten and foaming water is thrown over and conceals them. in short the rocks seem to be most happily fixed to present a sheet of the whitest beaten froath for 200 yards in length and about 80 feet perpendicular. the water after decending strikes against the butment ... on which I stand and seems to reverberate and being met by the more impetuous courant they roll and swell into half formed billows of great hight which rise and again disappear in an instant. this butment of rock defends a handsome little bottom of about three acres which is deversified and agreeably shaded with some cottonwood trees; in the lower extremity of the bottom there is a very thick grove of the same kind of trees which are small, in this wood there are several Indian lodges formed of sticks. a few small cedar grow near the ledge of rocks where I rest. below the point of these rocks at a small distance the river is divided by a large rock which rises several feet above

Thwaites, *Original Journals of the Lewis and Clark Expedition,* 2:147–50, 153–56.

212

the water, and extends downwards with the stream for about 20 yards. about a mile before the water arrives at the pitch it decends very rappidly, and is confined on the Lar.d side by a perpendicular clift of about 100 feet, on Star.d side it is also perpendicular for about three hundred yards above the pitch where it is then broken by the discharge of a small ravine, down which the buffaloe have a large beaten road to the water, . . . for it is but in very few places that these anamals can obtain water near this place owing to the steep and inaccessible banks. . . . about 300 yards below me there is another butment of solid rock with a perpendicular face and abo[u]t 60 feet high which projects from the Star.d side at right angles to the distance of 134 y.ds and terminates the lower part nearly of the bottom before mentioned; there being a passage arround the end of this butment between it and the river of about 20 yards; here the river again assumes it's usual width soon spreading to near 300 yards but still continues it's rappidity. from the reflection of the sun on the sprey or mist which arrises from these falls there is a beatifull rainbow produced which adds not a little to the beauty of this majestically grand senery. after wrighting this imperfect discription I again viewed the falls and was so much disgusted with the imperfect idea which it conveyed of the scene that I determined to draw my pen across it and begin agin, but then reflected that I could not perhaps succeed better than penning the first impressions of the mind; I wished for the pencil of Salvator Rosa [a *Titian*] or the pen of Thompson, that I might be enabled to give to the enlightened world some just idea of this truly magnifficent and sublimely grand object, which has from the commencement of time been concealed from the view of civilized man; but this was fruitless and vain. I most sincerely regreted that I had not brought a crimee [camera] obscura with me by the assistance of which even I could have hoped to have done better but alas this was also out of my reach; I therefore with the assistance of my pen only indeavoured to trace some of the stronger features of this seen by the assistance of which and my recollection aided by some able pencil I hope still to give to the world some faint idea of an object which at this moment fills me with such pleasure and astonishment; and which of it's kind I will venture to ascert is second to but one in the known world. . . .

LEWIS   FRIDAY JUNE 14TH 1805.
. . . after passing one continued rappid and three small cascades of ab[o]ut for or five feet each at the distance of about five miles I arrived at a fall of about 19 feet; the river is here about 400 y.ds wide. this pitch which I called the crooked falls occupys about threefourths of the width of the river, commencing on the South side, extends obliquly upwards about 150 y.ds

then forming an accute angle extends downwards nearly to the commencement of four small Islands lying near the N. shore; . . . the water glides down the side of a sloping rock with a volocity almost equal to that of it's perpendicular decent. just above this rappid the river makes a suddon bend to the right or Northwardly. I should have returned from hence but hearing a tremendious roaring above me I continued my rout across the point of a hill a few hundred yards further and was again presented by one of the most beatifull objects in nature, a cascade of about fifty feet perpendicular stretching at rightangles across the river from side to side to the distance of at least a quarter of a mile. here the river pitches over a shelving rock, with an edge as regular and as streight as if formed by art, without a nich or brake in it; the water decends in one even and uninterupted sheet to the bottom wher dashing against the rocky bottom [it] rises into foaming billows of great hight and rappidly glides away, hising flashing and sparkling as it departs the sprey rises from one extremity to the other to 50! I now thought that if a skillfull painter had been asked to make a beautifull cascade that he would most probably have p[r]esented the precise immage of this one; nor could I for some time determine on which of those two great cataracts to bestoe the palm, on this or that which I had discovered yesterday; at length I determined between these two great rivals for glory that this was *pleasingly beautifull,* while the other was *sublimely grand.* I had scarcely infixed my eyes from this pleasing object before I discovered another fall above at the distance of half a mile; thus invited I did not once think of returning but hurried thither to amuse myself with this newly discovered object. I found this to be a cascade of about 14 feet possessing a perpendicular pitch of about 6 feet. this was tolerably regular streching across the river from bank to bank where it was about a quarter of a mile wide; in any other neighbourhood but this, such a cascade would probably be extoled for it's bea[u]ty and magnifficence, but here I passed it by with but little attention; determining as I had proceded so far to continue my rout to the head of the rappids if it should even detain me all night. at every rappid cateract and cascade I discovered that the bluffs grew lower or that the bed of the river rose nearer to a level with the plains. still pursuing the river with it's course about S.W. passing a continued sene of rappids and small cascades, at the distance of 2½ miles I arrived at another cataract of 26 feet. this is not immediately perpendicular, a rock about ⅓ of it's decent seems to protrude to a small distance and receives the water in it's passage downwards and gives a curve to the water tho' it falls mostly with a regular and smoth sheet. the river is near six hundred yards wide at this place, a beatifull level plain on the S. side only a few feet above the level of the pitch, on the N. side where I am the country is more broken and immediately behind me near the river a high hill. below this fall at a little distance a beatifull little Island well timbered is situated about the middle of the river. in this Island on a Cottonwood tree an Eagle has placed her nest; a more inaccessible spot I beleive she could not have found; for neither man nor beast dare pass those gulphs which seperate her little domain from the shores. the water is also broken in such manner as it decends over this pitch that the mist or sprey rises to a considerable hight. this fall is certainly much the greatest I ever behald except those two which I have mentioncd below. it is incomparably a g[r]eater cataract and a more noble interesting object than the celibrated falls of Potomac or Soolkiln [Schuylkill] &c. just above this is another cascade of about 5 feet, above which the water as far as I could see began to abate of it's volosity, and I therefore determined to ascend the hill behind me which promised a fine prospect of the adjacent country, nor was I disappointed on my arrival at it's summit. from hence I overlooked a most beatifull and extensive plain reaching from the river to the base of the Snowclad mountains to the S. and S. West; I also observed the missoury streching it's meandering course to the South through this plain to a great distance filled to it's even and grassey brim; another large river flowed in on it's Western side about four miles above me and extended itself th[r]ough a level and fertile valley of 3 miles in width a great distance to the N.W. rendered more conspicuous by the timber which garnished it's borders. in these plains and more particularly in the valley just below me immence herds of buffaloe are feeding. the missouri just above this hill makes a bend to the South where it lies a smoth even and unruffled sheet of water of nearly a mile in width beating on it's watry bosome vast flocks of geese which feed at pleasure in the delightfull pasture on either border. the young geese are now completely feathered except the wings which both in the young and old are yet deficient. after feasting my eyes on this ravishing prospect and resting myself a few minutes I determined to procede as far as the river which I saw discharge itself on the West side of the Missouri convinced that it was the river which the Indians call *medecine river* and which they informed us fell into the Missouri just above the falls.

Epilogue
The Legacy of the
Lewis and Clark Expedition

The discoveries of the Lewis and Clark expedition turned a western wilderness of guesswork and rumor into a distinct part of the continent. Even though it demolished the dream of a convenient water passage through North America, the corps found a route from the Mississippi to the Pacific. The expedition opened a new world to Americans, who eagerly responded to its promises and opportunities. Later attempts to harvest fur and transform forests, prairies, and savannahs into fields, meadows, gardens, and cities culminated in claiming the continental boundaries of the United States. By exploring the breadth of the Louisiana Purchase, the Lewis and Clark expedition proved its significance to the future of the young republic.

To a considerable degree the success of the Corps of Discovery derived from Jefferson's design. His vision, support, and instruction raised the expedition above the concern of interest groups to a national undertaking. He conceived of an exploring expedition as a political and scientific instrument. Its task was to trace the course of an emerging empire stretching from the Atlantic to the Pacific and to increase the sum of useful knowledge through the collection of geographical, ethnological, zoological, and botanical information.

The success of the Lewis and Clark expedition backed the claim of the United States to the entire Columbia basin, dating from 1792 when the Boston sea captain Robert Gray sailed his ship across the river's bar. In subsequent decades, Americans derived their title to the Oregon Country to a great extent from the explorers' topographical descriptions and maps. Their reports about natural resources drew trappers and traders to the Missouri and Columbia Rivers. Their presence added to the legitimacy of "the rights of discovery."

The Corps of Discovery established official relations between the United States and Indian nations of the Great Plains, the Rocky Mountains, and the Pacific Northwest. The exploration introduced U.S. citizens to Native Americans unfamiliar to them: Shoshoni, Flathead, Nez Perce,

Walla Walla (Walula), Yakima, and E-che-loot (Wishram). Although they had difficulties with at least six trans-Mississippi linguistic families and the limitations of sign language, the explorers' journals abound with rare descriptions of nations that soon after succumbed to epidemics, starvation, and violence. A valuable fraction of their cultural beliefs, political organizations, economic activities, and social life are preserved in these accounts. Time and again the reports of the Lewis and Clark expedition on Native American affairs serve as benchmarks for an understanding of the complexity of the Indian world.

The contributions of the expedition to American geography, zoology, and botany opened the eyes of East Coast residents to the magnitude and riches of the West. They learned that the North American continent was wider than they had imagined and that the source of the Missouri was more distant from the outposts of the viceroyalty of New Spain in New Mexico. They recognized that there was much more to the western parts of North America than they had anticipated, including two major mountain ranges, the Rockies and the Cascades, separating them from the Pacific.

Clark's map of the expedition's route from Camp Dubois on the Mississippi to the Pacific Ocean has been praised by modern cartographers as an outstanding contribution to the geographic knowledge of western North America. Many of the topographic features along the trail that Clark meticulously recorded in his series of maps substantially aided orientation by putting names on the rivers, valleys, and mountains of a vast, previously uncharted area. In a way, these new place-names amounted to taking possession of and staking claim to the land by the United States.

Lewis's masterful descriptions of birds, fish, shrubs, and flowers presented to the world previously unknown animals and plants. He collected zoological specimens and species of live animals unknown to his contemporaries and shipped his finds back East. Lewis is also credited with using ecological study methods by describing the relations of western animals to their environment.

The risks entailed in the bold journey made the day-by-day progress of the first national scientific expedition a great adventure as well. Lewis and Clark devoted mind and body to the challenge. For twenty-eight months they fused planning with their gifts of improvisation. Successes and failures marked the course of the expedition; the captains coped evenhandedly with joy and despair.

Most important, their sense of mission reinforced their determination and strengthened their resilience in all aspects of the trip. The men's awareness that they were part of a national enterprise, not a trade venture or a trapping party, also hastened the transformation of a disparate group of people into a special army unit. Recognizing the significance of their task, they accepted military discipline as a means to reach the goals of the expedition. In particular, the explorers' sense of mission helped them to benefit from the knowledge of Native Americans, to cope with the results when their assumptions proved mistaken, and to live with the emerging reality of an awesome range of mountains.

Despite their mental and physical resources, at times the explorers felt helpless in the face of natural forces. The journey tested their mettle, but they endured, enthralled by the adventure and lured by their curiosity. Sacagawea, for example, would not be left out when Clark planned a trip to see a beached whale. At Fort Clatsop on January 6, 1806, Lewis reported that Sacagawea "observed that she had traveled a long way with us to see the great waters, and that now that monstrous fish was also to be seen she thought it very hard she could not see either." Her intense desire sums up the attitude that kept all members of the expedition on the move.

The sense of mission that inspired the explorers during their moments and stretches of drudgery contributed decisively to the success of the expedition. Lewis stated this conviction, and Clark echoed his words, on June 20, 1805, during the portage of the Great Falls. Clark's account exposes the layers of difficulties overcome by the entire expedition's sense of mission:

JUNE 20 th THURSDAY 1805
. . . Not haveing seen the Snake Indians or knowing in fact whither to calculate on their friendship or hostillity, we have conceived our party sufficiently small, and therefore have concluded not to dispatch a canoe with a part of our men to S! Louis as we have entended early in the Spring. we fear also that such a measure might also discourage those who would in such case remain, and migh[t] possibly hazard the fate of the expedition. We have never hinted to any one of the party that we had such a scheem in contemplation, and all appear perfectly to have made up their minds to Succeed in the expedition or perish in the attempt. We all believe that we are about to enter on the most perilous and dificuelt part of our Voyage, yet I see no one repineing; all appear ready to meet those dificuelties which await us with resolution and becomeing fortitude.[1]

[1]Thwaites, *Original Journals of the Lewis and Clark Expedition*, 2:175–76.

Lewis's pledge on his thirty-first birthday, August 18, 1805, among Cameahwait's Shoshoni is at once the most intimate and the most determined expression of the corps's sense of mission.

SUNDAY AUGUST 18th 1805.

... This day I completed my thirty first year, and conceived that I had in all human probability now existed about half the period which I am to remain in this Sublunary world. I reflected that I had as yet done but little, very little, indeed, to further the hapiness of the human race, or to advance the information of the succeeding generation. I viewed with regret the many hours I have spent in indolence, and now soarly feel the want of that information which those hours would have given me had they been judiciously expended. but since they are past and cannot be recalled, I dash from me the gloomy thought, and resolved in future, to redouble my exertions and at least indeavour to promote those two primary objects of human existence, by giving them the aid of that portion of talents which nature and fortune have bestoed on me; or in future, to live *for mankind,* as I have heretofore lived *for myself.*[2]

In his report to Jefferson after the return of the expedition to St. Louis on September 23, 1806, Lewis placed the results of the expedition in a global geopolitical context. Each detail of his letter reverberated the explorers' dedication to the cause, the national purpose of the expedition, and the benefits accruing to the United States from its success.

St LOUIS SEPTEMBER 23rd. 1806.

SIR: It is with pleasure that I anounce to you the safe arrival of myself and party at this place . . . with our papers and baggage. no accedent has deprived us of a single member of our party since I last wrote you from the Mandans in April 1804. In obedience to your orders we have penetrated the Continent of North America to the Pacific Ocean and suficiently explored the interior . . . to affirm that we have discovered the most practicable communication . . . across the continent by means of the navigable branches of the Missouri and Columbia Rivers. . . . notwithstanding the Rocky Mountains thus present a most formidable barrier to this tract across the continent a passage is practicable from the last of June to the last of September. . . . the Navigation of the Columbia and it's branches is good from the 1st of April to the middle of August when their waters subside and leave their beds obstructed by a great number of difficult and dangerous shoals and rapids. . . . we vew this passage across the continent as affording immence advantages to the fir trade but fear that advantages wich it offers as a communication

[2]Thwaites, *Original Journals of the Lewis and Clark Expedition,* 2:368.

for the productions of the East Indias to the United States and thence to Europe will never be found equal on an extensive scale to that by the way of the Cape of good hope. . . . That portion of the Continent watered by the Missouri and all it's branches from the Cheyenne upwards is richer in beaver and Otter than any country on earth particularly that proportion of it's subsiduary streams lying within the Rocky mountains. . . . altho' the Columbia dose not as much as the Missouri abound in beaver and Otter yet it is by no means despicable in this respect and would furnish a profitable fur trade, in addition to the otter and beaver considerable quantities of the finest bear of three species affording a great variety of colours, the Tyger catt, several species of fox, the Martin and Sea Otter might be procured beside the rackoon and some other animals of an inferior class of furs. If the government will only aid even on a limited scale the enterprize of her Citizens I am convinced that we shall soon derive the benifits of a most lucrative trade from this source. and in the course of 10 or 12 Years a tour across the Continent by this rout will be undertaken with as little concern as a voyage across the Atlantic is at present. . . .

. . . I have brought with me several skins of the Sea Otter 2 skins of the native Sheep of N. America. 5 skins and skelitons complete of the Bighorn or mountain ram, and a skin of the mule deer besides the skins of several other quadrupeds and birds natives of the country through which we have passed; I have also preserved a pretty extensive collection of pla[n]ts in Horteo have obtained 10 vocabularies. have also prevailed on the principal Chief of the Mandans to accompany me to washington, he is now with my worthy friend and Colleague Capt. C. and myself at this place, in good health and spirits. With rispect to the exertions and services rendered by this estimable man Capt. Wm Clark on this expedicion I cannot say too much, if sir, any credit be due to the success of the arduous enterprize in which we have been engaged he is equally with myself entitled to the consideration of yourself and that of our common Country. . . . I am very anxious to learn the state of my friends in Albemarle particular[l]y whether my mother is yet living. I am with every sentiment of esteem your most Ob^t Servt

MERIWETHER LEWIS
Capt. 1st U' S. Reg^t Infty.[3]

With one exception, peace prevailed during the voyage of the Lewis and Clark expedition. Jefferson's words on treating Native Americans, the corps's sense of mission, and its task to work for peace and trade forestalled aggression. Its small size meant that Indian nations did not consider the group a serious threat to their safety. A Native American woman

[3]From original manuscript in Lewis and Clark journals, Codex S, reprinted in Thwaites, *Original Journals of the Lewis and Clark Expedition,* 7:334–37.

with a child accompanying the explorers reassured them of the group's peaceful intentions.

Between 1804 and 1806, during centuries of hostilities between white and red people, an interlude of peace occurred on the expedition's trail from the Mississippi to the Pacific. On their journey a party of white men interacted peacefully with Native Americans. The explorers returned safely. Their reports, in turn, supported nascent dreams of a continental empire, stimulated an irresistible exploitation of natural resources, and unwittingly reinforced the white assault against Indian nations.

Questions for Consideration

1. What attracted European nations to the Pacific Northwest at the turn of the eighteenth century?
2. Why has the Lewis and Clark expedition been called Thomas Jefferson's brainchild?
3. How was Jefferson's purchase of the Louisiana Territory related to his sending an exploring expedition West?
4. What are the most important features of Jefferson's instructions to Meriwether Lewis?
5. How did Lewis and Clark turn a diverse group of men into a special army unit?
6. What did Sacagawea contribute to the success of the expedition?
7. Which stretch of the expedition's route proved to be most difficult?
8. How did the captains unravel the riddle of the Marias River?
9. What major difficulties did Lewis and Clark face in their relations with Native Americans?
10. Why could Lewis and Clark not establish lasting peace among the Indian nations along their route?
11. How did the lifestyles of some of the Native American nations along the route differ?
12. How did Lewis make contact with the Shoshoni Indians?
13. What role did Clark's Indian cures play in the progress of the expedition?
14. Which large animal had the explorers never met before, and why did they seem unable to leave it alone?
15. What enabled the captains to write detailed descriptions of birds and plants despite their lack of scientific training?
16. What did the citizens of the United States learn from the expedition?
17. What explains the ongoing fascination many Americans have with the Lewis and Clark expedition?

Suggestions for Further Reading

Allen, John Logan. *Passage through the Garden: Lewis and Clark and the Image of the American Northwest*. Urbana: University of Illinois Press, 1975.

Ambrose, Stephen E. *Undaunted Courage: Meriwether Lewis, Thomas Jefferson, and the Opening of the American West*. New York: Simon and Schuster, 1996.

Applemann, Roy E., ed. *Lewis and Clark: Historic Places Associated with Their Transcontinental Exploration, 1804–06*. Washington, D.C.: U.S. Department of the Interior, National Park Service, 1975.

Bakeless, John, ed. *The Journals of Lewis and Clark*. New York: New American Library, Mentor Books, 1964.

Bergon, Frank, ed. *The Journals of Lewis and Clark*. New York: Viking, 1989.

Bettes, Robert B. *In Search of York: The Slave Who Went to the Pacific with Lewis and Clark*. Boulder: Colorado Associated University Press, 1985.

Burroughs, Raymond Darwin. *The Natural History of the Lewis and Clark Expedition*. East Lansing: Michigan State University Press, 1961.

Clark, Ella Elizabeth, and Margot Edmonds. *Sacagawea of the Lewis and Clark Expedition*. Berkeley: University of California Press, 1979.

Clarke, Charles G. *The Men of the Lewis and Clark Expedition: A Biographical Roster of the Fifty-one Members and a Composite Diary of Their Activities from All Known Sources*. Glendale, California: Arthur H. Clark, 1970.

Cutright, Paul Russell. *A History of the Lewis and Clark Journals*. Norman: University of Oklahoma Press, 1976.

———. *Lewis and Clark: Pioneering Naturalists*. Urbana: University of Illinois Press, 1969.

DeConde, Alexander. *This Affair of Louisiana*. New York: Scribner's, 1976.

DeVoto, Bernard, ed. *The Journals of Lewis and Clark*. Cambridge: Riverside Press, 1953.

Dillon, Richard H. *Meriwether Lewis: A Biography*. Santa Cruz, California: Western Tanager Press, 1988.

Hosmer, James Kendall, ed. *Gass's Journal of the Lewis and Clark Expedition: By Sergeant Patrick Gass, One of the Persons Employed in the Expedition*. 1811. Reprint, Chicago: A. C. McClurg, 1904.

Howard, Harold P. *Sacajawea*. Norman: University of Oklahoma Press, 1971.

223

Jackson, Donald. *Thomas Jefferson and the Stony Mountains: Exploring the West from Monticello.* Urbana: University of Illinois Press, 1981.

————, ed. *Letters of the Lewis and Clark Expedition with Related Documents, 1783–1854.* 2nd ed. 2 vols. Urbana: University of Illinois Press, 1978.

Lamb, W. Kaye, ed. *The Journals and Letters of Sir Alexander Mackenzie.* Cambridge: Published for the Hakluyt Society at the University Press, 1970.

Nasatir, Abraham P., ed. *Before Lewis and Clark: Documents Illustrating the History of the Missouri, 1785–1804.* 2 vols. St. Louis: St. Louis Historical Documents Foundation, 1952.

Ronda, James P. *Lewis and Clark among the Indians.* Lincoln: University of Nebraska Press, 1984.

Swanton, John R. *The Indian Tribes of North America.* Washington, D.C.: Smithsonian Institution Press, 1952.

Wheeler, Olin D. *The Trail of Lewis and Clark, 1804–1806.* New York and London: Putnam's Sons, 1904.

Index